COUNTRY COMES TO TOWN

A volume in the series

American Popular Music

Edited by
Rachel Rubin
Jeffrey Melnick

COUNTRY
COMES TO
TOWN

**The Music Industry and the
Transformation of Nashville**

JEREMY HILL

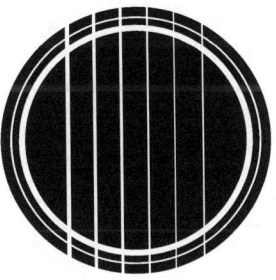

University of Massachusetts Press

AMHERST AND BOSTON

ISBN 978-1-62534-172-3 (paper); 171-6 (hardcover)

Designed by Dennis Anderson
Set in Adobe Caslon Pro by House of Equations, Inc.
Printed and bound The Maple-Vail Book Manufacturing Group

Library of Congress Cataloging-in-Publication Data

Hill, Jeremy, 1975– author.
Country comes to town : the music industry and the transformation of Nashville /
Jeremy Hill.
pages cm. — (American popular music)
Includes bibliographical references and index.
ISBN 978-1-62534-172-3 (pbk. : alk. paper) —
ISBN 978-1-62534-171-6 (hardcover : alk. paper)
1. Country music—History and criticism.   2. Music trade—Tennessee—Nashville.
1. Title.
ML3524.H56   2016
781.64209768'55—dc23
2015035259

British Library Cataloguing-in-Publication Data
A catalogue record for this book is available from the British Library.

Contents

Acknowledgments

THIS BOOK could not have been written without a tremendous amount of help from the following people and institutions. First, the American Studies department and Columbian College of Arts and Sciences at the George Washington University provided me with the time, money, and intellectual support needed to develop this book. Ideas first discussed in seminars and other gatherings prepared me for the project of writing a cultural history. Beyond that, the countless hours spent reading, writing, re-reading, re-writing, and most especially discussing ideas and theories of how to understand culture and history were their own reward, and I affectionately thank all the professors and fellow students who made the experience so stimulating and challenging. In particular, Chad Heap, Gayle Wald, Alex Dent, and Phyllis Palmer pushed me to select a subject I would actually want to stick with for going on ten years and helped me throughout the research and writing of this book. As well, I want to thank the George Washington University Seminar in U.S. Urban Studies for a travel grant in the early stages of the project that provided me with the opportunity to kickstart my research.

My graduate school writing group helped shape the book and reenergized my faith in the project numerous times during and after our time at George Washington. For that, I affectionately thank Dave Kieran, Lars Lierow, and Kevin Strait. In the final hour, Dave also came through in the clutch with much needed edits of my thorniest final chapter drafts, for which I am very grateful. I am also extremely happy to thank the following group of loyal grad school comrades for their support and levity over the years: Kyle Riismandel, Sandra Heard, Julie Passanante Elman, Stephanie Ricker Schulte, and Cameron Logan. It was quite a ride.

In order to write this book, I utilized a wide array of research institutions, and I want to thank their staffs and all those who keep libraries and archives going with their hard work and/or deep pockets. At the Country Music Hall of Fame, I met John Rumble on my first day of research in Nashville. John's exhaustive knowledge of the library's archives and endless enthusiasm for the songs of country music greatly enriched the project. I also thank Michael Gray for tracking down numerous sources and helping me navigate the library's extensive collections. I wish to thank Brenda Colladay at the Grand Ole Opry Museum, Marilyn Swing at the Nashville Metropolitan Court Clerk's Office, and the staffs of the Heard Library at Vanderbilt University, the Tennessee State Library, and the Metropolitan Archives. For having such a wonderful facility and helpful group of people, the Nashville Public Library deserves a special mention. In Washington, I also want to thank the staff of the Performing Arts and Newspaper and Periodical Rooms at the Library of Congress, and Wendy Shay at the Archives Center of the Smithsonian's National Museum of American History.

At the University of Massachusetts Press, Brian Halley and Carol Betsch helped me navigate an unfamiliar process. Rachel Rubin's ideas, insights, and suggestions made the whole manuscript better, but her particular attention to the third chapter, which continually gave me fits, was especially appreciated. I also wish to thank the two anonymous readers who helped focus and refine the manuscript. Margaret Hogan's inspired and meticulous copyedits made the whole thing much more legible, and I am tremendously grateful.

Throughout this project (as well as long before and hopefully well after!), my family has provided me with the fullest support imaginable. Emotionally, logistically, intellectually, and financially, they have made this endeavor possible. I wholeheartedly thank my parents, Mary Loots and Scott Hill, as well as Kathryn Hill, Madelyn Petty, and John and Joan Hill.

Finally, the biggest thank you, by a long shot, goes to Inge Stockburger. She helped me through this process in so many ways, and I can't even believe how happy it makes me to say thank you. It's no secret that this kind of writing project can be harrowing, and there's no one I'd rather have talk me down off the ledge. Luckily, that's just the tip of the iceberg when it comes to the ways in which she enriches my life.

AN EARLIER version of chapter 2 first appeared as "Country Comes to Town: Country Music's Construction of a New Urban Identity in the 1960s," *Popular Music and Society* 34, no. 3 (2011): 293–308. An earlier version of chapter 4 first appeared as "Country Music Is Wherever the Soul of a Country Music Fan Is: Opryland U.S.A. and the Importance of Home in Country Music," *Southern Cultures* 17, no. 4 (Winter 2011): 92–111, southerncultures.org.

Introduction

SOMETIME IN the early 1950s, or so the story goes, country music icon Hank Williams told a reporter, "You got to have smelt a lot of mule manure before you can sing like a hillbilly."[1] The line has been repeated many times over the years, presumably for its blunt humor value but also because it speaks to the authentic "country" credentials that the genre's performers were expected to display. Twenty years later, another icon of a different kind, Richard Nixon, issued a presidential proclamation decreeing that October should be National Country Music Month. Nixon was neither the first president nor the last to offer such a proclamation, but in contrast with Williams's claim, the text accompanying the presidential edict was striking for its loose interpretation of "country." Nixon claimed that, for country music, "Now the term describes not just a locale but a state of mind and style of taste, as much beloved downtown as on the farm."[2] Putting country as a "state of mind" on equal footing with country as a place, the declaration provided a more expansive understanding of who could perform and consume country music. Two decades later, in the 1990s, the undisputed king of country music was a son of Yukon, Oklahoma, which, despite its frontier-sounding name, was actually a suburb of Oklahoma City.[3] Garth Brooks had little experience on a farm. He had gone to college and earned a degree in marketing, and he put on live performances featuring pyrotechnic displays and light shows that rivaled the most extravagant rock concerts. Yet very few within country music culture disputed that he was an authentic country star, in fact the biggest star in the genre's history.

From mule manure to a marketing genius, the trajectory was never this simple or unidirectional, of course; there were those that contested Williams's more rigid claim about country authenticity in the 1950s and some who balked at Brooks's level of artifice in the 1990s. But this book shows that the transformation in country music's associations with particular spaces and places has played a central role in expanding the commercial and cultural power of the genre. Much of country music's early power derived from its connection to the nation's agrarian past, so it might seem strange to find so many instances of the idea that country music can be perfectly at home in other spaces. I argue, however, that the geographic *portability* of country music has been central to the genre's success. The suggestion that country music does not have to be rooted in "the country" has always been a potentially controversial idea, but its evolution over at least the last sixty years has been crucial to its evolving identity. If "country" can signify a mindset, the character of an individual, or an abstract set of virtues, rather than simply a geographic particularity, then the genre can speak to and for a wider range of actors. This book thus traces the efforts of a diverse set of country music figures to shape the built environment of Nashville and create a visible home for the industry there, while also exploring changes in a larger set of ideas about the country, the city, the suburbs, and music's relationship to all three. This attention to both the material and cultural landscapes of country music reveals that, by the end of the twentieth century, the genre's commercial and cultural power has been enhanced by the industry's development within Nashville and the use of ideas about country music's relationship to different kinds of spaces.

ONE OF the more striking things about studying country music is how quickly you realize that much of the genre's history has been about charting the trajectory of rural people *away* from the "country." Between 1920 and 1960, millions of southerners moved out of rural spaces and into the cities and suburbs of the West, North, and South.[4] As other scholars have deftly demonstrated, for the many Americans who migrated from rural spaces to urban and suburban areas over the course of the twentieth century, various incarnations of hillbilly music provided a place for mediating this process of migration. The Grand Ole Opry, for instance, the genre's longest-running radio program and eventual flagship for many decades, affectionately kept a vision of rural life alive and visible, while at the same time reassuring rural migrants that they would still be able to find their way in the "modern world."[5] Because of the demographic and geographic changes that unfolded during the genre's formative years, I want to demonstrate that most incarnations of what has come to be called "country music" have been bound up, to various degrees, in cultural conversations about social class, modernization, geography, and authenticity.[6]

In the middle of the century, producers, performers, and promoters of what was starting to be called "country music" had to wrestle very directly with the spatial associations (and their connotations of social class) attached to the legacy of "hillbilly music." Much of the music's appeal stemmed from its connection to the rural past, what some perceived as a "disappearing past," while at the same time powerful negative stereotypes about "hillbillies" persisted in the national discourse. These ideas assumed that the music was produced by untutored and uncouth people from the backwoods, farms, and "hills and hollers." The characterizations were not entirely negative, though, for, as Anthony Harkins has shown in regard to the hillbilly stereotype more generally, the hillbilly figure has also been perceived as a repository of traditional values and a positive bulwark against the purported ills of modernization and urbanization.[7] While disparaging city dwellers dismissed country folks' inability to assimilate into city life, other rural traditionalists claimed that country-to-city migrants lost an essential piece of their character in the migration. Practitioners of country music who hoped to be commercially successful had to carefully straddle this dichotomy.

To some degree, this is still true today. In various ways and for various reasons, members of the country music industry and its culture have had occasion to emphasize the music's distance from its rural past. Oftentimes this was because of the negative associations attached to rural space and folk, but it also represented concerted efforts to expand the geographic and cultural reach of the genre. Many individuals in country music, however, have eventually realized that this logic can be taken too far; it is generally beneficial, if one is going to affiliate with the phrase "country music," to maintain some sort of connection, tenuous as it may be, to rural space, culture, or people. Fans, journalists, and even some stars have pushed back at the direction the industry has taken, critiquing efforts to distance the music from rural and rustic figures. I argue that the notion of country character, or country as a state of mind, has played a crucial role in resolving this tension.

Rather than thinking that country music's appeal has been rooted in its geographic particularity, I suggest instead that the genre has gained increasing cultural power (measured in terms of both commercial success and politico-cultural clout) as it *de-territorialized* the space of country, transforming it into a state of mind rather than a specific physical space, and simultaneously rewriting the definitions of categories such as "ordinary folks" and "the people," which have always served as powerful markers of the music's appeal and fan base. This long cultural transition has required an evolution in the definition and location of "country" (a change really in what country could be, and who it could signify), from a notion of the genre and its people as at least those with roots in the agricultural economic system in the first half of the century, to a widely accepted understanding by the final quarter of the century that "country people" could live anywhere and that intrinsic but indefinable country "character" mattered more than geographic or socioeconomic identity. Whereas the rural culture of early "hillbilly" music was more deeply structured by associations with a life tied to the land (even as the specter of urbanization and adapting to urban migration simultaneously played key roles in the music), notions of country identity had become more divorced from geographic restrictions by the end of the century, a process that began decades earlier.

One of the most prominent sites for this conversation was the Grand Ole Opry's 1974 move from the Ryman Auditorium in downtown Nashville to a new theme park complex in the suburbs, the topic of this book's fourth chapter. Several months after the move (a departure that was roundly supported by almost every public Opry figure), Opry hostess Carolyn Holloran provided a summary of the Opry's new home that drew on tried and true language about the essential nature of country folk: "It's true you can take the boy out of the country but you can't take the country out of the boy, and the same goes for Country music. Country music is wherever the soul of a Country music fan is!"[8] Even though some fans have argued that true country music could not be just *anywhere* a country fan happened to be, but instead had to be rooted in the country and tied to the land, by the mid-1970s, the notion that country music fans could carry the soul of country music with them wherever they went was fairly commonplace. I argue, though, that the foundation for this line of thinking was facilitated by ideas and assumptions used to describe the migration of country folk to the cities and suburbs, and in particular the industry's urban development in Nashville. Proof of country music fans' compatibility with urban and suburban communities, and their ability to appreciate the essence of the music in new environments, helped to break down the notion that country music had to be confined to rural spaces, and this eventually led to the notion that it could be "anywhere."

Assumptions about the hillbilly nature of country musicians, almost always held by figures *outside* the industry, were not new in the midcentury, but they were all the more striking because they existed alongside a growing body of evidence to the contrary about the country music business. These powerful stereotypes overrode common knowledge about the workings of country music as an often urban industry. Rather than thinking of country music as an avatar of the past, somehow outside of America's postwar transformations, many industry figures increasingly insisted not only that country music fans and performers were also experiencing these changes but that the music and genre had something unique to say about how to deal with this period of change. It is easy to assign the "country folk" of country music the role of reluctant modernizer, but industry figures were quick to point out that they were dealing with the expansion of the suburbs, the decline of the city, and the subsequent gentrification of urban space along with everyone else. Rather than thinking of country music solely in terms of a traditionalist "lament the loss of the country and bemoan the modern city" narrative, country music figures produced multifaceted approaches to demographic and geographic change. Some were majority voices that resonated widely across the genre without being significantly questioned or threatened; others were minority voices that still offered salient critiques of orthodox thinking. The performance, production, and consumption of country music in the postwar United States could not possibly exist outside of the larger transformations of the social and cultural landscape of the nation. The cultural and commercial power of country music increased as the genre's practitioners successfully responded to these transformations, finessed the consequences of a declining rural population, and effectively affiliated the genre with the values of the nation's mainstream.

Finally, the term "country music" can never refer to a homogenous, clearly demarcated genre. Such boundaries are not firm or clearly established, and, in fact, contentious discussion over who and what gets to be included can often be one of the more pleasurable aspects of fandom. At any given point in time, "country music" has been home to multiple unique individuals with their own agendas, perspectives, and political leanings, as well as sharply different subgenres, all with their own casts of characters, studio locations, and sonic stylings. Likewise, the change over time, from a genre with roots in "hillbilly music" to the most commercially successful American music category, is immense. With that in mind, this book stays for the most part focused on two things: First, it considers the development of various pieces of the country music industry within the city of Nashville, including the locations of the homes of country stars, the construction of studios and record label offices, the placement of live music venues, and the interactions among the many individuals affiliated with these sites and the other business and civic elites of Nashville itself. Second, the book examines the production, circulation, and reshaping of ideas about the country, the city, and the suburb in texts associated with country music, including song lyrics, album liner notes, promotional material, music industry media, fan club newsletters, and public proclamations from the people of country music—the singers, songwriters, session musicians, producers, and fans. There is a significant overlap between the ideas circulating about different spaces within country music culture and the transformations of Nashville's built environment produced by the many pieces of the industry. The material and cultural landscapes worked together to produce powerful new images and identities for this very broad thing called country music.

OVER THE course of the 1940s, the popularity of what was often referred to as hillbilly music grew throughout the nation. But negative stereotypes about the backwoods hillbilly permeated national discourse on this booming musical phenomenon. In national magazines and other media sites, writers and illustrators depicted hillbilly performers and fans as simple in both their desires and musical ability, childlike in terms of responsibility and intellect, and particularly alien to the residents of urban America. Chapter 1 demonstrates the reach and depth of this prejudicial discourse, but also shows how hillbilly performers' own more nuanced self-presentations invoked but also undercut stereotypical assumptions. This chapter suggests that Nashville itself offered an appealing blend of rural and urban, North and South, modern and traditional. Opry stars and personalities such as Roy Acuff and Sarah Colley (who played one of the program's most iconic characters, Minnie Pearl) settled there and advanced public presentations that fully blended rustic roots and contemporary urban competence. Acuff even ran for governor on the strength of his business skills, challenging those who would write off himself and his fellow hillbilly musicians as simple country bumpkins.

Chapter 2 analyzes a shift in the marketing of country music that built on the earlier mix of urban and rural iconography: the new strategy fully embraced the notion of country "coming to town." Starting in the mid- to late 1950s, in order to counter still-prevalent ideas about the typical country music fan as a poor hillbilly located far outside the modern consumer economy, the Country Music Association and other industry boosters argued that their listening audience comprised primarily rural-to-urban migrants who not only lived modern lives but also constituted a new group of middle-income *urban* consumers. In tandem with this shift in marketing and ideas, the new "Nashville Sound" found significant commercial success with its more pop-oriented style of country, noted for orchestrated string sections, smoother lead vocals, and innocuous background choral groups, all of which also carried urban connotations. Key figures in the industry embraced the prevalent journalistic conceit of "country coming to town" (a phrase that was often used to describe country's increasing commercial success) and emphasized the urban location of Nashville's Music Row as well as the presence of country music fans in urban spaces all across America. In response, some critical fans and performers argued that the new sound was too "urban" and that city people, with their greed and commercialism, had ruined the inherently pastoral music, a shift emblematized for many by the transition from fiddles to violins on country records. As Music Row developed about two miles from downtown Nashville, industry leaders hoped that the proposed urban renewal plans to create Music City Boulevard could establish a clean, modern, tourist-friendly neighborhood that would highlight country music's commercial success and "countrypolitan" sound. The funding did not come through, and the industry blamed what they saw as persistent anti-hillbilly prejudice and disdain for country music on the part of city government and prominent Nashvillians.

The abstract discourse of "coming to town" adopted by the genre's promoters was continually complicated by the reality of their particular home town of Nashville. The third chapter shows that the lofty discourse of coming to town found in many country music texts (such as album promotional materials, song lyrics, interviews, and industry periodicals) did not correspond to the industry's approach to the much messier reality of the industry's adopted home town. Most notably, the civil rights movement in the 1960s fought battles for racial equality practically on the industry's doorstep. African American activists picketed the segregationist policies of a grocery store on Music Row, urban renewal projects displaced low-income residents from neighborhoods near Music Row, and the uprising in Nashville after the 1968 assassination of Martin Luther King, Jr., cancelled the Opry for the first time ever. Despite repeated claims that country songs represented the true experience of "ordinary Americans," country music discourse for the most part ignored or elided the travails of the civil rights movement, both nationally and within the city of Nashville itself. This avoidance developed in tandem with an emerging notion of country music as the soundtrack of the lives of the "ordinary folk," which suggested a universalism for country music that could only hold if the particularity of certain experiences was downplayed, implicitly suggesting that it was *white* ordinary folks for whom the genre spoke. Quite provocatively, assumptions about country music's racial identity and homogenous whiteness were in some ways reinforced by the prominence of the genre's first black star, Charley Pride. He was generally discussed as the exception that proved the rule, someone who, according to one text, "sounds like us but looks like them."⁹ Pride's success suggested that anyone could sing country music, regardless of race. At the same time, however, the media coverage and other texts surrounding his rise within the genre repeatedly emphasized the oddity of his race and served to reinforce in turn the essential whiteness of everyone else who sang country music. This chapter shows that, around the time of Pride's emergence within country music, various texts constructed country music as the "white man's blues," envisioning a parallel but clearly distinct lineage that obfuscated the long history of interracial cultural borrowing, influence, and interest shared by rural and working-class southerners regardless of race.

The fourth chapter argues that, by the late 1960s and early 1970s, as the Opry prepared to leave downtown for the new Opryland complex, the industry's efforts to promote country music and situate its listeners in the mainstream of American life had shifted once again—this time employing suburban rather than urban iconography. During the discussion (and mild controversy) over the Opry's move to Opryland, many observers speculated on what the move meant, and the Opry's leading figures responded by positioning the suburbs of Nashville as a safer alternative to the downtown space, which they marked as dangerous, unpredictable, and not enjoyable or safe for families. This argument resonated with that found in the broader country music discourse, which suggested that the "ordinary folk" were now in new kinds of country homes outside of the actual country. Country stars and leaders claimed that the Opry's new home was analogous to those found by many country fans who had moved from their rural homesteads into urban and then suburban homes over the previous decades. The phrase often repeated during this period to describe the Opry's move, "out of the barn and into a home," signified this transition. Industry leaders, writers, performers, and fans suggested that "country people" could retain their unique country character regardless of which American spaces they inhabited. In song lyrics, essays, interviews, and other public proclamations, country stars and fans collectively argued that wherever you happened to live, you could retain country values, thus creating a potent blend of unmarked spatial identity and authentic country character.

Despite Opry stars' dismal claims about the "slums" around the Ryman in the mid-1970s, the fifth and final chapter shows that the urban neighborhood never fully lost its hold on country music fans, and live music venues and souvenir shops, along with tours of the Ryman itself, persisted in keeping travelers interested in downtown Nashville. Class tensions manifested in debates about the future of the neighborhood and whether the honky-tonks and their clientele should be a piece of the city's vision of the future, but eventually the importance of country music heritage won out. In the late 1980s and early 1990s, private-public investments, driven by a coalition of interests, brought new retail and entertainment properties to the neighborhood, leading the Gaylord Entertainment Group, the new owners of the Opry and Opryland, to re-invest in the Lower Broad neighborhood, including reopening the Ryman Auditorium. Along with shifting ideas about Nashville's downtown and urbanity, these investments once again made Lower Broad an attractive destination, as industry leaders again looked to the neighborhood as the ideal nexus of live music, retail shopping, and living country music history.

Country music became a commercial phenomenon on an unprecedented scale during the last part of the twentieth century, but changes in the nature of the music and its production caused some observers to wonder, once again, whether it was too much like pop music and not enough like true, authentic country. The downtown neighborhood helped provide a resolution by providing a home for live music that kept the honky-tonk tradition alive and brought to the area steady streams of fans who could appreciate both the slick production of country albums and the more ragged sounds of up-and-coming hopefuls. Seventy years after the Opry first performed on the stage of the Ryman, the sound of steel guitars and fiddles still echoes around the corner of Broadway and Fifth, and nighttime brings crowds of country music fans to the blocks surrounding the old auditorium, just as it did in the 1940s. This continuity is a remarkable feat of preservation but also provides a window onto how much social and spatial change the neighborhood, and country music as a whole, has experienced.

"Nothing but Realism"

Early Hillbilly Music's Blend of
Rural and Urban

COUNTRY MUSIC's oldest and most famous institution got its name on a Saturday afternoon in late 1927. "Solemn Old Judge" George Hay's old-time music variety show was set to follow the NBC network's Music Appreciation Hour on Nashville radio station WSM. Toward the end of NBC's classical show, noted conductor Walter Damrosch declared there was "no place in the classics for realism." When Hay's program came on the air, he responded to Damrosch by declaring, "for the last hour, we have been listening to music taken largely from grand opera and the classics, and heard Dr. Damrosch tell us there is no place for realism in that kind of music. In respectful contrast to Dr. Damrosch's presentation, for the next three hours we are going to present nothing but realism." Later in the program, Hay continued to play off the contrast between his own show and the preceding classical program when he followed a performance by African American harmonica player DeFord Bailey with a reference to the Grand Opera of the previous show and triumphantly claimed, "From now on we will present the Grand Ole Opry."[1] At the moment of its christening, Hay publicly advocated for "nothing but realism," but even then "realism" was an elastic concept.

Despite his claim to provide "nothing but realism," Hay's Grand Ole Opry was not a recording of a barn dance in the country but an urban representation of a rural barn dance heard by radio listeners both urban and rural. Even with this commonly available knowledge, the Opry still resonated with millions of fans because of its ability to capture the *spirit* of rural culture, a quality that was crucial to hillbilly and, later, country music's success over several decades and throughout myriad stylistic and spatial shifts.

The Grand Ole Opry was part of a wave of radio programs that combined old-time music styles with vaudeville-style comedy and stage play.[2] WSM's program was not the first, and was in fact modeled on the WLS National Barn Dance, which was broadcast out of Chicago. In the first part of the twentieth century, Nashville developed as a central location for the insurance industry of the Southeast. Two major companies, National Life and Casualty and National Life and Accident, developed in Nashville, selling, among a range of items, industrial policies to the working classes of the rural and urbanizing South.[3] Edwin Craig, the son of National Life and Accident's founder, suggested developing a radio station that could be used for promotional and advertising purposes. The station's call letters themselves, WSM, advertised the mission of the insurance company: "We Shield Millions." The company prided itself on its capacity to insure a wide range of individuals. Beginning in 1925, the station hosted a live variety show every Saturday night whose audience extended across much of the Southeast and beyond, aided by WSM's clear channel signal. The company's salesmen in small towns and rural communities attempted to target WSM listeners as possible new customers, and one of the most important programs for executing this strategy was the Opry. Thus, the Opry itself developed within a network of modern urban commercial interests, as part of the insurance company's larger marketing campaign, and was in fact suffused with advertisements for mass-produced commercial products. The rise of radio provided a format for broadcasting these barn dance variety programs, and they appeared throughout the Southeast, as far west as California, and in northern cities as well. Chicago's National Barn Dance on WLS was nearly as popular as the Opry, but the Opry attracted a live audience almost immediately, first in the in-house WSM studios and then in larger venues around Nashville.[4]

The Opry's musical acts included old-time string bands, instrumentalists (banjoists, fiddlers, harmonica players), and, beginning in the late 1930s, close-harmony vocal groups. The weekly show started in 1925 but did not get its name until two years later, when Hay introduced Bailey and used the Grand Ole Opry moniker. Hay's act of naming depended on a kind of wordplay, changing Opera to "Opry" and Old to the more colloquial "Ole," which highlighted a tension between mocking the hillbilly genre and undercutting purportedly more sophisticated genres.[5] This was also true of many of the names of the bands that appeared on early Opry shows. For instance, the Skillet Licker Orchestra's name questioned the elite status of supposedly more sophisticated art forms (as in, even skillet lickers can perform in an orchestra!) while also simultaneously validating rural music's artistry by comparing it to that of an orchestra. The band names contained both of these trajectories, and performers and fans could emotionally connect to both associations. Fans were able to understand the duality, and this understanding contributed to the program's appeal.[6]

Beginning in the early 1930s, however, there was a shift in the Opry's presentation, and various Grand Ole Opry figures began to self-consciously highlight country's rustic roots, donning hillbilly costumes, tailoring names of instrumental and singing groups to an old-fashioned idea of rural life, and inhabiting country characters on stage and in films.[7] These self-conscious *performances* of hillbilly generated much of the Opry's wide appeal. In the interest of projecting a particular rustic image, the Opry's managers (most notably George Hay) encouraged these urban musicians to eschew their usual formal dress in favor of hillbilly costumes, and changed some of the group names to make them sound more rustic than urban. Dr. Bate's Augmented Orchestra, for instance, became Dr. Bate's Possum Hunters under Hay's direction.[8] The first phrase, "Augmented Orchestra," suggested urban associations while the change to "Possum Hunters" unequivocally signified rural life. Hay also personally named the Fruit Jar Drinkers and the Gully Jumpers, two other prominent groups in the Opry's first decades with pointedly rural band names.

Even as they performed in bands with such rural names, most of the early Opry performers had other professions within the city of Nashville. These string band performers, when they were not fiddling or singing for WSM on Saturday nights, were auto mechanics, wood workers, barbers, cigar makers, and oftentimes insurance salesmen for the parent company itself.[9] The Gully Jumpers were composed of two garage mechanics, a National Life employee, and one farmer. The Fruit Jar Drinkers also featured two mechanics and one barber.[10] Despite the humorously exaggerated rusticity of the band names and costumes, the musicians' urban connections were hardly a secret. Opry fans apprehended the performance of possum hunting, gully jumping, and fruit jar drinking that the group names and their members' stage play enacted. Fans who understood that barbers were playing rustic figures also presumably understood that not just *any* barber could play a gully jumper, that these particular Opry performers had something unique in their character and life experiences that allowed them to believably function in both worlds, or at least be able to enact appropriate performances of each. A figure such as Dr. Bate, raised in the country but living in the city, could play both a possum hunter and an orchestra leader (and a doctor). His hillbilly identity remained relatively intact, even within an urban setting. The Opry stars' country roots were crucial to their ability to play hillbilly and function in the hillbilly music industry.

Nashville and the Growth of Hillbilly's Commercial Viability

In the 1920s and into the 1930s, the live radio programs, in tandem with individual string band performances on local radio stations, built on an existing audience for the music and increased demand for recordings of hillbilly music, which, like blues records, were generally sold on the "race" divisions of record labels.[11] The many fifty-thousand-watt radio stations that broadcast hillbilly music in the 1930s also helped build an audience for the genre. In 1933, a portion of the Chicago-based National Barn Dance on WLS was broadcast on NBC's radio network. In 1939, the Opry achieved network status on NBC radio stations for a thirty-minute portion of the show every Saturday night as well. The presence of portions of these shows on national network radio expanded the geographic awareness and appreciation of the variety of musical styles they played. Several radio barn dance programs throughout the nation (including Chicago's National Barn Dance, Renfro Valley Barn Dance, and Louisiana's Hayride) featured musicians and stage performers from a rural milieu, but of these only the Opry lasted past 1960.[12] One of the main reasons for this was WSM management's early decision (1934) to form the Artists Service Bureau. The bureau aggressively booked package shows and large-capacity venues for their artists while maintaining an extensive network of business contacts. As a result, many Opry stars achieved national reputations and toured constantly while still performing on the Opry most Saturday nights.[13]

By the 1940s, the Opry's success and WSM's ability to believably wrap an urban production in rustic packaging played key roles in establishing Nashville as a viable center for the developing country music industry. The initial success of WSM and the Opry, combined with the presence of many prominent hillbilly musicians and songwriters in the Tennessee area, produced the first roots that would eventually make Nashville the most sensible location for existing record labels, as well as new entrepreneurs breaking into the market, to build studios, publish sheet music, or operate talent agencies. Historian Jeffrey Lange refers to the "centripetal forces of the Opry and the Nashville industry" that gradually brought more and more stars and session musicians into their orbit.[14] Nashville's central geographic location in the Southeast also played its part by drawing in a large live audience from surrounding states who saw a visit to the Opry as a kind of cultural pilgrimage. In turn, the accessibility of the live shows for rural residents of the Southeast helped deepen the Opry's place in the hearts and minds of the program's many listeners.

The Opry maintained its lineup of traditional string-band, folk, and novelty performers, but musical innovations that developed in other parts of the country also helped popularize different versions of hillbilly music. For instance, western swing evolved in Texas and California in the 1930s, combining jazz, European, and Latino styles and producing music with roots in southern rural performance styles that reached a wider audience through hybridization, amplification, and electrification, as well as a danceable beat.[15] In the 1940s, Texas performers such as Ernest Tubb and Hank Thompson used electric guitars because they were playing urban barrooms and needed amplification to be heard.[16] Most of these stars considered their own styles to be distinct from those of the Opry, but western swing and electric honky-tonk performers from Texas made guest star appearances on the Opry after releasing hit singles, further proving the Opry's position as the program with the widest scope and audience.[17]

In addition to concurrent changes in the sound and style of the music itself, several other social and economic factors facilitated the rise of commercial country music. The advent of World War II spurred a new wave of internal migrations, bringing rural and southern consumers and workers to urban areas and intermingling servicemen with different musical backgrounds and interests in a variety of military spaces. The rural South lost 20 percent of its population during the war, as rural migrants headed either north or west, or, in a migration much less discussed, to cities and coastal towns of the South itself.[18]

One of the most important structural factors in the emergence of a strong viable country music industry, though, was a dispute between broadcasters and the licensing agency, the American Society of Composers, Authors, and Publishers (ASCAP), which created a window of opportunity for the proliferation of new country songs and songwriters. ASCAP demanded that radio stations pay fees for each song broadcast over the radio (charging that by playing licensed recordings, stations were unfairly acquiring free content), and stations argued that their broadcasts to mass audiences provided enough free advertising for the publishers' product to justify skipping the licensing fee. In order to protest ASCAP's policy, broadcasters engineered a mass boycott of ASCAP songs beginning January 1, 1941. Broadcasters had already astutely formed their own licensing organization, Broadcast Music, Inc. (BMI), whose compensation structures and less restrictive membership requirements opened the doors to many new and already established hillbilly artists.[19]

The broadcasters' boycott of ASCAP and subsequent creation of BMI gave "hillbilly" songwriters a new route for promoting their songs to a wider audience. This helped raise the visibility of the music while also creating new compensation structures for its performers and writers. The licensing organization battles played out in New York City mostly, but the consequences were felt around the nation, and Nashville-based industry figures were some of the first to capitalize on the openings generated by these corporate wars. BMI recognized the centrality of Nashville early in its existence and located a branch office in Nashville well ahead of ASCAP.

The creation of BMI inspired Nashville publisher Fred Rose to partner with Grand Ole Opry performer Roy Acuff, and their publishing company, Acuff-Rose, was tremendously successful throughout the 1940s. The partnership between Rose and Acuff, one of the most popular Opry stars, solidified the importance of Nashville within the consolidating field of country music, providing yet another anchor to the city and simultaneously lending credence to the notion that hillbilly artists were in fact professional musicians. Acuff-Rose in the beginning outsourced the actual sheet music publishing to a Chicago firm, but very quickly moved production to Nashville and began renting larger offices from National Life.[20]

Much of the Opry's sway over popular hillbilly artists came from the knowledge, as Acuff found in 1946 when he briefly left the Opry, that a star's power was constituted in tandem with the Opry, at least in the 1940s. The stars were most popular when they appeared weekly on the Opry. Even though WSM paid Opry performers a very small wage for their actual appearances on the radio show, the powerful ability of the Opry's "brand" to help book lucrative appearances for their stars elsewhere made the appearance requirements tenable.[21] As such, as World War II came to an end, the Opry, and by extension the city of Nashville, were already poised to become the center of the hillbilly music world.

Nashville billed itself as "The Athens of the South," and in fact funded the construction of a life-sized replica of the Parthenon at the turn of the century, first as a temporary structure for the centennial exposition in 1897 and then restored and made permanent in the 1920s.[22] The nickname referenced the city's self-positioning as a center of erudition and sophistication, and the city's "interest in the arts, education, and many buildings of classic design," according to the Nashville Chamber of Commerce.[23] But even as white-collar industries such as state government and insurance drove its economy, Nashville's civic leaders preserved and incorporated various elements of the region's history and "premodern" character in their promotional and marketing efforts. In the 1940s and 1950s, the city's boosters argued that Nashville could blend the rural and urban, the past and present, by modernizing the city's economy without losing an essential "downhome" character. In describing why so many people chose to live in Nashville, one promotional writer declared, "Many are impressed with the tempo of the modern city, with its thousands of people engaged in trade, the students and teachers in its many colleges, and its artisans who work in busy factories turning out hundreds of products for national defense and domestic purposes." The same text, however, continued by suggesting an entirely different aspect of the city: "To others, colorful scenes of the Old South, faithfully preserved throughout the Nashville area, call to mind the days and deeds of an era resplendent with charm and romance, that is linked inseparably with the story of America."[24] The text implicitly endorsed the South's racist past ("colorful scenes of the Old South") but also positioned the city as part of a modern industrial economy, attempting to find an appealing middle ground. Chamber of Commerce promotional materials in this same period emphasized Nashville's "middle-ness" in virtually every way, including its size, climate, topography, and specifically the region's geographic relation to the rest of the country: "midway between the Great Lakes and the Gulf of Mexico, and approximately half way between the Atlantic Coast and the plains states of the Middle West."[25]

The city's desire to look both forward and backward required a delicate balance when dealing with the Opry. The radio program contributed to the city's gentle nostalgia but also threatened to overrun it with potentially unseemly hillbillies who could serve as reminders of the region's not-so-glorious premodern past.[26] Chamber of Commerce publicity materials mentioned the Opry without emphasizing its presence, although in the early 1950s, this began to change and local businesses began to recognize the economic potential of the industry.[27] The industry's increasing contributions to the region's service economy eventually convinced the city's political and business leaders of the industry's value to the region. In fact, Nashville civic boosters positioned the city and region as a welcoming combination of southern hospitality and northern advancement in the same period that the Opry similarly blended a modern business sensibility that increasingly contrasted with its fabled agrarian and hillbilly past. In the public presentations attached to their Nashville-based enterprises, country businessmen and -women blended rural character with an urban cultural production and created an image that resonated with fans precisely because of this yoking of rural and urban. Successfully pulling off this performance depended on making a believable claim to authentic rural roots while also establishing a believable claim to their comfortable place within Nashville's urban professional classes.

The size of the Nashville metropolitan region distinguished the city from spaces such as New York and Chicago. Opry stars operated in or near downtown, and the city provided urban amenities and associations while still offering accessible rural spaces of residence, easy mobility, and spatial versatility.[28] In the early 1950s, the size of the downtown and the distribution of the area's access routes allowed stars like Roy Acuff, Minnie Pearl (Sarah Colley), Red Foley, and Ernest Tubb to live in neighborhoods outside of the city, or in unincorporated areas on the edge of the city limits, which were, even at peak time, within a fifteen- to twenty-minute drive from downtown.[29] In choosing to own homes in the outer limits of Nashville, these Opry stars enacted membership in a white-collar commuting class. The scale of Nashville's geography also facilitated a far-flung network of industry locations and sites within its boundaries, with publishing houses Acuff-Rose and Cedarwood opening up shop on the main arteries leading out of town.[30]

In 1943, after being asked to leave the War Memorial Auditorium, the Opry moved into the Ryman Auditorium in downtown Nashville.[31] Thomas Ryman had built the auditorium in the 1890s and ceded the venue to the city of Nashville, expressly stating that the auditorium was to be used for the enjoyment of all citizens of Nashville. Originally more like a church, with a rostrum in the middle surrounded by circular rows of pews, the building had been converted into a performance venue by cutting the stage in half to create a backstage space. The Ryman loomed over a strip of two-story buildings housing furniture stores, corner liquor stores, and eateries along Broadway. The stretch of Broadway between the Ryman and the Cumberland River was referred to as "Lower Broad" because it was this stretch of Broadway that rolled down the final hill to the river, but also because the street served as a dividing line between downtown to the north and less glamorous neighborhoods to the south. Hotels, restaurants, and office buildings dominated the area north of Broadway, whereas the blocks south of the avenue consisted of service and filling stations, used car lots, body shops, and parts and tire stores. Downtown Nashville's parking and traffic problems were legendary, and this automobile-centric neighborhood catered to the needs of these downtown commuters. But as suburban development increased in the Nashville region, and the number of downtown office workers declined, the neighborhood's traffic lessened.

By the end of the 1940s, Nashville boosters looked to remake its urban spaces through urban renewal and present the region as a medium-sized and accessible city equally amenable to northern capital, national tourism, and southern rural migrants. WSM and the Opry hoped to benefit from the city's drive for modernity and the "improvement" of downtown and the Ryman's surrounding neighborhood. Nashville's planners put forth rhetoric that promised to clear the entire central business district of "blight" and "slums" leaving the Ryman in a prime downtown location. The renewal plans for the blocks closer to Lower Broad, however, never made it off the planning books and into concrete Housing Authority plans.[32]

The Opry thus found itself on the fringe of downtown; the Ryman sat only two blocks north of the Greyhound bus station, generally a sign of a neighborhood on the slim edge of respectability but also perfectly placed for the guitar-toting dreamers who were disembarking from their journeys and pilgrimages.[33] In the late 1940s and early 1950s, the Opry and its fans (as well as adept downtown business owners) began to fully cultivate a home for the show in the downtown space of Nashville, enlarging the scope of a typical Opry visit and locating the Opry within an intricate network of country music establishments. The Ryman's location just off of Lower Broad, enmeshed in a denser constellation of hotels, restaurants, transportation hubs, and retail shops, facilitated this development. Opry star Ernest Tubb moved his record shop to Broadway in 1951, half a block and around the corner from the Ryman.[34] In addition to actually selling albums over the counter (as opposed to the previous shop's reliance on placement of orders), the new venue sold Opry-related souvenirs and included a performance space in the back. With these new additions, Tubb's shop and its second performance space (and Tubb's midnight radio show, which he broadcast from his shop directly after the Opry) greatly increased the level of Opry-oriented traffic on Lower Broad.[35] Around the same time, local restaurants and hotels began advertising to country fans in newspapers and country journals, marking Lower Broad and the surrounding blocks as an enlarged space of Opry-related tourism, which cemented the Opry's presence within Nashville and eventually created an intriguing and highly visible imbrication of rural visitors and urban space.[36]

Most Opry visitors had traveled from out of state, many of them from rural spaces or small towns, and thus the Opry as a live music event produced a particular spatial encounter. Country fans came to downtown Nashville to watch rustic performances that were in turn broadcast by clear channel radio across the nation. Before the show these tourists shopped in souvenir and record shops, stayed in hotels located in varied Nashville neighborhoods, and mingled with other fans in the taverns and restaurants of downtown Nashville. On stage, Opry personalities enacted a vision of this same country rube in the big city encounter through their performances, even though many fans clearly understood that the performers themselves were urban businessmen and -women offstage, and that many of the fans had experience with urban spaces as well.

"Rural Rhythm" and Opry Stars' Efforts to Counter Hillbilly Stereotypes

During and after World War II, as the wealth and fame of hillbilly music stars increased, national discourse still firmly located the performers in the hills, backwoods, or mountains, and, as a result of this geographic isolation, still unfamiliar with even the smaller towns and the cities of the South. The coverage elided the deep historical connections between urban and rural economies, reductively narrating a journey in which hillbilly musicians brought their music out of the hills and into the cities for the very first time.[37] In so doing, national journalists promoted a specific vision of hill or mountain life rooted more in early twentieth-century stereotypes, and understood hill people themselves as either currently degraded, or previously degraded (uneducated, fecund, closer to nature), but now modernizing (learning about money and manners). Despite the circulation of an urban self-presentation, national commentators repeatedly focused only on performers' inherent rustic nature, falsely imagining a musical style that could only have emerged from the nation's backwoods and hill country, and which was entirely alien to urban Americans. In national magazines, the convenient signifiers of hillbilly rusticity overwhelmed the more complex realities of the hillbilly music business. Elid-ing the fact that most "hillbilly" musicians had been professional per-formers for decades, national media drew a distinctive spatial journey and set of assumptions about hillbilly music's commercial ascendance—sug-gesting that the music literally came down from or out of the woods, hills, and farms to reach the urban centers of America.[38]

These articles responded to and perpetuated persistent assumptions that the music was natural and wild, untamed, uncorrupted by modern urban hands. The stories maintained a spatial distance or hierarchy, leav-ing the music degraded and ridiculous in a way, but they also served to help the industry market the music as authentic in its "capture" at its true place of genesis. A 1944 *Saturday Evening Post* article on talent scout Art Satherley described the process of finding the hidden talents of hillbilly music: "When Satherley is told that there is somebody in an out-of-the-way place who has a very original ballad and that this native artist is too shy to come to town, he will pack his recording equipment into suitcases and head into regions where no city shoes have ever trod before."[39] The comment envisioned a music produced in the hidden corners of the coun-try, incomprehensible to urban eyes, from which inhabitants emerged like children, intimidated by the clamor of the "town" and shyly willing to per-form for Satherley only if he journeys to *their* virgin territory. The marked depth of the woods through which the information traveled to reach the "folksters" implied a distance not just spatial but cultural as well.[40] Further positioning hillbilly music production at a remove from the city, the article described the lengths to which Satherley would go to find his talent with the phrase "and on foot where there are no passable roads."[41] Despite the fact that "hillbilly" performers of the late 1940s, such as Little Jimmy Dickens and Minnie Pearl, repeatedly referenced their presence in world capitals like Paris and Hollywood, these articles focused mainly on an origin narrative in which raw talent percolated deep in the woods and had to be sought out or seized on in those rare instances when the wild-eyed primitives stumbled out from the woods.

Mid-1940s coverage of the Opry and hillbilly music strongly associ-ated the genre with inherent rusticity, and the phrase "rural rhythm" was often used to describe the style up through the end of the decade. Such a phrase indicated that one of the most elemental components of the songs was somehow intrinsically rural, a product of the space itself.[42] Na-tional journalists also commonly used botanical metaphors to suggest the music emerged directly from the land: "The general practice is to take a recording outfit into the territory where such songs grow."[43] A 1944 *Saturday Evening Post* article referred to Grand Ole Opry performers as "bucolic singers and bands." The same article broadly declared, "All hillbilly music sounds monotonously alike to the urban eardrum."[44] These journalists routinely assumed that such a thing as "the urban eardrum" existed, and that hillbilly music itself was entirely antithetical to urban ears.

These commentators mapped very clear spatial assumptions onto the music. The persistent belief in an "urban eardrum" that could not tolerate a "rural rhythm" played out in particular descriptions of the *sound* of hillbilly music too. Initially, trade magazines rarely described the music itself in much detail, except as a series of trimmed gerunds evoking a chaotic country party, as in "pickin'," "twangin'," and "wailin'," eliding artistic and creative efforts and positing more natural sounds and expressions as the source of the music. A 1946 *Collier's* writer described the music as something country people had previously "been doing mostly for fun," until the commercial success of a couple of hillbilly tunes had convinced them to try to sell their product.[45]

Into the 1950s, journalists conceptualized country stars as "great, natural musicians," emphasizing their general lack of classical training but also suggesting, again, that the music emerged unmediated and organically from hillbilly culture and an agrarian lifestyle.[46] An article from early 1946 argued that hillbillies had become more savvy and recently learned the commercial value of their music (such as it was): "Reports are coming in from more and more waxers that the boys from the hills have been wised up. They're not hillbillies anymore; they don't come cheap or naïve; they know the value of their product and they're collecting for every nasal twang or corn-jug burp."[47] Suggesting that hillbillies just make the sounds and collect the checks, such demeaning references implied that hillbilly music was simply the collection of natural sounds of the hillbillies themselves and their agrarian lifestyle, erasing any sense of original creative artistry on the musicians' part and marveling at the fact that these sounds could make a profit.[48] A 1953 article in *Nation's Business*, on the European appeal of what the article refers to as "hillbilly and western," emphasized the lack of musical training and raw expression of genuine emotion and experience: "Some of them do not know a note of music, but their great appeal as entertainers is in the rawness of their emotions and their sincerity in conveying them."[49] These descriptions completely missed the professional nature of the industry and elided the fact that Acuff-Rose had been publishing sheet music for a decade. Cleary, Acuff and Rose found plenty of country songs created with notation in mind and fully believed that hillbilly fans would buy and utilize the sheet music. Instead of focusing on this aspect of the music industry and culture, writers emphasized those who "do not know a note of music." The reality was much different. Acuff's publishing house presented a professionalized, transmittable vision of the songs and songcraft, countering the stereotype found in the national media, of untutored hillbillies making "natural" sounds that only later were turned into profitable music.[50]

In addition to his highly profitable publishing operation, Roy Acuff embarked on a series of ventures that ultimately worked to counter the stereotype of hillbillies as country rubes stumbling across profits by selling their "natural" music making. Capitalizing on his name recognition and goodwill with fans, Acuff developed Dunbar Cave on the site of an unused two-hundred-acre resort owned by the town of Clarksville, which he purchased in the late 1940s. Acuff constructed a multifaceted entertainment space on the grounds offering the cave itself as an attraction, fishing and boating on the lake, regular live music performances, and an old hotel that gave way to cabins for lodging. Acuff successfully charged a ten- to twenty-cent admission fee and individual fees for each activity on top of that.[51] He also opened up a museum exhibit of his own collection of hillbilly artifacts.

Acuff's supporters nominated him for the Democratic gubernatorial primaries in 1944 and then in 1946 for the Republican side, but he declined to run both years and eventually discouraged voters from voting for him while acknowledging that he appreciated the sentiment. In 1948, however, when friends and supporters once again nominated him, Acuff told the party that he would avoid actively campaigning in the primaries but that, if nominated, he would run in the general election, seeing it as the will of the people. Acuff won the Republican primary and between the end of August and November 1, 1948, he crisscrossed the state with Republican Senate candidate Carroll Reece. Acuff's and Reece's campaign featured much music, and in the slightly condescending words of Reece himself at their first joint campaign appearance, "You have heard some delightful entertainment by Roy Acuff and his Smoky Mountain boys. Also he has spoken to you briefly about his desire to serve you as the governor of this great state."[52] Treating Acuff as his campaign's musical entertainment and Acuff's own campaign as an afterthought, Reece saw the stage as his own. By contrast, however, Acuff presented himself as a serious campaigner who was certainly well qualified to govern the state.

Acuff's political ambitions received a great deal of press, some of which re-narrativized his initial interest in the governorship. Beginning with a claim made in a 1944 article in the *Saturday Evening Post,* Acuff's gubernatorial aspirations were repeatedly misconstrued as a reaction to then-governor Prentice Cooper's decision to refuse to attend an Opry celebration in 1943, and his pointedly singling Acuff out for turning Nashville into the hillbilly capital of the world.[53] The slight, if it in fact actually happened, may have played some role in Acuff's eventual decision, but in none of the election years did he actively put himself on the ballot. Instead, friends and supporters and, in one case, *Nashville Tennessean* journalists placed him on the ballot to disrupt the status quo. But by the end of the 1948 campaign, Acuff did feel that he had encountered anti-hillbilly prejudice and responded with a passionate defense of being a hillbilly singer, pointing out that the incumbent governor, Gordon Browning, had "tried to make fun of me by calling me a hillbilly fiddler and sideshow performer. I am a hillbilly singer and fiddler, and if that is a crime, I'll have to plead guilty to it. I'll even go further than that and tell you that I am proud of it."[54]

Acuff continually emphasized his competence as a business owner as a qualification for the governorship, refusing to be pigeonholed as a hillbilly singer and fiddler. Instead, he presented himself as a singer who could still retain authentic hillbilly character while making impressive sums of money and competently managing several business operations. Pointedly referring to the fact that he paid more in taxes each year than those who presumably poked fun at him made all year, he declared, "The fact is, friends, that the taxes I pay to the Federal Government and to the state . . . taxes on my business operations which I run myself . . . are enough to support some of the people who have been writing this kind of ridicule since the campaign started."[55] His assertion revealed Acuff's confidence that he could campaign as a hillbilly with money. He referred to himself as the "man with the fiddle" who spoke for the "poor man" against the "fat politician" while simultaneously trumpeting his acute business acumen and hundreds of thousands of dollars of annual income as adequate qualifications for the job. Acuff could speak for the poor without being one. Acuff relied on a self-presentation that emphasized both his homespun common sense and genuine affection for the "little guy" while using his business savvy to prove that he would be a good administrator. Throughout, however, he maintained allegiance to his hillbilly roots while consistently presenting himself as a successful modern businessman.

Probably the second most popular Opry performer in the 1940s, perpetually lovesick small town gossip Minnie Pearl, was played by Sarah Colley, widely known to be a well-heeled Belmont Conservatory attendee and daughter of one of Tennessee's wealthiest lumbermen. On stage, Colley played the exaggerated rustic role of Minnie Pearl, but offstage, she repeatedly made clear in journal and magazine articles that she was an urban-educated woman *playing* the shy small-town country girl. Her invented name itself (and fans' awareness of the stage name as frequently found in feature articles on "Pearl") called into question the pure veracity of the performance, allowing readers of country music journals to understand her stage work as a performance so strikingly different as to require a different name. In articles, Colley claimed that some of her rich relatives stopped talking to her when she started "being a hillbilly."[56] Her suggestion of a process of becoming a hillbilly cemented Colley's dual identity. She elaborated that she went to college for two years but did not think it "marked her too much." She used publicity materials and interviews with country journals to highlight the distance between her onstage performance as a goofy and perpetually lovesick country girl and her offstage life as a well-educated Nashville socialite. The title of a long 1953 article on the popularity of the Pearl character, in the first issue of *Pickin' and Singin' News,* unequivocally claimed that Colley "mimicks the country ladies."[57] Rather than believing that she unfairly portrayed small town country girls, however, the article highlighted Colley's roots in a small town, ostensibly the background necessary for her successful mimicry. Media coverage referred to her clothes as her "costume," and Colley alluded to the *construction* of Pearl, referring to the fact that she "plays" hillbilly and foregrounding those biographical details of her personal history that sharply jarred with the fictional details of Pearl's life. In so doing, she created a space for fans to apprehend both her personae simultaneously.

Like the barbers and mechanics who "played" gully jumpers and possum hunters in the Opry's first two decades, Acuff and Colley both created dual presentations, whose subtleties the audience could certainly apprehend, but the reception outside of the Opry community was not always so nuanced. One national journalist recognized this dichotomy but came away with a drastically different interpretation than that presumably favored by the "hillbilly" performers: "Opryites are extremely sensitive. They can stand being called hillbillies on the stage, but in real life they consider the term derisive. Some of them only have a childlike sense of responsibility, don't understand the difference between business and personal affairs, and can't stand being scolded."[58] The leap between the second and third sentences encapsulates much of the national discourse on the music, in essence chastising hillbillies for an unjustified desire to be taken seriously as urban professionals.

Opry dialogue and comedy bits certainly invoked exaggerated rustic stereotypes but also provided a more nuanced understanding of rural people's worldliness alongside these caricatures. The Opry's frequent and popular comedy bits revealed a stance or persona that was split between two worlds. Host Red Foley bantered with various Opry personalities in between songs, including Minnie Pearl, Rod Brasfield, and Opry announcer Grant Turner. On the eve of an Opry troupe's visit to Europe in 1949, the talk revolved around Pearl's and Brasfield's confusion and lack of knowledge about French language and customs, as they conceptualized or tried to understand the language through a decidedly rural lens. Brasfield asked Pearl what "à la carte" means, and she responded, "Ala Carte? It means on the wagon!"[59]

The following exchange also traded on the notion that international travel was entirely alien to Pearl and Brasfield's personae.

> R: Say Minnie, ain't you excited about goin' over to Europe?
> M: I sure am, Rodney. But I'm a little bit skeered about goin' over the ocean in a airyplane
> R: Shucks, Minnie—It's jes' like settin' in a rockin' chair.
> M: Mebbe so, Rod. . . . But I ain't never heerd o' anybody havin' to bail out of a rockin' chair![60]

Even as Minnie Pearl played the rube character, it was not one of total abjection. She astutely questioned the viability and safety of transoceanic jets, and her assertion that no one ever had to bail out of a rocking chair resonated with and endorsed those who chose (or had no choice but) to remain outside of the international tourist economy. The humor is gentle rather than biting, but the assumptions permeating the performance are still firmly rustic.

The performers' more grounded awareness of the realities of the modern world came in the form of Opry host Red Foley, who concluded the network portion of the program by describing the trip without idiomatic country expressions: "Well, we've got to say so long for now . . . as we mentioned before, we're goin' a few thousand miles overseas for two weeks."[61] Foley performed as "himself," Pearl and Brasfield were characters produced on stage. Foley was the "straight" foil and in fact had been handpicked for his crossover appeal by NBC network executives to host the Opry when Acuff left in 1946. Foley was from Chicago and more in the country-pop crooner mold, though he did emphasize gospel tunes appreciated by traditional audiences (whereas Acuff's own singing style leaned more heavily toward old-time string band).[62]

Opry singers' song lyrics likewise strengthened this suggestion that country people would retain their country character even as they traveled the world, made large sums of money, and further lost daily interactions with the farms and hills of the past. Jimmy Dickens foreshadowed this stance in his 1949 song "Country Boy." The song appears to be a straightforward celebration of country life and assertion of country identity, in opposition to those "folks that think that they're so doggone high falutin'." But a somewhat incongruous line in the first verse tips off the listener to Dickens's actual position: "I'd be the same in Hollywood / Or right in my own kitchen." The reference to Dickens in Hollywood acknowledged that the Opry star was no longer *just* a country boy; rather, it reassured listeners that his poor rural upbringing shaped his everyman disposition and allowed him to be a country boy no matter where stardom would take him. The song's references to feed sacks and plow lines function as unambiguous signifiers of the rural childhood that formed the narrator's sensibility; Dickens's song focused on his upbringing and his inherent character while slyly nodding to Opry stars' globetrotting ways.

The Hillbilly in the Cultural Imaginary of the 1950s

In contrast with the nuanced self-presentations produced by Opry and other hillbilly music stars, stereotypes about the music and its people persisted into the 1950s. Potentially in response to the industry's more nuanced and sophisticated self-presentations, beginning in the early 1950s, *Billboard* used the term "country music" to describe the music and "hillbilly" much more sparingly. A series of articles in other national lifestyle magazines about the new hillbilly phenomenon, however, retained the older terminology. In fact, these articles repeatedly took pains to highlight the distinctiveness of the genre's culture and participants through the use of the term. Just at the moment when the emerging genre of "country" music moved closer to the mainstream of the pop music industry, these articles returned to an exaggerated rustic cliché. In magazines like *American Magazine, Nation's Business,* and *Collier's,* for instance, self-identified city writers conjured images of "funny little men chasing each other with pitchforks and banjos" to describe and marvel at the hillbilly phenomenon.[63]

During this period, journalists often used the industry's commercial success to humorously figure hillbilly's rusticity. For instance, a hyperbolically titled article, "Thar's Gold in Them Thar Hillbilly Tunes," expressed surprise that the industry "has its own big hillbilly stars who individually make up to $300,000 a year, its own hillbilly music publishing companies, even its own handsome young hillbilly singing stars who set hillbilly bobby-soxers to squealing."[64] The author repeatedly used the older term to describe various aspects of country music culture, thus constructing a parallel hillbilly world that contained some of the same recognizable features as the "normal" world of the 1950s. The coverage also frequently played the idea of commercial success of country rubes for humorous effect. For instance, one author juxtaposed the hillbilly performers' extensive revenues with their hopelessly simple tastes and desires, suggesting that "some stars, making hundreds of thousands of dollars a year, will eat the same meal three times a day—fried potatoes, fried eggs, and fried pork chops."[65] Another author spelled out the precise sums hillbilly stars made through personal appearances, records, and publishing rights, and opined, "For guys who were skinning mules not too long ago, this is a lovely bale of hay."[66] The humorous possibilities of the country stereotype were too much for these urban writers to resist.

Even if these authors sometimes recognized the sophistication of the Opry performers, their caricatured descriptions of the Opry's fan base allowed for no such sophistication. Articles on the Opry phenomenon frequently depended heavily on the comedic juxtaposition of Opry fans as country bumpkins entirely out of place in a city like Nashville: "In Nashville hotels, they often bed down eight to a room, and bring along their own food. They clean their hotel rooms, never having heard of maid service. Many of them never heard of tipping either. Bellboys and elevator operators, when the management isn't looking, may make up for this oversight by charging ten cents per elevator ride."[67] Positioning Opry fans as distinct from more savvy Nashville hotel employees, and assuming a readership well versed in hotel etiquette in explicit contrast with the Opry fans, the article simultaneously described the fans' devotion to the Opry and their poverty.

The Opry existed in a bustling downtown space to which it contributed tourist dollars and some small amount of prestige, but much of the iconography of the Opry and hillbilly culture told a different story. The front page image of a 1952 article in *American Magazine* strikingly featured a barn with an attached Grand Ole Opry banner amid a series of pastoral hills, without any other building around, and a flock of country people incongruously carrying individual lanterns to the building/dance.[68] The image represented the Opry as a country barn dance, not the urban phenomenon it truly was. The caption, "from the hills and hollers," suggested a country-to-city journey, but the image firmly located the Opry itself in the country. The article also described the Opry's early growth as a process in which "other natural entertainers drifted in from the hills and hollers on succeeding Saturday nights."[69] This kind of language, suggesting that the "natural" entertainers just happened to drift into the Opry, as if borne by the wind, removed the agency and intentionality of the professional musicians who appeared on the program.

These articles distorted the nuanced self-presentations of Opry and other hillbilly stars through a spatial lens, firmly locating the "hillbilly" in non-urban spaces. Despite the fact that many Opry performers had lived in Nashville and maintained urban employment for decades (even those Gully Jumpers and Fruit Jar Drinkers from the 1930s), national discourse still drew on a city/country divide and assumed WSM personnel were urbanites while the hillbilly performers had to be entirely rustic. One writer positioned WSM personnel as "city folks" creating order out of the chaos of a sea of country rubes on the Opry's stage: "Several city fellers kept weaving purposefully through all the turmoil and bedlam, apparently looking for lost actors or propelling tardy ones to the mike."[70] Again, the article positioned the performers as childlike, in need of a push from WSM personnel to keep them on task. The radio station personnel and station managers were the city folks (collecting the gate receipts presumably, too) while the articles figured Opry performers as rural.[71]

In tandem with this paternalistic discourse, national media coverage often used subtle (and sometimes not so subtle) animalistic imagery to describe the musicians. A 1952 *Newsweek* article noted, "Mr. Pellettieri . . . looks like he should be conducting a symphony instead of herding hillbillies," and "the stage swarms with some 125 singers, guitar players, fiddlers, comedians and the like."[72] The author represented the Opry performers as creatures who swarm across a stage, in need of herding, blatantly juxtaposed with members of a symphony orchestra who need no such paternalistic maintenance. This was part of a larger characterization of hillbilly music industry that missed the mark: the performers were not children or animals requiring paternalistic control from WSM. Instead, the "chaos" on stage was part of the show's production and created much of the appeal for fans. The author's misapprehension (willful or not) speaks to the discursive positioning of hillbillies that the magazine articles enacted. Hillbilly readers would presumably understand the nature of the chaos on the Opry's stage (enjoyable in part because of the stance the performers take) as something more performative than an expression of their inherent inability to follow orders.

THE MISAPPREHENSION on the part of some writers for national urban publications matched or mirrored some of the industry's own shifting self-presentations. Roy Acuff claimed you had to be a "country boy" to sing or write country music, but as his own example proved, Acuff understood that country boys no longer had to live in the country, as long as the music still "came from the heart" and drew on rural experience.[73] In the 1940s, the Opry presented a dichotomy whose nuance many commentators missed, in the process perpetuating some of the unsavory aspects of the hillbilly stereotype. *Pickin' and Singin' News,* started in 1953 and published in Nashville, was the first publication to cover the country music industry specifically from an insider perspective (but still with claims to impartiality). Similar to the blend of rural and urban embodied by figures such as Acuff and Minnie Pearl, the pages of the journal contained an uneasy tension between celebrating the music as appealing across geography and recognizing or perpetuating assumptions about its innate rusticity.[74] In its early issues, the journal still aligned itself with a particular "downhome" milieu and style. It featured regular columns with rustic titles such as "Lowdown on the Hoedown," which provided small bits of information on country performers' musical happenings, and "Over the Cracker Barrel," which offered more gossipy bits on the performers' personal lives as well as information on other country personnel such as disc jockeys from around the country. But these features disappeared in the publication's second year, suggesting that anti-hillbilly sentiment had won out. In the late 1950s and 1960s, a new wing of the country music industry would more forcefully split open this blend of rustic and urban, and the next chapter examines this development and the increased emphasis on urban space and iconography.

"Country Comes to Town"

A New Urban Identity for Country Music in the 1960s

IN THE mid-1950s, Nashville was home to a great many talented musicians but had few studios and no standout places to record music. WSM, the radio home of the Grand Ole Opry, had a strong roster of musicians, engineers, and producers, and in the 1940s and early 1950s, these talented individuals also brought their talents to other musical outlets. For instance, three WSM engineers had created Castle Studios in the downtown Tulane Hotel in the late 1940s, and had recorded both pop and country hits in the studio. But in 1955, WSM president Jack DeWitt decreed that WSM employees could not moonlight for other operations, and the side operations, including Castle Studios, shut down.[1] This sudden vacuum was fortuitous for a pair of brothers who had been trying to establish their own studio operation in Nashville. In 1954, Owen and Harold Bradley purchased a duplex in a location chosen for its combination of lower price and proximity to downtown Nashville, in a residential neighborhood recently zoned commercial.[2]

Harold Bradley was a talented guitarist who would go on to play on a number of classic rock, country, and pop songs. Owen was a band leader, producer, and, as it turned out, whiz at acoustic engineering and studio construction. Owen's efforts to tweak and reshape the duplex and Quonset hut the Bradleys set up in the backyard wound up creating a string of hits that would reshape the sound of country music and its place in the mainstream of national pop music in the 1950s and 1960s. Owen converted the residential home into a recording studio by knocking out the first floor and

31

turning the basement into a studio with an eighteen-foot ceiling. He hung burlap bags and blankets on the wall of his studio, creating acoustics that quickly became appealing to a wide range of performers and producers. When he and his brother purchased the duplex, the site was chosen mostly for pragmatic reasons, such as cost and accessibility. The success of the studio, however, and of those who followed in the Bradleys' footsteps and constructed studios, publishing houses, and record label offices, created a new neighborhood with powerful associations for the genre of country music. This new neighborhood would spark the start of a new chapter in country music's evolution, as various figures attached to Music Row hoped to use the urban neighborhood to produce and shape a different image for the genre and its people.

Country Goes "Pop"

Over the course of the 1940s, the careers of crooners like Frank Sinatra, Bing Crosby, and Tony Bennett had boomed while the big band era waned, and this trend toward coherent lyrics and the primacy of the lead vocal had helped to propel hillbilly songs as well. Beginning especially with the songs of country icon Hank Williams, pop stars such as Tony Bennett and Patti Page covered straight country songs for the pop charts, lending the songs a newfound degree of respect in popular music and foreshadowing the commercial potential of these combinations.[3] The lyrics and melodies of country songs seemed to fit squarely within the mainstream of pop music, and Hank Williams's tunes in particular resonated with millions of Americans. But many other hillbilly artists performed highly successful concert tours during this time as well. Even as high-profile postwar honky-tonk artists such as Hank Williams and Ernest Tubb captured the media's attention, other country singers like Red Foley, Eddy Arnold, and even Hank Snow were offering up smoother sounds as early as the late 1940s.[4] Eddy Arnold's career had already straddled the line between hillbilly and pop, but in 1948, his singles still dominated the country side of the charts. That year, the top four country singles were all Arnold songs; nonetheless, in September of that year Arnold left the Opry to capitalize on his early glimmers of crossover potential and make movies and television shows for a broader audience.[5]

Even without the Opry, though, Arnold still dominated the country charts. In 1955, he recorded an album with the Hugo Winterthaler Orchestra in New York City's Webster Hall. His version of "Cattle Call" from this recording session sold 500,000 copies.[6] Arnold's smoother vocal in front of an orchestrated string section proved extremely popular, and this song would become something of a model for the next wave of "country-pop." Arnold had recorded mostly in New York from 1945 through 1955, until the construction of the new RCA Victor studio on Music Row brought him back to Nashville full time.[7] Roy Acuff, with his more traditional sound, had left the Opry in 1946 but had returned within a year after finding it harder to tour without the regular Opry performances. By contrast, Arnold never came back. He represented a new breed of country star who could exist without the Opry and was evidence of country music's growing commercial influence beyond the Opry and beyond the previous confines of "hillbilly music."

Industry leaders hoped the popularity of stars such as Williams and Arnold would lead to sustained commercial success for other country artists, but two different developments dealt setbacks to the genre just as it was fully coming into its own. Most famously, rock and roll shook up the entire pop music landscape. But the proliferation of the Top 40 format within the radio industry also impacted country artists' profits. Radio stations looked to capitalize as much as possible on the emerging emphasis on recording-driven, chart-measured hits, as recordings were cheaper than live performances. Standardized playlists made the collection and selection of songs easier while making the stations' prepackaged sets more attractive to advertisers.[8] Because these standardized playlists cut across multiple genres, this shift dramatically reduced the number of country-only radio stations. But it also accommodated a new emphasis within country music at large, an emphasis on recordings over live performance that gave the studios on Music Row and the labels and performers a venue for making money and building a reputation without the Opry itself.

Rock and roll emerged out of both Tennessee music capitals, Nashville and Memphis, despite Memphis's place in the historical imagination as the location of Sun Studios and Sam Phillips's first Elvis Presley recordings. In the early 1950s, black R&B artists began covering what they referred to as "hillbilly" songs and white artists with some country connections began covering R&B songs.[9] Other early rock artists recorded in Nashville, and Presley himself performed on the Opry and recorded with the Jordanaires, the background vocalists who also appeared on numerous Nashville Sound recordings later in the decade and into the 1960s.[10] He toured with Opry legend Hank Snow and was referred to as a "hillbilly" singer in the mid-1950s, but by the end of the decade, Nashville's country music establishment wanted no part of him.[11] Rockabilly's instant popularity had caused many previously honky-tonk and country-pop artists to release rockabilly songs, but then ultimately triggered a retrenchment within the industry and led industry figures to position country music as adult, dignified, and (given rock's southern associations) national.[12]

In 1955 and 1956, country disc jockeys began to argue that country stars and fans need not panic over the possible death of country music at the hands of rock; instead, they argued that country artists should sing country songs and not try to imitate other styles.[13] They chastised country artists for trying to record rock records and instead advocated remaining true to "country," but what that meant exactly was still up for grabs and subject to much contestation. Quality, simple songs sung with some minor pop instrumentation changes would, in these jockeys' minds, retain the true country audience. Indeed, as rock began to fade slightly and shift direction (rhythm and blues solidified as its own genre and white rock had some of the rougher edges sanded off), country stars rebounded with successful country-pop singles and the pessimistic outlook diminished. Nashville record producers operating in the country genre thus found success with the national adult market because of a conscious attempt to modernize the sound of the genre, an effort that had been incrementally underway since at least the mid-1940s.[14] The tantalizing goal of crossover success hinged on the "downhome" appeal of country artists harnessed with a less twangy vocal and instrumental sound that could reach those record buyers turned off by the sounds of hillbilly music.

Disc jockey and producer Connie Gay explained the marketing idea fairly transparently in 1957 when he used the past tense to describe "hillbilly music" to a journalist: "Hillbilly music was banjos, guitars, fiddles. We've added a sweet touch to it and taken out the twang. You don't get the raucous plink, plank, plunk of a couple of decades ago." Gay used the notion of a switch from hillbilly to country not just in name but in style too, conceptualizing hillbilly music as something substantively distinct from country in sound and bearing. He claimed, "Can't can't be can't in hillbilly music—it's cain't. But can't *can* be can't in country music."[15] This conceptual change was mirrored in a style emerging simultaneously with the development of a new urban neighborhood of studios and publishing houses not too far from the Opry's home in downtown Nashville.

Music Row and the Development of the Nashville Sound

When Owen Bradley first constructed the studio on Sixteenth Avenue, the demand for recording Nashville performers had exceeded the availability of quality recording space, but major labels were still reluctant to invest their own capital in new recording space. Bradley saw an opening and struck a deal with Paul Cohen, the head of the Decca record label, wrangling a guarantee of at least one hundred recording sessions a year from Decca artists in exchange for access to Bradley's high-quality production site.[16] The deal was central to the initial investment in Music Row, and the studio's immediate success bred more success and more studio construction. Other combinations of country and pop had emerged and flourished for several years before the Bradleys purchased their duplex on Sixteenth Avenue. But the syncretic blend of country and pop, and its particular Nashville flavor, came from the session musicians hired for early Music Row sessions. These musicians created what came to be known as the Nashville Sound, playing, along with backing vocal group the Jordanaires, on many of the top recordings coming out of the Row. The remarkable efficiency of the Music Row studios and the availability of these session musicians meant that the sounds they produced appeared on hundreds of country records across performers, labels, and sometimes even genres.[17]

Each of these musicians made a distinctive contribution to the Sound itself. Floyd Cramer, for instance, experimented with and then honed a "slip note" style, which he later said was like "making an intentional mistake, then recovering."[18] Cramer pointed out that this was quite similar to how steel guitar players "found" their notes as well. This style of piano playing often stood in for the steel guitar that producers increasingly left off of country records. In this way, the new sound preserved a form of continuity with country's hillbilly past while still maintaining the desired association with a more modern approach. The Sound also depended on the close harmonies of the Anita Kerr Singers and the "oohs" and "aahs" of these singers and the Jordanaires. In tandem with a common use of echo chambers improvised in the original studios and later built into the new Music Row studios, this new vocal style surrounded the singer's lead vocal and definitively marked a Nashville Sound record.

In 1957, Ferlin Husky's softer, lusher, version of the country song "Gone" was the number one country single and spent ten weeks at the top of the country charts. Husky's recording, made in Bradley's studio, gained attention for its more ethereal sound (what background singer Millie Kirkham referred to as "kind of a soprano floating around in the clouds"), achieved through the use of a background choir of voices and the echo chamber in which they were recorded.[19] These became defining features of the country records produced at Bradley's studio. Along with larger developments within country pop (including Eddy Arnold's use of a full orchestra), numerous imitations of Husky's sound eventually crystallized into a recognizable new style. The general musical components of the Nashville Sound were the use of background choir groups and orchestrated strings instead of steel guitar and fiddle, and a lead vocal that consciously avoided the nasal twang often associated with country vocals.[20]

As the neighborhood of Music Row developed and expanded, the phrase "Nashville Sound" gained even more traction from this easy spatial association with the congregation of recording sites within Nashville. Music Row thus developed simultaneously with country's distillation of the new pop-country sound and its attendant commercial success.[21] A wide range of figures began using the phrase to describe both the new country-pop direction put forth by the studios of Music Row and the general sense of rising commercial success that the recordings generated. The phrase was used as early as 1958, and was common enough to be referenced with little expository description by 1963.[22] Pinning down an exact definition, though, would prove difficult. In 1963, Chet Atkins (who along with Owen Bradley was one of the admitted architects of the Sound) ambiguously described it as a "state of mind reflected in the spontaneous enthusiasm of the product."[23] Over time, the Nashville Sound came to take on negative connotations, though the tradition of referring to the Sound in terms of a vague "feeling" continued into the 1970s. Paul Hemphill, in his 1970 journalistic tract on the phenomenon of the Sound, portrayed it as "the loose, relaxed, improvised feeling found on almost anything recorded out of Nashville today."[24] The Nashville Sound quickly became the symbol for a new incarnation of country music: slick, overproduced, and expressly commercial. Regardless of one's feeling about this development, it was clear that these characteristics would have been impossible to associate with country music even as late as the end of the 1950s; as chapter 1 showed, prejudicial depictions and understandings of hillbilly music still dominated national perspectives throughout the 1950s. Earlier industry figures undoubtedly played a role in the production of these images and roles, but they had done so in a more or less self-conscious attempt to create an appealing and in some cases marketable blend of rural and urban, contemporary and rustic. Given the prevalence, however, of a national discourse that missed this subtlety, the next generation of country music promoters would be much less likely to see the value of such a syncretic urban and rural blend.

The Country Music Association and "Country Comes to Town"

As the genre coalesced and expanded in Nashville, leading figures within the industry increasingly looked to the idea of the city as a way to distance the genre from the continuing negative associations of its rural past. They themselves presumably understood the ability of country stars to blend rural and urban but were worried that outsiders did not. Before 1958, the beginnings of the Nashville Sound germinated out of a combination of individual experimentation in the studio and a kind of free-floating dialogue about the future of country music playing out on the pages of trade journals and in the larger music industry press. Producers experimented with adding certain instruments or flourishes to their records, and journals editorialized or more indirectly commented on the relative value of these changes. The Country Music Association (CMA), established in the late 1950s, however, began to outline a strategy to take these shifts in the nature of the music and use them to enlarge country's audience and reach. The CMA formed out of the meetings of various concerned individuals within the network of country music institutions and specifically sought out members from every corner of the industry. The original board of directors contained two slots each for the following nine categories: publishers, artists, management, disc jockeys, radio, records, trade journals, composers, and nonaffiliated individuals.[25]

The industry had only very recently coalesced around certain generic features as well as institutional sites within Nashville. Prior to the CMA's formation, the industry lacked a formal leadership organization. The Opry itself, along with its host station, WSM, had previously charted a course for the nascent industry (though it was hardly the only powerful player) by virtue of the show's unmatched audience and the gravitational force that the Opry exerted on most hillbilly musicians and singers. The CMA, of course, recognized the significance of the Opry but did not necessarily assign it more importance than any other radio program. The association's executive director, Harry Stone, in his 1960 published summary of the evolution of the industry, pointed to the many different cities with their own live country programs, rather than singling out WSM and Nashville. In fact, nowhere in his fairly detailed summary of the genre's history did the word "Opry" appear.[26]

But despite their differences, the association's development was actually facilitated by structures in place because of the Opry. One example was the WSM Disc Jockey Festival, which in 1958 became a site for the CMA's first pronouncements on its public relations strategy. The organization had formed its charter only months before and was still struggling with fundraising by the time of this 1958 meeting. The festival's keynote speaker (and former program manager at WSM), publisher Jack Stapp, established national exposure for country music as the organization's prime goal: "If country music does not become more accepted nationally . . . if we do not saturate the country with good publicity, if we do not educate the public, we must be prepared to suffer the consequences."[27] The recent decline in the number of country stations across the nation (a product of both the rock-and-roll boom and the trend toward Top 40 formats) figured prominently in the CMA's vision of a genre in struggle. In 1953, 65 percent of the nation's radio stations played country music at some point in the day; by 1961, the CMA estimated that only 36 percent were playing any country at all.[28]

Stapp and the other founders of the CMA saw inherent commercial potential in the sonic developments that had already begun to transform the genre, and realized the organization's prime concern would be convincing key players in the broader national music landscape of this possibility. They chartered the CMA to begin the "fostering, publicizing and promoting of country music, by bringing the commercial possibilities of country music to the attention of advertisers, advertising agencies, station managers, and radio and TV networks."[29] For instance, *Broadcasting* still relied on older, stereotypically comical notions of the music; a 1959 article on Connie Gay's uncanny ability to sell country music to city people scornfully described the music as "a deafening mixture of scraping fiddles, wheezing accordions and the wails of a love-struck mountain maiden singing through her nose."[30] The phrase "mountain maiden" evoked a much earlier time period, and the aural cacophony these lines suggested did not resonate with the songs of the early Nashville Sound era. Such a description might have been commonplace fifteen years earlier, but with the changes of the Nashville Sound already well underway, the language was jarring.

The CMA resented persistent assumptions about the intelligence, taste, and even hygiene of the musicians and their fans, which came to the fore at a series of congressional hearings in the late 1950s.[31] The CMA believed (quite often correctly) that even as country stars moved ever closer to pop (both in terms of sound and commercial reach), these outdated ideas about hillbilly music still held sway with national journalists, station managers, and, importantly, advertising agencies. The CMA's leadership set out to further persuade networks and advertisers to overcome their misguided assumptions about the income, intelligence, and geographic location of country's fans in order to make the genre a truly national phenomenon. They circulated numerous mailings and press releases, gave presentations at agency meetings, and corresponded directly with disc jockeys as well. The CMA looked to emphasize that country fans were no longer rural hillbillies but were in fact modern urban consumers, and because of this, new country stations could be profitable for their sponsors.

As part of this central strategic decision, then, the CMA endorsed the musical changes already afoot on Music Row. The CMA's 1960 mailing to advertising agencies in fact carried an implicit endorsement of the stylistic changes associated with the emerging Nashville Sound and explicitly connected the new sound to reaching new urban audiences: "No longer the toe-tappin', fiddle-twanging music of the backwoods, country music has emerged from the darkness to become a highly commercial format for local radio. This modern 'folk' music can be programmed to a vast consuming audience in any metropolitan city."[32] This description harshly used the stick of country music's present to beat its past. The mailing explicitly rejected two key elements of the traditional country sound with one crucial hyphenated phrase ("fiddle-twanging"), and located the older style of country music temporally in the past and spatially in the "darkness" of the backwoods. For the CMA, it was not just that the audience for the traditional music had expanded, bringing the music of the backwoods *to* the city; rather, the music itself had been transformed. This transformation was underscored as well by the modifier "modern." The CMA acknowledged the historic prejudice against backwoods hillbilly music while at the same time quite clearly geographically distancing contemporary country music from the hillbilly music of the past.

The CMA endorsed the new Sound and then attempted to persuade country disc jockeys on the best way to sell the music. The CMA approached disc jockeys to ensure that country shows and country stations did not devolve into corny schlock that drew on and in turn perpetuated hillbilly stereotypes. Rather, its leaders sternly encouraged stations to treat country music with sincerity and sophistication. These exhortations invoked the dominant national hillbilly stereotype that had so exaggerated the Opry's rusticity a decade previously.[33] The CMA directly invoked the older set of hillbilly stereotypes as part of their argument for the need to reevaluate country performers and their fans. A CMA letter specifically lecturing disc jockeys and radio station managers on the importance of country radio show titles made the perceived prejudice against which they were fighting explicit: "There may be some frankly ashamed to admit that they listen to 'Corncob Hoedown.' The industry has come a long way in recent years and no one can deny that Country & Western has grown up. We are not a group of raggedy, country boys and girls with missing front teeth. We have acquired status. In choosing a title for your show, make it one that a listener would not hesitate to tell a friend about."[34] Clearly worried about the rustic associations conjured by a title like "Corncob Hoedown," the letter emphasized country's new class distinction. The CMA saw a serious, respectful presentation of its music as the best way to approach the adult market.[35]

Four years later, Tex Ritter told an audience of sales and marketing executives, "But the Country and Western entertainer has grown up. To think of today's Country artist as an illiterate rube with a long beard, bare feet, and a crock jug would be as big a mistake as comparing a quiet country lane to the Pennsylvania Turnpike. He is a big time entertainer."[36] These frequent references to missing front teeth, corncobs and hoedowns, bare feet, and jugs of liquor drew on a caricature of the hillbilly that the CMA still believed to be the dominant association with its music. The CMA's direction to radio station personnel in some ways ideologically disagreed with the ethos behind the Opry's stage presentations of the 1940s and 1950s (like the exaggerated rustic stylings of the Minnie Pearl character, for instance). In fact, the new approach adopted by the CMA and taken up by many other industry figures argued that clinging to comical or idyllic visions of the genre's rural past was holding the genre back commercially. Instead of fully deconstructing the stereotypes, however, this project ended up reifying them in a way by suggesting that country performers and fans were *no longer* barefoot, drunken rubes. This discourse did not dispute the stereotypes but instead displaced them onto the genre's past.

In order to counter these persistent hillbilly stereotypes, the CMA aggressively highlighted the *urbanity* of both country fans and stars. Its efforts to convince advertising agencies of the commercial viability of country radio stations centered on highlighting the fans' residence within metropolitan areas around the nation and not just the farms of the Southeast or the hills of Appalachia. Unlike some traditionalist country fans, the CMA did not buy in to the notion that country belonged in the country, that rural Americans had any kind of exclusive claim to country music; in fact, the association's promotional materials repeatedly argued the reverse. As with the CMA's official declaration that country music was no longer the fiddle-twanging of the backwoods, the organization's vision of country fans firmly located them in metropolitan areas. In the 1960s, the CMA began to claim more forcefully that country music fans were the backbone not just of America's rural spaces but more crucially of its urban areas. As a 1960 CMA mailing to three hundred advertising agency executives and time-buyers proclaimed, the country music audience was composed of "the every-day working people of any city large or small—the housewife, mill worker, fisherman, truck driver—in short, the people the advertiser wants to reach."[37] The mailing kept the idea of "every-day working people" (the very much still beating heart of country music's identity) but removed any trace of the rural. The jobs were still blue collar but did not involve working the land. The geographic locale of this imagined audience was urban and national.

In the end, the promotional endeavors and geographic cultural positioning of the CMA worked. In terms of both commercial success and urban locations, country music had of course been "coming to town" since the beginning of its commercial career. But the early 1960s witnessed a large-scale awareness of that fact, and the language most often chosen to express this awareness invoked the migration from country to city.[38] This trajectory was frequently captured with the phrase "country comes to town," which was openly used in this period to celebrate country music's commercial success in journal articles, advertisements, and album liner notes.[39] The phrase was ubiquitous, but the geographic journey that it imagined missed the mark slightly; country music had been imbricated in urban spaces since its beginnings as a commercial genre in the 1920s.[40]

No matter that country music had been previously recorded in New York, Chicago, and Los Angeles, the level of sophisticated production on the Nashville recordings conditioned an understanding of the music as *newly* urban. The discourse was referring to an urban sensibility as much as it was an urban geography; the music was figured as more technologically urban even as it was now recorded more often in the less demographically urban Nashville. In this context, a series of album titles in the first half of the 1960s played with a mildly ironic city-country pairing, including Nashville Sound pianist Floyd Cramer's *Country Piano, City Strings;* Roberta Sherwood's *Country Songs for City People;* and Slim Whitman's *Country Songs, City Hits.* Whitman's 1960 album title in particular suggested that the songs could become a "hit" only in the city, that they were purely (and merely) songs out in the country. The back cover essay began, "To paraphrase an old saying: 'You can take the song out of the Country, but you can't take the Country out of the song.' Actually, *nobody wants to;* Country songs are too good as is and, besides, they're doing too well in the city! This album is proof of that statement; every one of these songs came from the Country, and every one was a big hit in the city—*all* cities, to be exact."[41] The essay fully endorsed the notion of a discrete city-country divide, replicating and rhetorically drawing on the easy but slippery assumption that the country was a place distinct from the city. But the essay tracked an explicit geographic journey that emphasized both the songs' origins in the country and their successful transition to the city. The text's emphatic declaration that the country songs had become hits in *all* cities paralleled the inclusive wording in the CMA's mailing to ad agencies, which referred to "the everyday working people of any city." Like the CMA's materials, the album liner notes essay contained no trace of regional difference or particularity. The essay pridefully announced the success Whitman's songs had with urban listeners while simultaneously making an argument that they remained, at heart, true country songs.

Whitman's formulation, with its use of the "can't take the country out of the boy" cliché, further contained a clear assumption that "country" as a category was not solely geographic. After all, the classic formula only works if "country" can also be something portable, an essence that remains intact even as its people are far from the farm. In this regard, "country" means actual rural space in the first part of the phrase (the country from which the boy leaves) but refers to country *character* in the second half (the country essence that remains inside him even in a bustling metropolitan space). As it had been for Acuff and Pearl, the trick was to balance both of these aspects of "country," to somehow prove intrinsic character borne out of authentic rural experience while also asserting a comfort level and success within the city. The sound of Whitman's album reflected this balance: the production borrowed much of the Nashville Sound instrumentation, such as the heavy use of choreographed background vocals, but Whitman still managed to slip in his trademark yodeling (on tracks such as "You're the Reason" and "Bouquet of Roses"), a nod to an older style of country vocals.

Despite these nods to more traditional country styles, however, not everyone agreed that the balance of new and old could still truly be called "country." The concerted push for an all-country radio station format was the CMA's response to the larger shift toward Top 40 that imperiled the country industry. The CMA measured success through statistics on the number of radio stations that programmed country at some point in the day as well as the number of country-only stations; by these measures, their efforts were entirely successful.[42] But whether the songs these stations played could truly be called country music was very much up for grabs. Country music culture was not uniform in its approval and enjoyment of the new sound; the Nashville Sound was being heard over more and more stations but much to the *dismay* of many fans. The main voices of dissent in the 1960s came from fans writing letters to trade journals such as *Music City News,* not from industry executives themselves or even prominent artists on the more tradition-minded Opry. Traditionalist fans took to letter to editor pages to bemoan both the specific changes wrought within the new studios of Music Row and the discursive shifts engineered by the CMA. These fans claimed instead that country music required fiddles and simple singing, and that, in fact, "city people" had no place in country. Such fans often blamed the influence of "city people" for the major shifts in the genre that, in their eyes, made country music less authentic. It was not just the association with pop music that tainted the new style in the eyes of resistant traditional fans but also the connection they saw between the new sound and urbanity itself.[43]

The instrumentation changes associated with the Nashville Sound gave rise to heated debates about whether or not the new sound could still be called "true country," and these debates often centered specifically on the geography of the fans and the locations where the new music was conceived and produced. One particularly passionate fan crystallized the oppositional sentiment by arguing that country music was the authentic music of the specifically rural and working-class people of America, and that the musical changes brought about by the Nashville Sound were destroying this connection. His 1965 letter to the editor invoked the key sonic touchstones of the Nashville Sound (horns, background choral groups) while pitting money-grubbing city folks against true country music fans:

Country Music belongs first to the laboring and rural people of this country. They have no musical training and often can't even read music, but when the day's work is done they can take down the old guitar, banjo, or fiddle and play the simple songs that tell about their way of life in a fashion that the finest symphony orchestras in the world can never imitate. They don't want your horns or drums—they don't want your chorus singing in the background or even your Jordanaires making little noises behind them. All that stuff is for the city people who jumped on the country music bandwagon when there turned out to be so much money in it.[44]

The writer belittled the much-celebrated Jordanaires and their "little noises," and drew a stark divide between the "laboring and rural people" (to whom country music truly belongs) and "city people" who were changing the music for, in the writer's opinion, blatantly commercial purposes. In specific contrast with the urban high art of classical symphonies, the letter writer argued that country music belongs to these people since it could be easily played within the home, after a hard day's work, with the simple instruments at hand and nothing else. This argument describes a form of "authentic" country music in opposition to that being produced through modern technology in the studios of urban Nashville. Although it was unclear if this fan specifically blamed the CMA for the original changes, or considered its leaders the "city people" who jumped on the bandwagon, this kind of letter did explicitly contradict the language and ideology of the CMA's promotional efforts. While the CMA had begun saying in 1960 that country music fans were the norm in American cities, this writer structured his lament around a different and more proprietary claim: that country music instead *belonged* to rural people.[45]

This letter's references to true fans' instrumentation preferences were common among other critiques of the Nashville Sound as well. Defenders of the traditional sound of country music often pointed directly to instrumentation changes as the new sound's principal sin. The switch from an older style of fiddle playing to the heavy use of orchestrated string sections or violins served for many as the main lens through which the changes were understood. Many of these fans invoked this shift even as they presumably understood that violins and fiddles are essentially the same instrument with different styles of playing, which made the strong preference for one over the other that much more striking. It was not that violins created intrinsically intolerable music, just that they could not be used for *country* music.

Another fan letter to *Music City News* in 1964 outlined rigid boundaries for country music and argued specifically that the Nashville Sound did not fit the criteria, again, in part because of the move away from the fiddle and toward nontraditional instrumentation: "Country music has gone so . . . Pop that we true Country Music fans don't know what a true Country record sounds like any more. Violins and chorole [*sic*] groups certainly don't belong on a country record. Indeed not—only guitars, steel guitars, fiddles, bass, singer and most of the time dobros. . . . Perhaps the Nashville sound does satisfy a lot of people's musical desires, but all of us true country fans can just look because you all are too busy to care about us."[46] For this fan, the new sound represented an unfortunate shift away from a treasured musical heritage, and the fan blamed city people and the industry's willingness to sidle up to them for commercial reasons. The use of orchestrated violins and other more classical string instruments had become the principal signifier of country music's twin demons of commercialization and urbanization. The CMA did not dispute this: in fact, their 1960 mailing to sponsors and radio stations explicitly rejected the older style of "fiddle-twangin'" music. The Nashville Sound was discussed favorably by stars and producers and belittled by traditionalist fans, but both sides understood the spatial dimensions of the situation.

In the early 1970s, after the commercial success of the Nashville Sound had peaked and many varied voices within country culture had begun to critique the new sounds, retroactive defenses of the Sound also tended to rely on spatial metaphors to associate the musical transition with geographic movement. They positioned the new sound as a necessary shift in the service of an admirable commercial aspiration that allowed country music's stewards to transport the genre from a kind of mythical originary rural space outward into the cities and beyond. In 1972, Eddy Arnold told an interviewer, "I stayed pretty much with the same kind of song. What I did was just change my background a little bit—from the down-home kind of fiddle and steel guitar to the violin. And we orchestrated them, so that we could appeal to Middle America rather than just appealing to the minority. You see, for many, many years country music only appealed to a minority."[47]

Singer-songwriter Dave Dudley defended the transformation in a similar way in a 1973 interview, stating that "they've made it up town or whatever the word might be. I think they've done that for a reason, I don't believe the songs have changed. I think that everybody including me would like to have more people like country music so we've made it more acceptable by putting on violins or whatever they do."[48] As with Arnold's argument, for Dudley the violins were a virtually interchangeable piece that could be added in without altering the core of the song or its genre identification. Dudley's dismissive phrase "whatever they do" shifted agency away from the country star and toward an unseen producer or engineer, suggesting that the song's true country authorship and authentic feeling remained intact despite the modifications made by someone else, the producers. This rhetorical move at least made vaguely plausible his declaration that he did not believe "the songs have changed." Arnold and Dudley openly admitted to wider commercial aspirations but did not attach the same negative connotations to commercialism as the irate letter writers who bemoaned the stylistic changes made in the name of increasing country's audience. Arnold and Dudley defended the Nashville Sound by minimizing the "background" changes while maintaining that the songs themselves were still true country songs, and in fact had not changed at all. They made this provocative claim despite the fact that, as letters from angry fans showed, many fans *defined* country music in terms of instrumentation choices.

Both artists also invoked geographic markers, "uptown" or "Middle America," in line with the need to appeal to wider audiences. Dudley's notion of "uptown" differentiated the modern music from its rural past, and Arnold's "Middle America" signified a desire to move away from associations with the rural South. The trick for the Nashville Sound's defenders was to suggest that country music, whose principal feature was often its authentic connection to "the people" (a connection often defined in terms of earnest lyrics and natural singing), could still retain this country character while adding clearly marked urban accoutrements and openly moving "uptown." Following a tradition established by performers like Little Jimmy Dickens and Roy Acuff, these defenders argued that inherent country character was not necessarily dependent on place or instrumentation. Inspired by "Town and Country" promoter Connie Gay as early as the late 1950s, one journalist described this idea by declaring, "Country music is not really a kind of music; it is a style, a way of playing. The one quality indispensable to a country music performer is 'down homeliness'—an amalgam of simple virtues of the kind that your sweet old Grandmother used to praise."[49] This powerful understanding of country music as a style or set of virtues resonated with descriptions of the Sound that persisted into the 1970s. But in the late 1960s, Nashville's Music Row offered country music an opportunity to combine the new sound with a new understanding of the possibilities of urban space.

"Shantytown USA": Music Row and Urban Renewal

Country had never really had a clear-cut urban "home," and the establishment of Nashville as country's primary base, in addition to creating a cohesive set of studios, musicians, and publishing houses, provided a platform for the industry to use its own neighborhood to promote the increasingly salient idea of country "coming to town."[50] Country music studios had been constructed on or near Sixteenth Avenue since the mid-1950s, but in the mid-1960s, the industry's leading promotional organization settled there as well. The CMA's journal, *CMA Close-Up,* set up shop in an office building across the street from Owen Bradley's studio in 1965, surrounded by multiple publishing houses, talent agencies, and outposts for major labels such as Decca and Capitol. The journal's masthead featured the downtown Nashville skyline as viewed from Music Row, and its columns and features covered local news events as well as business and personal notices about Nashville-based recording artists. The spatial orientation of the journal mirrored the consolidation of Music Row as a self-conscious industry neighborhood. The cover design of another industry journal, *Music City News,* also employed a shot of the downtown Nashville skyline from the perspective of Music Row, with some of the Row's more modern buildings in the foreground. This was a particularly urban and modern vision of Nashville, which established a specific geographic identification for the area.

As Music Row grew both geographically and commercially, Nashville's metropolitan government began to show more interest in the industry and work with Music Row leaders to smooth the neighborhood's growth. Municipal leaders began to attend more country music functions to show the industry its due respect. Also, the CMA worked with the metropolitan government to secure land for the genre's first hall of fame. The metropolitan government leased a prime piece of real estate at the north end of Music Row for the construction of the building, and in 1967, country music's first hall of fame opened. Over the course of the 1960s, and especially with the hall's construction, businesses in the surrounding neighborhood increasingly began to recognize the importance of Music Row's presence.

More neighborhood service and retail shops changed their names to reflect the area's emergence as a distinct neighborhood landmark, and music-themed souvenir shops also opened in response to the increased flow of fans who were starting to discover the neighborhood and include it on their country music–themed pilgrimages. Businesses across the street and around the corner from the hall started using the moniker "Music City" in their names; signs for Music City Motors, Music City Service Center and Gas, and Music City Esso had all cropped up by the end of 1967.[51] Even though the moniker "Music City U.S.A." had been coined in 1950 and did not necessarily refer only to country music, the increased density of the industry's presence in the late 1960s created this spatial association.

The explosive growth of Music Row over the course of the late 1950s and early 1960s gave the industry a material investment in the urban space of the neighborhood as well as a cultural investment in transforming the urban space to construct a particular image for the genre. As Music Row developed and consolidated, many industry leaders hoped to use country's new neighborhood as yet another opportunity to refute tired hillbilly stereotypes. In much the same way that the CMA and promoters of the Nashville Sound hoped to show that country music did not have to be rustic and backwoods, those with an investment in the future of Music Row hoped to use the neighborhood to demonstrate that the genre could easily make a home in a clean, modern, upscale urban space.

Given this interest in promoting a specific image for the neighborhood, various figures were concerned about its structural and aesthetic integrity. Don Davis, whose Wilderness Music offices were in the heart of Music Row (operating since 1965 out of a house two blocks from Bradley's original studio), invoked fairly extreme poverty and dilapidation when he publicly speculated, "Sometimes I wonder if Metro wouldn't rather just take our tax money the way they're doing now and let us stay here in 'Shantytown' from now on."[52] The reference to Shantytown contrasted sharply with the plans for modern office and studio construction that were either in the planning stages or already underway. An article in the 1968 *Country Song Roundup Annual* invoked a similar image of dilapidation when it described the prospect of a visitor coming to Music Row to get a glimpse of the "magic" and finding something else entirely: "Some of the buildings are old with wrinkled faces that tell their age by loose hinges and sagging windows. The streets and byways are narrow, as well as dimly lit. And the general look of the neighborhood isn't the best."[53] It was this emphasis on the aging structures and infrastructure in the purportedly deteriorating neighborhood that Music Row planners were working to counter in the public's imagination. Another article from earlier in the decade referenced "rickety homes" and "low-rent apartments" as reasons for renovation.[54] Popular songwriter Tom T. Hall, in describing his first days in Nashville living on Music Row, disparagingly referred to the neighborhood with the ultimate marker of urban poverty: "The first apartment I had here was on 16th Avenue—when it was really a slum."[55] Like Davis's reference to "Shantytown," Hall's provocative use of "slum" strongly suggested that an urban neighborhood, without proper maintenance and planning, could be a poor fit for modern country music.

It is also possible that Music Row figures had another neighborhood in mind when they made these dire proclamations. Music Row developed on the edge of a mostly white neighborhood that bordered a predominantly African American residential area. The census for the tract east of Sixteenth indicated the population was 90 percent African American in 1960, while west of Sixteenth was 95 percent white.[56] In the push for Music Row Boulevard, industry figures who were advocating for renewal referred to the dilapidation of the neighborhood, but the greater preponderance of dilapidated structures were on the eastern edge of the historic African American neighborhood of Edgehill, several blocks east of Sixteenth.

Instead of thinking of country's urban locale as contradicting their ideal image of country music simply for being urban, key industry figures instead saw it as the *wrong* kind of urban space and looked, as did many other municipalities and groups, to urban renewal to fashion the right kind of space for their neighborhood. The dilapidation of the neighborhood did not fit the industry's idea of itself nor did the industry see it as an inevitable product of coming to the city; their support for urban renewal showed a belief that a city could in fact provide a comfortable home for country music. In fact, as late as the fall of 1968, investors (led by Eddy Arnold) planned on building a fourteen-story office building in the heart of Music Row. The building would have housed record labels, publishing offices, and talent agencies as well as a restaurant and a rooftop with a swimming pool and heliport.[57] This was hardly an effort to keep the Row "downhome"; instead, it was part of a collective effort to build the neighborhood into a more dense urban space. Industry leaders looked to expand vertically, tearing down older buildings and replacing them with bold new construction, to fully differentiate the Row as a modern urban space. Music Row leaders' vision of the future found its most perfect outlet when Nashville's urban planners first included the neighborhood in their plans for the larger area's renewal.

Nashville was one of the first American cities to fully utilize federal funding to embark on several large-scale projects between the late 1940s and the mid-1960s.[58] Nashville civic leaders used urban renewal beginning in 1949 to raze blighted housing and remake three neighborhoods: the downtown area, a large portion of East Nashville, and Edgehill. When Congress passed the 1949 Housing Act, Nashville's already existing Housing Authority seized the opportunity for garnering federal funds, razing ninety-six acres of low-income housing north of Capitol Hill in order to construct a leg of interstate highway and commercial and retail development. Nashville then began the East Nashville Renewal Project, which involved both the replacement and rehabilitation of substandard housing.[59] Although not near Music Row, the success of these two projects led the municipal government to apply for federal funding for even more renewal, and savvy industry figures saw an opening for their own neighborhood.

Music Row's immediate neighbor to the west, Vanderbilt University, began looking to expand its campus in the early 1950s. In fact, university officials had been somewhat quietly buying proximal properties as they came on the market.[60] The Nashville government, however, soon saw Vanderbilt's desire for expansion as a way to bring federal urban renewal funds to the city.[61] A clause added to the federal 1954 Housing Act regarding universities, hospitals, and other public amenities promised that any purchases these institutions made for land expansion would count toward the one-third local contribution which federal urban renewal regulations required.[62] This made privately planned university expansion an attractive and inexpensive way for cities to secure federal funding for improving the infrastructure and housing base of the university's surrounding neighborhoods. Private spending could count for the local share of public funding. Despite assertions by many community members that the areas around Vanderbilt were not really deteriorating and did not need renewal, the Nashville Housing Authority approved the school's expansion plans as part of a larger municipal project, and the nearby Music Row was, at least initially, swept along in its wake.

The Nashville Housing Authority, which was in charge of urban renewal in addition to public housing, announced the plan in December 1960 along with projects in three other areas. As a smaller part of this larger project, the Housing Authority saw a potential boulevard through

Music Row as the answer to traffic congestion between the city's south-western residential neighborhoods and the major east-west thoroughfares that funneled in to downtown. Twenty-First Avenue South was one of the city's most congested streets, in part because of the university and in part because it was one of the few arteries connecting the two parts of the city, and the boulevard between Sixteenth and Seventeenth Avenues was intended to divert much of that traffic.[63]

The prospect of an impressive new boulevard running through the heart of Music Row, part of a much larger urban renewal project in the planning stages, led industry figures to believe that renewal could turn their neighborhood into a more tourist-friendly urban space with less substandard housing, better infrastructure and sewage systems, and open sight lines to make the space more aesthetically pleasing.[64] In these efforts, industry boosters did not downplay the urbanity of Nashville but in fact trumpeted the urban possibilities of Music Row. Conscious of the notion of their historical role as barely tolerated hillbillies in a city that billed itself as "The Athens of the South," industry leaders, artists, and fans hoped that "Music City Boulevard" would solidify country's place as the premier industry, both symbolically and economically, in Nashville, as well as making Nashville itself a premier American music city. Nonetheless, despite the industry's own ambitions for the project, the boulevard was never planned as or designed to be "Music City Boulevard." It was not until the industry seized on the idea and began to bill it as such that the urban renewal project and country music became linked, and the boulevard's informal name and attachment to country music became salient.[65]

In April 1967, however, funding limitations forced the federal government to break the project down into two phases; the first stage was the land specifically associated with Vanderbilt's growth and the second that of Scarritt and Peabody Colleges, which were much smaller but closer to Music Row.[66] Thus, the piece of the boulevard designed to go straight through Music Row was delayed until the second phase. With the bulk of the university purchases now attached solely to the first phase, and therefore fewer university dollars counting toward the local contribution, the debate over the boulevard became a debate over whether *local* funds would be used to renovate Music Row. The music industry focused its attention on pressuring the metropolitan council to allocate the money, even as the project had been driven from the beginning by Vanderbilt's expansion plans.

The ambitions held by Music Row leaders never fully factored into Housing Authority planning, despite the industry's important and growing presence in the neighborhood. Music Row leaders were looking for a new way of arranging the visitor experience, in line with their discursive presentation of the new Nashville Sound and the promotional efforts of the CMA, which could showcase modern attractive features, not the dilapidation associated with their hillbilly past. Linked to this was the sense that local support for the boulevard would prove the city's interest in presenting the neighborhood and country music as viable tourist attractions. Municipal support for country music had always been seen as tenuous at best, and industry leaders and rank-and-file members were keen to be given more visible shows of support from the Nashville establishment.

In these efforts, the music industry in fact had wide support among the Nashville business community; key members of the community saw the boulevard and its effect on country music enterprises as a good investment for the city. Edward Jones, the Nashville Chamber of Commerce's executive director, argued for the boulevard by pointing out, "People write us and tell us they came to see Music City (row) and then couldn't find it."[67] Jones was not affiliated with the industry but still argued that country music provided a benefit to the greater Nashville economy. Likewise, Metropolitan Trustee Glenn Ferguson, a longtime advocate of the music industry, argued that the building of the boulevard would pay for itself in increased tax revenues and suggested, "It seems strange to me that everyone the world over—except the city administration—recognizes the importance of this industry."[68] Ferguson used the worldwide commercial appeal of country music (which the CMA had frequently couched in urban terms) to argue for lucrative spatial changes in the Music Row neighborhood. As with the CMA and the promotional discourse around the Nashville Sound, this argument highlighted country music's success with fans from beyond rural America. In fact, Ferguson positioned the metropolitan government, not country music, as out of step with the times.

In the end, though, the University Center Urban Renewal Project, as its title indicated, was principally driven by the expansion of Nashville universities, most notably Vanderbilt University. While the Row was ultimately excised from the project, the urban renewal debates did provide a platform for discussing the kind of neighborhood Music Row could and should be. At this point, industry figures and their supporters in local business and politics saw the boulevard project as an opportunity for the city government to make a crucial investment in renewing their neighborhood. The Metropolitan Council publicly debated the boulevard issue in October 1970, giving the industry a platform to make its case.[69] Industry figures looked to increase their capital and symbolic investment in Nashville but did not fully have the backing of the city at this point. Mayor Beverly Briley had initially supported the boulevard plans but reversed his stance several months before the council vote, suggesting instead that they convert the two already existing streets to one-way streets. Although key community voices such as Jones and Ferguson had argued that the boulevard was necessary for the city, as country music was such an important part of the city by this point, Briley took the opposite stance, saying at the time of the vote, "Music Row is only one of hundreds of projects desperately needed in our city." Councilman James Tuck echoed Briley's sentiment, noting, "There are 35 other (councilmanic) districts which need projects also."[70]

By contrast, both local newspapers were in favor of the boulevard and couched their support in terms of how crucial country music was to the city. When Briley reversed his stance ahead of the council vote, the *Nashville Tennessean*'s editorial, "Music Row Promise Ought to Be Honored," referred to Briley's flip-flop on the issue as a "breach of faith with one of the community's largest and most appreciated industries."[71] U.S. Representative Richard Fulton echoed this line of thinking in a telegram to Mayor Briley: "The music industry people have just been too good to Nashville to let this matter drag on. They have certainly helped us, and now, when they need it, I feel that we should give them all the help we can."[72] The notion of reciprocity and symbolic support at times seemed to outweigh the economic arguments as the most compelling reasons for building Music City Boulevard.

Ultimately, the Metropolitan Council did not buy the industry's arguments on the economic or symbolic importance of the boulevard, to Nashville or to country music. Once the boulevard was moved to phase two of the University Center Project, and federal funds were no longer guaranteed, the council balked at the inflated price tag of the needed property. Furthermore, land speculation in the neighborhood ahead of the renewal project had increased the land values and driven up the city government's price tag for the entire project.[73] Despite the vocal community support from the chamber of commerce, the city's two newspapers, and other government figures such as Ferguson, the council vote went against the boulevard in October 1970.[74] In the aftermath of the vote, music industry figures focused on the council's lack of willpower. The defeat on the council vote led to widespread disillusionment with the metropolitan government among country music leaders, and industry leaders stopped attending council meetings and planning sessions for the future of Music Row.[75]

Two multistory plans for new office buildings were on the books but were both cancelled when boulevard plans fell through. Also, media coverage suggested that, with the boulevard plans stalled, there were "slums creeping up around Music Row."[76] For all the rhetoric of "country coming to town" and the multimillion dollar success of the Nashville Sound, the industry was unable to convince the city of Nashville that its new urban home needed any substantial modernization. Even as the CMA's efforts to convince radio and advertising industries that country fans were urban consumers were wildly successful, out on Music Row, in spite of the increasing recognition of country music's importance to the city of Nashville, country music leaders were ultimately unable to fully remake their neighborhood into the clean, modern, showcase to which they aspired.

This failure may in part have been tied to persistent assumptions about the music that ran counter to the CMA's and Music Row leaders' vision of country music as a modern urban phenomenon. For instance, even media coverage in support of neighborhood renewal relied on rural iconography to describe the plight of an industry that was trying to distance itself from the negative associations of such imagery. An editorial cartoon in the *Nashville Tennessean* two months after the eventual council vote against the boulevard juxtaposed two images; the first showed a well-dressed gentleman in an automobile driving past a sign that read "Nashville: MUSIC CITY, U.S.A., World Famed Home of 'The Nashville Sound.'" The second showed the same visitor encountering what looked to be a farmhouse, with a nearby shed; one lone, dead tree; and a sign tacked onto a bent stick in the ground reading "Music City's Music Row."[77] The headline, "A Tale of Two Cities," highlighted the contradiction between the world-famous Nashville Sound and its dilapidated neighborhood, but the image suggested *rural* poverty instead of the density more often associated with an urban neighborhood. Even as country figures used the language of urban poverty ("a slum") to describe their neighborhood, the notion that country's home base must be inherently rundown, dilapidated, and above all *rural* still persisted.

Despite the commercial progress country music had made, and despite the deliberate efforts on the part of the CMA and others to paint country as a plausible urban genre, pervasive hyperbolic rhetoric continued to associate country music with unredeemable rusticity, even in publications produced by the industry itself. In an article in the 1970 *Country Music*

Who's Who, for instance, Jack-Warren Ostrode insisted that the "credit for the appeal to present-day audiences really belongs to the pioneers of yesterday who wrote their songs from the privacy of their souls and sang them lustily behind a rusty plow on an ancient, barren hill. Blessedly, their talents have been constantly re-born in each new generation of Country Music artists."[78] The image of a "lustily" singing plowman played on stereotypes of simple, earthy, plain folk and the bizarre description of an "ancient, barren hill" further distanced these primordial country performers from the modern world. The image was over the top but represented a persistent idea that country music promoters still had to address in their push to market the genre as contemporary and urban.

DESPITE COUNTRY music's long association with rural poverty and humble origins, in the 1960s, the CMA looked to provide the genre with a markedly new socio-spatial identity while still preserving the music's rural spirit and deep connection to "ordinary" Americans. Artists and commentators described the Nashville Sound as more urban or "uptown," country marketers looked to situate their expanding audience in urban areas, and the new constellation of recording studios emerged in a neighborhood that industry figures believed could be turned into an appealing tourist destination through urban renewal. These three developments were linked by their shared investment in the notion that country music and its fans were becoming more urban, and that country's newfound urbanity was preferable to its previous geographic and class markers. For these cultural actors and industry stewards, to make country music more modern meant making it more urban. They associated "the country" with the past and looked to cities as the future of the genre. But as the next chapter shows, urban Nashville contained its own set of complications, and the "country comes to town" discourse that imagined urbanity going hand in hand with modernity and middle-class comfort quickly bumped up against a city experiencing segregation, poverty, and the civil rights struggles which these conditions sparked.

"You Sound Like Us but You Look Like Them"

The Racial Politics of Country Music in the City of Nashville

THE SAME year that the Music Row Boulevard dreams died at the feet of the Nashville Metropolitan Council, a different urban renewal project, this one fully endorsed by the city government, displaced a mostly forgotten figure from the Grand Ole Opry's past. It was the Edgehill Renewal Project, and the storied Opry performer was DeFord Bailey, an African American musician who played harmonica on the Opry from its inception in 1925 until he was unceremoniously fired from the program in 1941. After his dismissal, Bailey lived in Nashville for the rest of his life, operating a shoeshine shop less than a mile from Music Row. This enterprise sustained him until the Nashville Housing Authority claimed both his home and the building that housed his shop, in 1970 and 1971 respectively, to make way for public housing projects. Even though a campaign to recognize Bailey's accomplishments and his importance to Opry history was begun later in the 1970s, in this moment his cause was not championed by the Opry or other prominent figures in the industry. Their silence can best be understood by analyzing the cultural investments in racial identity categories held by many different players within country music culture.

Although many figures within country music culture in the 1960s were quick to suggest that the genre's appeal stemmed from its ability to speak for the everyday concerns of ordinary people, the pressing everyday concerns (decent housing, education, and employment) of African Americans in this era were not found in the public discourse of country music culture. The development of Music Row, the emergence of the Nashville Sound, and the music's subsequent commercial success occurred simultaneously with major transformations in both urban space and racial equality that affected every American city, including Nashville. Nashville was one of the first American cities to take advantage of federal urban renewal dollars, as well as one of the first sites of nonviolent demonstrations for equal access to public accommodations for African Americans. Most figures within the Nashville-based country music industry were no doubt aware of these developments, but by and large, country music discourse did not acknowledge their importance. This separation was intricately tied to prevalent ideas about the presumed racial identities of the genre's performers and fans.

Country Music as a "Ledger of Life": But Whose Life?

At least since the 1950s, hyperbolic descriptions of the power of country music have continually centered on the music's purported ability to tap into the quotidian truth of ordinary Americans' lives.[1] In 1958, the Grand Ole Opry's manager referred to country music as a "ledger of life," boldly declaring of the genre's lyrics, "The words are those that filter through the mind after an exhausting day of honest toil. . . . They're the phrases that bubble through the laughter of a gay holiday . . . or push through gritted teeth when a man lies face down to sob out real grief into the fragrant earth."[2] Songwriter Teddy Bart similarly provided a nearly impossible summary of country's appeal in 1964: "Country music is a simple, uncomplicated music whose lyrics cover practically everything that ordinary people are involved with in their daily lives."[3] Bart suggested that country music was very simple but at the same time somehow encompassed *everything* an ordinary person encountered in her or his daily life. This is, of course, highly improbable: the range of topics covered must be constrained by some kind of parameters and must be linked in some way for any kind of description of the genre's lyrical content to be coherent.

This equation for the lyrics of country music depended on two things that in some ways were mutually incompatible: these figures claimed, on the one hand, that country music detailed the absolute truth of "real life," and, on the other, that the music supposedly spoke for and to "everyone." The particularity necessary to make music speak to real life requires the privileging of certain experiences over others, and the notion that a country song could contain universal truths ignored the quotidian details of ordinary lives that vary across class, race, gender, and geography, among other things. Claims that the music could represent the entire range of everyday experiences were made even more dubious as the 1960s progressed, and massive resistance to segregation and institutional racism affected the daily lives of millions of black and white Americans in the U.S. South. This chapter places the claims about country music's universalism in stark contrast with the genre's avoidance of the central issues affecting African Americans in Nashville and elsewhere during this very period. For example, in a 1965 *Music City News* letter to the editor, disc jockey Jon Swope celebrated the new appeal and sweep of the Nashville Sound, arguing that "country music is music for the people . . . people in the towns, and in the country . . . young and old . . . rich and poor . . . white collar or blue."[4] Swope set up a series of clichéd dichotomies that in 1965 could have easily included "white and black," but which in this case pointedly did not.

In the middle of the century, Nashville boosters were heavily invested in the idea of promoting Nashville as a kind of "middle space," marked more by moderation and a greater embrace of modernity than that purportedly found elsewhere in the South. This was also true in the 1950s on the issue of civil rights, at least in terms of how the civic elite framed the debates. Municipal leaders trumpeted the city's reputation for moderation, and there was some evidence to support their claims. Mayor Ben West in the early 1950s supported an ordinance that changed the city council electoral process from at-large elections to mostly district-by-district representation, enabling two African Americans to be elected. He also successfully argued that black police officers should be on the force.[5]

In the late 1950s, though, public school integration was the issue where Nashville most vocally trumpeted its progressivism. Three years after Owen Bradley set up his recording studio, the Nashville Board of Education drew up what came to be known as the Nashville Plan, in accordance with the ruling in *Brown v. Board of Education,* to be implemented in the fall of 1957. Nashville's proposal was one of the first in the country and called for a gradual integration of one grade per year, starting with the first grade, while also granting parents of both races the chance to opt out via written request if their child was zoned into a school in which they were the minority.[6] The plan met with a mixed response.[7] A diverse set of Nashville interests, including business, retail, and newspaper concerns, wanted to avoid the kind of ugly and destructive clashes that had marked civil rights movements in other parts of the South. Roughly six hundred mostly white citizens had formed the Nashville Community Relations Conference, an integrated mixture of businessmen, clergymen, and teachers who did not necessarily support the principle of integration but were publicly opposed to extralegal efforts to fight it.[8]

Nashville's black press saw the support of the white community as crucial to the movement, though they understood white support to be generally rooted more in traditionalist support for the rule of law than out of any particular belief in black equality. Even an African American newspaper generally very critical of the municipal government, the *Nashville Globe and Independent,* supported the integration efforts of the city's civic leaders, praising West and the pro-integration forces within Nashville while emphasizing the significant role that outside agitator John Kasper (of the White Citizen Councils) played in resisting Nashville's 1957 integration plan. The paper argued that Kasper and his followers were outnumbered "at a time when the best element of Nashville's people have become reconciled to carrying out desegregation along the lines recommended by the United States Supreme Court."[9] In fact, Kasper was jailed multiple times by the Nashville police for incitement to riot, and when finally released the third time, left Nashville for over a year.[10]

After the schools began to be integrated, the next arena in the battle for equal rights was public accommodations, starting downtown. Even though other sit-ins became more famous, the Nashville sit-ins had their genesis before the more famous Greensboro, North Carolina, protests of early 1960. The presence of black universities in Nashville was a crucial factor in the early beginnings of this movement.[11] A group of students from Fisk University had organized the previous year to apply civil disobedience to the problem of integrating Nashville's public accommodations. They performed test sit-ins in the final months of 1959, sitting at lunch counters but leaving when asked. Between February and May 1960, massive organized sit-in efforts forced downtown Nashville businesses to integrate their lunch counters and other public spaces. The protestors faced violence from white counter-protesters, jail time, and, in one case, expulsion from Vanderbilt University for their role in the movement.[12] Generally regarded as the most philosophically grounded and well-organized of the sit-in movements, the Nashville protests succeeded after only three months in persuading the Nashville government and downtown business interests to agree to promote the integration of downtown public spaces.

The key event was the segregationists' bombing of black activist Alexander Looby's house. The following day protesters marched on City Hall and a shaken Mayor West agreed, when asked, that segregation was wrong.[13]

Race relations and civil rights struggles in Nashville have rarely been associated with the country music industry's presence there. In fact, it is nearly impossible to find any trace of country music as an economic, demographic, or cultural force in histories of the civil rights movement within Nashville.[14] This is the case even though the neighborhood of Music Row developed near key sites of struggle in the movements. As the previous chapter shows, the first studios on what would become Music Row were constructed on the cusp of a salient racial boundary. Furthermore, Music Row was less than a mile from a triangle of black universities—Meharry Medical College, Fisk University, and Tennessee State University (TSU). Villa Place, the street that ran parallel to Sixteenth a half block to the east, was remembered later as being the home of several of TSU's jazz musicians in the late 1950s. With so many musicians in town, Nashville's night clubs did become sites for integrated jam sessions, though not without incident or unequal restrictions on participation. In the 1950s, white country session musicians like Hank Garland and Buddy Harman could play in black clubs, but the reverse situation happened with much less frequency.[15]

The first studios on what would become Music Row were constructed even before the integration of Nashville's public schools and before the sit-in movement began. It did not take long, however, before the movement made a highly visible foray into the surrounding neighborhood. In addition to the downtown sit-ins, which were front-page news in Nashville for months, Music Row also became a site of civil rights resistance when the integration movement expanded to other commercial ventures. The blocks to the west and east of Bradley's and other studios were primarily residential, but the nearby commercial district one block south on Sixteenth Avenue served both black and white customers.[16] In 1961, integration efforts began to address hiring practices, and Student Nonviolent Coordinating Committee (SNCC) leaders in Nashville targeted an H. G. Hills grocery store two blocks from Bradley's studio, at the corner of Sixteenth and Grand. For three weeks, integrated groups of picketers protested the store's discriminatory hiring practices, encountering violent opposition from groups of white youth as well as arrests and beatings courtesy of the Nashville police force.[17] This incident and others transpired almost literally on Music Row's doorstep but was nowhere to be found in the industry's public discourse.

Even as Nashville's municipal leaders promoted the city's support for integrating public accommodations, the city was still structured by unequal access to jobs, education, and housing.[18] Music Row figures could not believably claim ignorance of these facts, as the Row actually bordered one of Nashville's principal sites of prominent black activism. On the east side of Music Row, in Edgehill, opposition to urban renewal provided another visible instance of inequality, as black activists focused on its effects on African American opportunities for affordable housing. Much of this activism centered on the Edgehill Urban Renewal Project, which in fact adjoined Music Row (and eventually displaced DeFord Bailey in 1970). This project demolished older single-family homes, to be eventually replaced with public housing units, and caused the relocation of over two thousand mostly African American families.[19] The metropolitan government contributed roughly $12 million to the project, seeing it as central to a larger, citywide battle to protect the city center and surrounding property values from encroaching "slums" and "blight." Housing authority documents pointed to the renewal of "steep and hazardous" streets and the building of amenities such as a new junior high school and a branch of the Nashville Public Library.[20] But the larger renewal project also allowed the housing authority to acquire properties and structures deemed substandard and construct new public housing projects, in effect becoming a landlord for many low-income residents.[21]

Because of these projected consequences, the Edgehill renewal project faced a wide array of organized opposition. A coalition of African American and neighborhood citizen groups (including the interracial Nashville Committee for Decent Housing, the NAACP, and the Nashville Christian Leadership Council) formally complained to federal civil rights agencies, asserting that urban renewal in Edgehill would mean intensified segregation, as displaced residents would be forced into segregated public housing or the few nonwhite neighborhoods in other parts of the city.[22] Furthermore, they argued, homeowners were not getting fair value for their homes: appraisals were unfairly lowered for homes within the Edgehill boundaries, compared to similar homes in other parts of the city. This disparity, compounded by the fact that African American home buyers often had to pay above-market prices for homes in restricted areas, meant that many homeowners were forced into renting by the urban renewal and housing authority policies. Avoiding this topic of discussion did not square with country music's claim to represent the daily struggles of "ordinary folks." The industry's geographic proximity, at least in the

form of the rapidly developing Music Row, makes country music's marked
indifference to the everyday concerns of African Americans in their neighborhood all the more provocative.

Over the course of the late 1960s, as renewal plans for Music Row
Boulevard intensified and Row figures had to lobby the metropolitan government for funds, music industry players often positioned themselves
and their industry as an underappreciated and marginalized piece of the
economy, scorned by the civic elites of Nashville because of the genre's
negative associations. But the debates over Edgehill's renewal project
showed that other groups, notably the black activists fighting the municipal takeover of the neighborhood, understood the music industry as a
privileged piece of the city's power structure.[23] Before hearings on the proposed renewal plan, African American real estate broker Inman Otey tied
a potential zoning change to the music industry's aim to adjust the nature
of the neighborhood from residential to commercial, declaring, "There
is a distinct segregation pattern being formed in urban renewal in south
Nashville. The University Area is on the other side of 16th Avenue. Part
of the south Nashville urban renewal project will be bought as residential
and will be reclassified as commercial. There will be a Negro reservation
created."[24] More explicitly, at a Metropolitan Council meeting in October
of 1965, councilman and NAACP branch president Mansfield Douglas
specifically referred to the "music industry complex on 16th Avenue South"
as a possible cause for the controversial shift in zoning on Hawkins and
Bigler Streets from residential to commercial.[25]

In the 1960s, as Music Row developed into a clear country music destination and industry hub, country music was in, but not necessarily of,
the city of Nashville. The industry was not integrated into the community
and not always eager to play up the complexities and specificity of its spatial location. Country music journals only sporadically situated coverage
of the industry within the urban landscape of Nashville, and referred to
the municipal government only when Mayor Beverly Briley recognized
country figures and accomplishments.[26] When they did address Nashville itself, Music Row publications often provided much of the same
municipal propaganda as other boosters, celebrating Nashville's role as a
pioneer in American urban renewal and extolling the city's growth and
stability without focusing on any tensions or problems.[27] In the spring
of 1968, this separation between the industry and its home base crystallized more clearly with the tragic assassination of Martin Luther King,

Jr., and his murder's reverberations through Nashville's African American community.

Martin Luther King's Assassination: "The Show Must Go On"

In the days following King's assassination in another Tennessee music city, the neighborhood of North Nashville became a site of clashes between enraged students of Tennessee A&I State University and police and National Guard forces. Over the course of the weekend, snipers held the guard at bay while fires and protests continued throughout the area.[28] The metropolitan government issued a curfew, and troops were separately sent to seal off the university's campus and protect the downtown area around the Capitol.[29] The curfew meant that night's Grand Ole Opry would have to be cancelled for the first time in its history. According to the *Nashville Tennessean,* however, even though the long lines of visitors waiting to see the program were absent from the downtown neighborhood, there were still some attendees who had not heard the news and showed up at the auditorium Saturday night hoping for a show. Still, Opry officials were on hand to greet the disappointed visitors, and opened up the theater so they could at least walk around, see the stage, and say that they had been there. A city fireman was even on hand, apparently to protect the building from the Opry guests, rather than the Opry guests from potential unrest.[30]

Even though the curfew forced the Opry to cancel the program, the program officials' seeming indifference to the details of the curfew suggested that they did not take it too seriously. In addition, to make it up to visiting fans, longtime Opry figure Roy Acuff engineered an impromptu afternoon show that day in a smaller private venue over his downtown storefront museum. The fact that Opry stars were able and willing to convene a private show in the immediate aftermath of a national tragedy suggests a certain amount of indifference, and the industry press coverage of this show further revealed a divide between Nashville's African American community and country music. The May issue of *Music City News* framed the event through the lens of Roy Acuff thankfully saving the day for the fortunate Opry fans, without even mentioning King's assassination as the cause of the possible unrest: "There's a rumor of a march uptown. A siren screams around the corner. Uniformed men, carrying rifles, and closing places up and down the street. Some people have come into town and looked, and left again. There's a feeling of uneasiness in the streets. But upstairs at Mr. Ed's there's laughter and applause. The lights are up. The show is on. And a small group of Country musicians put on a show a lot of Music City visitors will remember . . . for a long, long time."[31] There is a stark contrast in this passage between the "uniformed men" and sense of uneasiness elsewhere in the city, and the laughter and gaiety of the small club performance. The article mentioned urban unrest in Nashville but distanced the action on the streets of Nashville from the private show at Mr. Ed's, even as the special show took place downtown. In essence, the article focused on the experience of *visitors* to Music City, those fans who had traveled great distances to see their favorite live radio program, reading the tragedy of King's assassination only through the lens of how it affected the Opry. The clear avoidance of the subject of King's death and the specific consequences of the tragedy was striking, suggesting that Opry fans were not emotionally affected by the killing and, furthermore, that white fans could use country music as a diversion from the racial unrest of the period.

A comparison with Detroit and the Motown record company is instructive. As Suzanne E. Smith has argued, the music and culture of Motown was both a product of and an agent in the larger matrix of civil rights struggles on both local and national levels. Motown released recordings of Martin Luther King's speeches and Langston Hughes's poetry (the Hughes album, done in collaboration with a local Detroit poet, was titled *Poets of the Revolution*), booked their artists before integrated audiences in the South, and attempted to resist the displacement of urban renewal by buying and utilizing downtown performing spaces. After King's death, the Motown label contributed performers and money to the Southern Christian Leadership Conference (SCLC) and publicly supported the Poor People's March.[32] Very few, if any, figures associated with the genre of country music made any such recognition of the event and the larger social issues that were entwined with King's assassination.[33] Unlike Motown within the city of Detroit, various pieces of the country music industry used Nashville but did not emerge out of a particular neighborhood or community within Nashville. A larger network of capital and resources with scattered historical roots in Nashville had emerged over time, and the city became a destination for a disparate group of musicians, investors, agents, writers, and producers.[34]

Perhaps more importantly, Opry stars and Music Row record labels were not selling civil rights in the same way that Motown was selling black culture and black liberation (even as Motown was conscious of its ramifications for a large white audience). Instead, country music's promoters were selling a very particular kind of ordinariness, everyday *white* life stripped of its particulars. The lack of any reaction to or recognition of Martin Luther King's death was not an anomaly but part of a larger pattern predicated on the genre's faulty assertion that the music spoke to and could only respond to "universal" experiences. According to this cultural logic, the genre of country music held a "natural" position of universality and thus did not need to address the experiences of particular groups, such as African Americans, who might feel a personal connection to King's death.

The Ordinary Folk and the Racial Identity of Country Music

By avoiding discussion of the pressing everyday concerns of African Americans, such as equal treatment before the law and equal access to jobs, housing, and entertainment, country music discourse was able to suggest that the music spoke for white "ordinary folks" without having to directly invoke racial preference. This interest in the struggles of ordinary white folks was directly invoked by country music booster (and later president of the Country Music Association) Tandy Rice, who, when asked in 1967 about the wide appeal of country music, explicitly connected civil rights to leftist cultural politics and contrasted these ideas and values with the concerns of the ordinary folk who enjoyed country music. He claimed, "Right now, country music is stable, like the great backbone of this country. The lyrics are simple, and sincere, not about civil rights and such. These folks don't go for the Bob Dylan, Joan Baez kind of thing. The lyrics are about what concerns everyday folks."[35] Rice's comment assumed that "ordinary" folks had moved beyond civil rights and suggested that the issues which Dylan and Baez advocated belonged on the margins. Rice created a particular construction of "civil rights" as something extra, gratuitous, or produced by outsiders, not based in the quotidian reality of everyday folk.

The emphasis on "everyday" and "daily" argues for a more fundamental and universal level of action and feeling that excluded historically contingent, though obviously extremely relevant, issues such as civil rights.

These claims about country music only make sense if "ordinary people" in their "daily lives" do not have trouble securing a spot at a lunch counter, voting without harassment, or fear being assaulted by the police or racist vigilantes. By contrast, even in Music Row's own backyard, Edgehill residents were dealing with the difficulty of finding decent affordable housing, seemingly one of the most "everyday" of concerns. Country music figures' silence about African American political struggles did not just stem from a general aversion to politics within the genre but instead from the larger ideological issues and the industry's emerging racial and class identity. What was at stake, whether it was ever articulated explicitly, was a notion of ordinary and everydayness that could draw on the genre's "everyman" appeal while still avoiding potentially divisive racial and class politics. This ideology of ordinariness, and the associations with the people or "everyday folk" that country music figures have often marshalled, became entwined with a renewed emphasis on country music's whiteness, which manifested itself across multiple texts throughout industry discourse in the late 1960s and early 1970s.

African American influence on country music has long been acknowledged within country music culture, but to various degrees and with no small amount of qualifications. Both Jimmie Rodgers and Hank Williams, the male giants of early country lore, were known to have personal connections to black musicians who supposedly inspired their more "soulful" work. But recent scholarship has also demonstrated that the African American impact on country music is not just limited to this kind of "creative muse" role for white performers or tied chronologically only to the early part of the twentieth century, but that black musicians and fans have always fully participated (or tried to fully participate, sometimes encountering barriers) in country music culture.[36] Historian and journalist Pam Foster has traced a long and rich history of black country music fandom, and anecdotal evidence from biographies of black stars such as Ray Charles and Charley Pride suggest that many rural black families listened to the Opry every Saturday night for decades.[37]

The history of African American participation in country (or hillbilly) music goes back as far as the genre's earliest roots. African American DeFord Bailey was one of the Opry's most popular acts in the program's early years, both in Nashville and on the road. His harmonica playing was rooted in an earlier tradition of string band music, which in the late nineteenth and early twentieth centuries was shared by rural southern whites and blacks alike. Bailey referred to the music he learned from his grandfather and others as "black hillbilly" music and saw himself as part of this longer tradition.[38] Bailey's talents were celebrated by the Opry and its fans, but WSM management and George Hay adopted a paternalistic attitude toward Bailey, managing his finances for him, paying him less per performance than white musicians received, and discursively presenting him as a "mascot" for the Opry. Hay wrote, in his own self-published history of the Opry in 1953, "Like some members of his race and other races, Deford was lazy. . . . He was our mascot and is still loved by the entire company. We gave him a whole year's notice to learn some more tunes, but he would not. When we were forced to give him his final notice, Deford said, without malice, 'I knowed it waz comin', Judge, I knowed it wuz comin'.'"[39] Hay, whose early radio career featured frequent minstrelsy performances, justified the move in this text by literally voicing Bailey's acceptance of the dismissal in simulated black dialect, and referred to Bailey's laziness as a racial trait. As mentioned above, Bailey lived the rest of his life in the Edgehill neighborhood, operating his own shoeshine shop less than a mile from Music Row for decades before the Edgehill Urban Renewal Project demolished the building that housed his shop. Fired by the Opry in the 1940s and displaced three decades later by the sweep of urban renewal, Bailey serves as an emblematic figure of the displacement of the African American experience enacted by both country music discourse and urban renewal in this period.

In the 1950s and 1960s, however, country music had complicated, overlapping relationships with other popular music genres, and black and white musicians did in fact play on the same records and cover each other's songs with regularity.[40] The slippery lines around genres in this time period may have created a window for an unusual amount of cross-racial interaction in the studios. Black soul artists both wrote and covered country songs (and vice versa), although racial assumptions about who could sing what kind of songs were still held both by white country producers and disc jockeys, as well as black R&B labels and radio stations.[41] Several Nashville Sound hits were written by black writers. Sonny James, in particular, recorded hit country singles written by African American writers and performers.[42] But even when black artists produced what seemed like country music, industry gatekeepers on occasion kept racial boundaries in play. Diane Pecknold has shown that the institutional context surrounding Ray Charles's album of country music cover songs, *Modern Sounds in Country and Western Music,* reveals a fairly strict policing of racial boundaries in effect in the early 1960s. According to Pecknold, the Country

Music Association and other industry players were happy to celebrate the success of Charles's album (and, in fact, the CMA used it as evidence of the genre's modernity and ability to appeal to urban middle-class audiences), but refused to think of Charles as a "country" artist.[43] The album was not played by country music disc jockeys and did not make the year-end lists of best country albums.

This tendency changed somewhat in the mid-1960s, however, as a black country singer did emerge on the Nashville Sound scene who was resoundingly described by his promoters as well as industry media voices as authentically country. In early 1966, Charley Pride signed with a major label, the first African American country singer to do so. His label's early marketing strategies downplayed or completely elided Pride's race, only releasing promotional materials featuring his image after his songs had been on the air for many months.[44] At the same time, Pride's handlers aggressively asserted his authenticity as a country singer from the beginning, seemingly preparing for resistance to the notion of a black country star. The label titled his first album *Country Charley Pride*, suggesting the expectation of a dubious audience. Likewise, a small article in *Music City News* foregrounded the need for "proof" that Pride was in fact country with the headline "Charlie Pride Album Proves He's 'Country.'"[45] This combination of surprise and doubt suggested that an implicit layer of whiteness covered country music. A 1968 article on Pride in *Billboard* made this explicit with the headline "Country Music Now Interracial."[46] The "Now" in the headline served to underscore the fictional assumption that the music had previously been solely white.

In 1967, Pride first appeared on the Grand Ole Opry and reportedly told the audience, "I've got a lot of reasons to be happy tonight, real happy. But I guess my biggest reason is that I'm an American."[47] This declaration strategically emphasized his Americanness over any racial identification, continuing a strategy of acknowledging but downplaying his unique position in country's racial order. His strategy on stage, which played well and was often highlighted in journalistic summaries, was to joke about his blackness, referring to it often as his "permanent tan," suggesting in a self-consciously playful way the possibility that underneath the tan he was white, and, in this context, permitting Pride to be discussed first as a country singer and only second as a black man (although the joke at the same time reminded the audience of his racial difference). Despite his efforts to minimize or downplay the importance of this difference, the black press enthusiastically supported him and repeatedly covered his successes. Black journalists, particularly those writing for the Baltimore *Afro-American,* celebrated his commercial and artistic achievements while pointing out the (undeserved) rarity of an African American country star.[48]

Pride's marketing team strategically established that he had always been a country music fan, in part by emphasizing his listening to radio broadcasts of the Grand Ole Opry as a child. An article in *Music City News* shortly after his major label signing pointed out that Pride's interest in country music began in boyhood and specifically mentioned his listening to the Grand Ole Opry. In addition, the article asserted that "Charley's background is made up of the 'stuff' that Country Music comes from, earthiness, hard work, high hopes and heartbreak. And his love for it is genuine, developed during boyhood."[49] His producer, Jack Clement, also tied Pride's country music bona fides to his childhood radio listening habits, telling a *Billboard* journalist in 1967, "He's sincere about it. Country music is all Pride knows. He grew up listening to the 'Grand Ole Opry.'"[50]

Pride's initial promotional discourse emphasized the authentic *country* sound of his voice and the potentially surprising fact that this sound involved absolutely no artifice: according to these texts, the "natural" way he sung just happened to sound country. For instance, in the liner notes to Pride's first album, Jack Clement wrote, "Charley Pride knows a lot about Country Music, but more than anything else, he knows how to sing Country Music." Another article summarized this idea by stating, "His voice and his style is perfected simplicity. He has adopted the very best of country music songs for his own and delivers them in a good, straightforward, honest voice, a voice that has to be the kind for which country music was written."[51] Again, without explicitly addressing the oddity of a black country singer, the article wrote against an implicit notion that Pride's voice was not country. The fervent description of Pride's vocal capabilities and "authentic" country sound suggested a potential belief that his voice was in fact the kind for some other, blacker type of music.

But Pride was not the only African American country singer for long. Sparked by his success, several other labels signed black artists. O. B. McClinton recorded on Enterprise, Memphis-based Stax's country imprint, and Stoney Edwards recorded for Capitol in Nashville. Shelby Singleton's unfortunately named Plantation Records signed black singer Linda Martell after she was discovered singing R&B in a South Carolina club.[52] None of their careers achieved the same kind of success as Pride's, but their albums were promoted in a similar fashion. The title of Edwards's first record, *Stoney Edwards—A Country Singer,* points to the contradiction seemingly inherent in a black country performer, as it attempts to persuade disbelieving record buyers that the black man on the cover is indeed a bona fide country singer. O. B. McClinton also recorded a country album on Stax Records in 1971, and, as with Pride's early publicity material, the front cover showed McClinton with his back to the camera (the back cover, however, did feature a close-up photo of McClinton).[53] Like Edwards and Pride, McClinton's first album title (*Country*) reinforced the idea that, despite the racial evidence, he was in fact a true country singer. Even more directly, one of the songs on the album, a McClinton original, was titled "Country Music, That's My Thing."

Pride eventually reached the upper echelon of country stardom, but his racial identity continued to hover near the surface of much of the discourse surrounding his music. Pride and other black country singers were marked as hillbilly singers who "just happened to be black," reinforcing country music's whiteness while at the same time staking out stark boundaries for a star like Pride: he would only ever be the "black" country star.[54] Despite Pride's commercial success and prominence on the Opry, the potential for his racial identity to disrupt this success crystallized in a seemingly harmless anecdote provided by the *Nashville Banner*. Their editorial quoted the star himself as saying, "I met a white man he says 'You know—you sound like us—but you look like them.'"[55] Despite the editorial's attempt to play the line for humor, it also served as a reminder that the frequently mentioned authenticity of Pride's voice (which was again and again described as "pure country") was the only thing keeping him in the country music world. In this editorial, he was explicitly marked as a black man in a white world, and while the us/them dichotomy was partially played for laughs, an undertone of menace still remained.[56] By reminding Pride that he looked like "them," the story suggested that, at any time, how he looked could trump how he sounded. He (as well as Bailey before him and less successful performers such as Edwards and McClinton later) was the exception that proved the rule for country music in the 1960s. Pride was continually marked as racially odd, and the careful treatment of his ability to sing country music almost in spite of his race helped to shore up the idea that country music, on some level, was a white musical form.

An ideology of universality, which multiple country music figures invoked, consciously or unconsciously, in many different ways, only worked if racial specificity (among other identity categories) was minimized or country music's whiteness was openly emphasized. In other words, discourse on the genre of country music could take one of two tacks, either elide discussions of race and implicitly present country music as white (while still maintaining a pretense to inclusive universalism), or explicitly stake a claim that country music was a soundtrack for the life of ordinary white people, just as the blues or R&B or soul could perform the same function for African Americans. Over the course of the 1960s, country music shifted from the former to the latter, as its texts increasingly aligned the genre with the constructed racial category of whiteness.

White Man's Blues: Country Music as a Counterpart to Soul and Blues

In the late 1960s and early 1970s, even as (or perhaps in part because) Charley Pride climbed to the top of the country charts, a description of country music as the "white man's blues" circulated through discussion of the genre. An early incarnation of this discourse could be found in a 1966 *Saturday Evening Post* article, which asked (and answered), "What is country music? It's soul in a rhinestone suit."[57] By that year, soul was clearly identified with black musical expression, suggesting that the author was drawing a racial parallel between white country music and black soul music.[58] In 1970, an article on the Grand Ole Opry in an issue of *Country Song Roundup* made this racial parallel more explicit. The author, Darrell Rowlett, hyperbolically began, "The heart of rural white America is found still pounding and straining, lashing out at urban living from its breast in Nashville, Tennessee. Its pulse can be measured by the nasal whines and wails, steel guitars, rickety banjoes, and crying fiddles." Continuing on, Rowlett staked a claim to country's status as a white form of soul or the blues, "as the Negro claims a soul sound in the Rhythm and Blues, the southern dirt farmer has his miseries preserved with country music, and the sagas are sung weekly at the hillbilly blues shrine, the Grand Ole Opry."[59] The passage claimed a shared experience of misery in need of expression through song, but suggested that blacks and whites had separate musical forms to express and preserve these experiences.

Rowlett referred to the Opry as a "hillbilly blues" shrine, and that construction (the blues with a marker of whiteness in front of it, also reminiscent of Elvis Presley's nickname, "the hillbilly cat") appeared in the subtitle of John Grissim's 1970 nonfiction account of the genre, *Country Music: White Man's Blues*. Grissim's title performed a similar sort of move, comparing but separating country and blues, yet the phrase "white man's" more insistently argued that country spoke for the *mainstream* of white culture, as opposed to the more marginalized "hillbillies." The phrase helped produce an assumption that country music was white. Conversely, the blues were assumed to be not-white, since why else would white men need to have their own version? They were parallel in the sense not only of being homologous but also of two lines that will never cross or come together. The possessive potentially lessened the need to address issues such as civil rights, for African Americans presumably had their own avenues of expression and motivation in the blues, soul, or gospel. According to this logic, country was the *white man's* blues and was thus intended for expressing the troubles of ordinary, hard-working whites.[60]

Country star Penny DeHaven followed this same construction in an interview for *Country Song Roundup*, when asked to define country music: "White man's blues. I just stole that from somebody, but it's the truth that's how I define it. You spill out your whole heart. You spill out your feeling inside. . . . When it comes to country music you've got to really feel it."[61] Like Rowlett's assertion about rural blacks and whites, the parallel here between country and blues (and white and black experiences) was strong: just like the blues, DeHaven seemed to say, country music provided a space to fully express the deepest, most heartfelt emotions. These declarations made the case that the two genres were similar musical forms but that country clearly and inarguably belonged to whites while African Americans had the blues. This delicate balance produced and required an understanding of country music as not racist, but not especially concerned with civil rights either, in effect arguing that blacks had their own musical culture to deal with their own daily struggles.[62]

In addition, the successes of the civil rights movements also led to what some historians have referred to as a "white ethnic" backlash (or revival, depending on your interpretation) in the late 1960s and early 1970s. The title of Matthew Frye Jacobsen's monograph, *Roots Too,* exemplifies the general thrust of this scholarship, which argues that, in addition to African Americans, aggrieved whites in the post–civil rights era wanted to discover and take pride in their ancestry.[63] The "white man's blues" discourse resonates with this development as well, even though rural southern heritage movements have not been discussed at length by scholars of the white ethnic revival movements.[64] Rooted in a response to the civil rights movement and, in particular, government-sanctioned affirmative action and busing programs, northern white ethnics claimed that they were being attacked by liberal elites for sins which they themselves had never committed. The associations between the language of the "white man's blues" within country music discourse and this strand of white ethnic reaction to civil rights were also explicit in country musicians' support for political candidate George Wallace. Such support, however, did not necessarily indicate affiliation with his race-baiting politics. Instead, there are powerful linkages between the language Wallace used to describe the "common man" and the prevailing discourse of "everydayness" that also played a significant role in the language and iconography in the genre of country music.

Wallace's campaign rhetoric focused strongly on a divide between "ordinary" workers and soft-handed elites, a group that for him included government bureaucrats, academic intellectuals, and wealthy layabouts. He claimed his critique of the civil rights movement and federal support of integration turned on this axis, rather than on simple racist ideology. For instance, he critiqued "limousine liberals" who supported integration but sent their own children to private schools. Wallace minimized the importance of civil rights and argued fervently against the constitutionality of federal intervention in state and local issues. He also, however, repeatedly claimed that he was not racist and pointed out his support for certain African American issues, even in his own state of Alabama (the Tuskegee Institute, for instance).[65] Even though very few mainstream country stars publicly advocated Wallace's more extreme stances on race, their support for him was driven by an affiliation with his language of the "little guy."

Like the lists of specific professions the CMA used to describe country music fans in the early part of the 1960s, Wallace identified his constituency through their occupations, with lists that included "the bus driver, the truck driver, the beautician, the fireman, the policeman, and the steelworker, the plumber, and the communications worker, and the oil worker and the little businessman."[66] His campaign literature in fact invoked two occupational categories strongly identified with country music, dirt farmers and truck drivers: "Can a former truck driver married to a dime-store clerk and son of a dirt farmer be elected President?"[67] In turn, many country stars actively supported him in the 1968 election. Minnie Pearl had appeared at his campaign rallies as early as 1958, and Wallace opened most of his rallies with music from a country band.[68] By 1968, the political appeal of country music had not gone unnoticed by other candidates as well. Nixon's campaign penned a ditty that they wanted a country star to sing for distribution on country radio shows, but most of the contemporary stars instead supported Wallace.[69]

It is quite possible that the association with and highlighting of country's whiteness was partially rooted in the idea that, at a time of civil rights attention focused on the plight of African Americans and other nonwhite groups in the 1960s and 1970s, poor whites, hillbillies, or just plain country people were forgotten (or caricatured). As Anthony Harkins has shown, mainstream media attention to the "discovery" of Appalachian poverty in the 1960s reintroduced the figure of the hillbilly to the national media discourse while simultaneously lampooning it. Harkins points to the heightened attention to representations of hillbilly poverty in mass-media advertising and television shows between 1962 and 1969, the same era in which journalistic and political attention to Appalachian poverty increased. In the 1960 primaries, John F. Kennedy's trips into Appalachia had elevated the visibility of (and purported national concern for) white rural poverty. This, in turn, Harkins argues, led to an increase in depictions of southern mountain inhabitants, both benign and highly derogatory.[70] In this regard, leaders of Nashville-based pieces of the country music industry were not only looking to invoke the music's heritage but also to redefine how that heritage was depicted and conceptualized.

Shantytown USA: The "Slums" of Music Row

It is in the context of both this increasing focus on country music's whiteness and the marked racial associations attached to the urban space of Nashville that we can fully analyze and understand the commentary on the nature of Music Row and the perceived need for urban renewal to renovate the neighborhood at the end of the 1960s. Industry planners, investors, and property owners wanted the concept of urbanity to signify "modern and cosmopolitan" for Music Row, but this idea did not match what they saw as "the slums" surrounding the Row. In the late 1960s, the dire conditions of the Edgehill neighborhood drew negative media attention, further pushing Row leaders to attempt to distance their own neighborhood from this racially marked zone of urban poverty. Music Row figures' invocations of "shantytown" or "the slums" were not just incidental or easy ways to describe the image of dilapidation they wished to project, but were intricately connected to the ideas about space and identity that various country music figures were still in the process of sorting out. Ultimately, the doomed Music City Boulevard promised an opportunity to more clearly demarcate the *neighborhood* of Music Row as a distinct entity from the surrounding spaces.

Even if Music Row leaders did not specifically invoke Edgehill, other country music commentators did, reinforcing the notion that the neighborhood was perilously marked in the public perception of the industry. Paul Hemphill's widely discussed 1970 book, *The Nashville Sound,* directly tied Music Row to urban renewal and Edgehill, describing the Row as "an eight-square-block area about two miles from downtown, in the urban renewal area around Sixteenth and Seventeenth Avenues South, near Vanderbilt University and a vast Negro section."[71] Hemphill's unspecified "vast Negro section" was undoubtedly Edgehill.

Similarly, John Grissim's account of the "white man's blues," published the same year, also foregrounded and frontloaded a discussion of Music Row and the "rundown" nature of the surrounding neighborhood. Grissim played with the contrast between what he saw as a poverty-stricken community in such close proximity to the vibrant music industry: "What is so amazing is that one can leave the company of such talented, wealthy artists and musicians working in such a technical environment, walk out the front door onto Seventeenth Avenue South, and see weed-filled lots, run-down buildings and private homes for senior citizens. In fact, the whole of Music Row (which technically refers to Sixteenth Avenue South) is part of a poverty-stricken Model Cities district."[72] Grissim's geography was wrong but in a very telling fashion. The Model Cities Program was a particular kind of urban renewal program designed to allow local communities to plan and implement a "total attack" to reshaping a neighborhood. It was in fact in place in North Nashville, not in either Music Row or Edgehill.[73] Instead, Music Row, at the time of Grissim's book, was sandwiched between an urban renewal project driven by Vanderbilt's expansion to the west and public housing construction in Edgehill to the east, neither of which were part of the Model Cities Program.

Model Cities neighborhoods, at least in Nashville, were predominantly African American, and Grissim's slipup here reveals how he understood the purportedly poverty-stricken neighborhood near Music Row as African American and simply used the terminology as a kind of shorthand. The way in which these two texts situated Music Row reveals the extent to which the neighborhood was often read as low-income and African American, forcing industry leaders to make decisions about how to depict and interact with this racialized space in this particular social context. How would country music discourse have been different if their approach had embraced an inclusive vision of "coming to town" and addressed the highly visible evidence of inequality and struggles for equal access to public space?

IN THE late 1950s and early 1960s, country music lyrics were talked about as a "ledger of life," or a description of the everyday life of ordinary people, despite the fact that the quotidian details of everyday life are different for everyone. This tendency was still dominant in the 1970s, and in fact was taken up by President Richard Nixon in a 1972 presidential proclamation that also strove for an impossible level of universalism: "Strong, simple, and moving, country reflects the joys, the sorrows and the ideals of our people. Love of family, love of country, faith in God, and the happiness and heartbreak of everyday life—these are the themes that run throughout our country music, and that bind us all together as Americans."[74] Nixon's proclamation equalized both the happiness and heartbreak of all Americans, suggesting that all sorrow was shared, rooted in a generic component of human experience rather than differentially distributed across a systemically unequal society. Tex Ritter, in a speech at the CMA awards banquet the next year, continued this discourse. Ritter opined that "the country song seems to be the most direct for the country writer knows no other way. His songs reflect the hopes and dreams of everyone as well as everyone's fears and failures. And his songs are a common meeting ground."[75] Ritter linked a universal set of hopes and dreams with those expressed in country song, setting forth an implicit argument that those who did not find their hopes expressed in country song did not fit the inclusive "everyone." This chapter shows that these elisions and absences were not incidental or coincidental but in fact resonated with a set of ideas and assumptions about the white racial identity of the music and its fans, despite a plethora of evidence of racial diversity within both the genre's influences and its contemporary producers and consumers. The next chapter explores the ways that, in the early 1970s, the Grand Ole Opry's move to Nashville's suburbs built upon and deepened this notion.

"Country Music Is Wherever the Soul of a Country Music Fan Is"

Opryland U.S.A. and the Importance of "Home" in Country Music

IN THE SPRING of 1974, the Grand Ole Opry left the nineteenth-century Ryman Auditorium in downtown Nashville and moved into a newly constructed amusement park complex in the city's suburbs named Opryland U.S.A. The size of the new complex, along with its multiple retail options, extravagant rides, and live animal shows, stood in stark contrast to the staid, cathedral-like auditorium that previously housed the show. Opry leaders were aware that the historic setting had been just as important to the program's enduring appeal as the list of performers who regularly plied their trade on its stage, and that the image of the new complex would have to be managed carefully. They realized that references to the Ryman as a "tabernacle" or "mother church" referred not just to the auditorium's early history as a home for religious meetings but also to the theater's central, sacred place in country music culture.[1] The Opry's corporate parent, longtime Nashville insurance company National Life and Accident Insurance Company, however, envisioned the new park as something bigger than just a home for the Opry; they saw it as a chance to expand the Opry's brand and profitability.

To justify the move to an expensive, modern entertainment complex, Opry stars and leaders employed a two-pronged strategy. First, Opry figures drew on a potent national discourse about urban space and railed against the "slums" of downtown Nashville to argue that the Ryman's urban location was inappropriate for the Opry's family-friendly audience and image. Second, they argued that even though the Ryman had been home to the Opry for over three decades, what really gave a home its unique flavor was its inhabitants, and that together the fans and stars would invest the new Opry House with the same downhome charm and character that they had brought to the Ryman. This rhetorical defense of the construction of the Opryland U.S.A. complex, and the decision to make it the new home for the venerated old radio program, drew on and perpetuated a larger matrix of beliefs and values about country music's ability to retain traditional characteristics while still embracing modern living spaces.

The Ryman and Downtown Nashville

Although the Opry's move out of the Ryman in 1974 was greeted with the bittersweet tears of leaving a childhood home, the Ryman had in fact not always been the home of the Opry. The program changed venues several times in the first decade and a half of its run. But in 1943, the Opry settled in the city-owned Ryman Auditorium, where it would stay until 1974. Despite a history of barely grudging acceptance on the part of Nashville's elite, by the mid- to late 1960s, the country music industry was supporting Nashville's economy, and the city institutionally supported the industry by emphasizing its potential to increase Nashville tourism. In particular, the city recognized that most Opry visitors came from outside of Nashville, and they brought their tourist dollars with them.[2]

By the 1960s, many Opry fans generally spent the afternoon ahead of the show shopping, eating, and drinking in Nashville's downtown establishments (some of the most popular destinations were Linebaugh's Restaurant and Ernest Tubb's Record Shop), expanding the ritualized space of an Opry visit to include not just the Ryman but the surrounding downtown blocks.[3] Before the show, fans waited in lines that stretched around the corner on to Lower Broad, the neighborhood's primary commercial strip. By the late 1960s, Tootsie's Orchid Lounge, whose back entrance abutted the Ryman's own back entrance, had become a world-famous watering hole for Opry stars before and after their sets. As a result, fans frequented Tootsie's and other hot spots in hopes of an up-close and personal glimpse of their favorite stars.[4] The density of downtown development facilitated this easy access to multiple retail sites and generated a festive atmosphere on show days, but it also created a more unpredictable, heterogeneous space.

Throughout the 1960s, urban tensions manifested in a major shift in how cities were lived and understood, in Nashville and across the nation. Suburban expansion had reduced the residential population near city centers, and new suburban retail centers (in tandem with never fully resolved traffic and congestion problems in inner cities) cut into downtown retailers' share of the market. Rather than acknowledging these shifts, business research publications and studies advocated continuing to chase after middle-class suburban women and generally disdained nonwhite lower-middle- and working-class residents who lived closer in, even though they were a loyal consumer base since they had fewer transportation and economic options. Lower-income ethnic and African American neighborhoods near downtown were not seen as an opportunity but as *the* threat in the late 1950s and 1960s.[5] In addition, retailers, investors, government officials, and journalists all saw downtown as under siege from "blight" and "slums," while popular culture imagined "The City" as a place of crime, poverty, and disease. Popular culture productions in turn demonized the inner city and presented downtown and other expressly urban environments as dangerous, diseased, and threatening to engulf the surrounding "better" sections.[6]

In tandem with these prevailing cultural ideas, the development and success of suburban office and retail centers threatened the profitability of downtown businesses, and Nashville retailers and city officials alike worried about the future of downtown.[7] In the late 1960s, these downtown retailers and developers looked to urban renewal as a way to revitalize the area and combat the flight of shoppers to the suburbs.[8] In the early 1960s, one design firm, explicitly recognizing the importance of the Opry to Nashville's economy, proposed including a Performing Arts Center (which could house the Opry) in their plans for a joint public-private redevelopment of the downtown area.[9] Thus, it was entirely conceivable that the Opry could have found a way to remain a central piece of Nashville's downtown. But the program's corporate stewards at National Life had other, more ambitious ideas. As WSM's chairman of the board, Edwin Craig, declared in 1968, "We always have been interested in enhancing the growth of the Grand Ole Opry concept."[10] As the somewhat ambiguous use of the term "concept" indicates, they were looking to capitalize on the Opry's brand.

The Ryman Auditorium, built in 1890, was by the late 1960s in major need of structural renovation, for reasons of both safety (reinforcing and fireproofing) and comfort (air conditioning and newer, more comfortable pews). WSM president Irving Waugh researched the financial investment needed to make the auditorium fire-resistant, improve air conditioning and heating, and expand the site itself to provide more space for dressing rooms for the stars and offices for WSM. Waugh determined that significantly investing in an auditorium renovation just to maintain a show that occurred only twice a week, and that had no other major mechanisms for generating profit, made little sense. It would be more sound to invest in a larger complex of facilities that would allow WSM to capture more of the Opry visitors' tourist dollars, as well as bring in visitors who were not Opry fans.[11] In order to achieve this, National Life needed a large plot of land and the ability to control and regulate the space.[12]

The language that the Opry's more vocal leaders deployed at the time of the move revealed the extent to which Opry stewards perceived, or attempted to portray, the downtown space as "under siege." Opry leaders used the words "protect" and "control" to valorize the new suburban site over the unpredictable downtown space. In 1975, Opry star Roy Acuff wrote in his introduction to journalist Jack Hurst's book on the Opry: "We are now in a beautiful spot at Opryland, and we have enough land out here to protect it."[13] Hurst quoted Waugh in the same book: "We decided that instead of rebuilding down there we should go outside the city to a place where we could control our own environment."[14] Waugh insisted they had to go "outside the city," suggesting it was not just downtown that was unsuitable; rather, there was no urban space that would allow them to protect and control Opryland the way they wanted to. Opryland offered controlled access both in terms of visitors (accessible only by car and located in a predominantly white and affluent neighborhood) and merchants (Opryland itself contained food, shopping, and accommodations for visitors). In this case, not surprisingly, suburban values meshed with suburban land opportunities.

National Life bought a total of 369 acres but only used 110 for the actual development of Opryland, leaving a buffer zone around the park to distance the visitor experience from the sights and sounds of unwanted commercial development—what the official National Life press release referred to as "sufficient acreage to provide for the Opryland park itself, parking, and enough additional area to permit control of the park environment."[15] The extra space had no necessary park function but allowed

WSM to control the visitors' entries and exits to Opryland. This was a major change from the Ryman, where "unprotected" visitors waited in lines on the street and in nearby alleys.

Opryland provided National Life with the opportunity to control not just the park but its surrounding commercial space. At the time of purchase, the Opry's new neighborhood contained a combination of undeveloped rural land and new residential construction for relatively affluent white suburban families.[16] With the Cumberland River on one side and the newly minted Briley Parkway on the other, the future site of Opryland was well protected from encroaching development.[17] The spatial arrangement of the complex established a buffer zone around the ring of the park to separate the visitor from the outside world, and the planners designed the park itself as a kind of surreal fantasy land to further distance the visitor from any particular kind of spatial associations.

WSM and National Life, knowing full well the importance of the Opry's "authentic" setting, went to great lengths to sell the new Opryland as a natural, realistic environment. Their initial press release stated, "The entire Opryland U.S.A. complex is alive with naturalness. There is NO animation. Instead, the total flavor is one of reality from live buffalo roaming the range to honest to goodness American antiques used throughout the scores of buildings." Opryland's stewards intended to retain "real" elements of the actual country, including open spaces, live animals, and trees, while openly merging these with many modern amenities, including a parking lot that could hold 3,800 cars and a dedicated retail complex called Opry Towne.[18] This kind of large undeveloped and controllable space was simply unavailable downtown.

But the Opry's decision to leave downtown Nashville was also made in the context of urban disinvestment and explosive suburban development. By 1968 when the decision to relocate the Opry was made, Nashville's urban spaces had seen several significant civil rights battles; activists had integrated many public leisure spaces, and Music Row had been a site of prominent civil rights protests.[19] In addition, urban renewal projects had deepened the segregation of the city and intensified income inequality. In 1967, just one year before the decision was made to relocate the Opry, both Coney Island's Steeplechase Park and Chicago's Riverview Park had closed their gates after decades of providing urban amusement to working- and middle-class whites. In both cases, declining attendance numbers were tied to integration and the unwillingness on the part of white families to share such spaces with African Americans. Eric Avila has argued that a significant shift was occurring which reduced the desirability of public space in urban areas in favor of a new kind of suburban commercial amusement structured around inaccessibility, not accessibility.[20]

Racially inflected understandings of dangerous urban space have often manifested themselves in discussions of crime and safety, and it was no different for Nashville and the Ryman. Country stars cited the importance of fan safety without mentioning specific crime or danger, instead using the term "slums" to describe the Ryman's neighborhood and presumably believing their audience would understand the connotations of the word. As with the use of terms such as "control" and "protect" to blatantly describe Opryland's security benefits, Opry stars made no attempt to mask their concerns about the downtown space. Physical danger, economic distress, and moral laxity were bound together in a general sense of undesirability loosely invoked by Opry figures with the term "slum." This invocation of slums suggested that the suburban Opryland area was simply "nicer." Opry veterans Acuff and Hank Snow both used this term to disparage the neighborhood, and Vic Willis ominously commented, "Thank God we're getting out of here. They should've built a new Opry House forty-nine years ago. They talk about atmosphere encircling this place. Well, let me tell you something. We don't need this type of atmosphere."[21] Although it is unclear precisely what atmosphere Willis feared, his use of the word "encircling" resonated with the commonly available notion of the slums as a "ring of blight" surrounding the nation's downtown areas.[22] This subtle intimation of danger and undesirable "others" worked to justify the move without the need for explicit evidence of crime and danger.

Opry star Porter Wagoner's criticism was more spatially pointed. He focused on the alley between the Ryman's back door and Tootsie's Lounge, a previously celebrated aspect of the Opry's environment, which famously facilitated star-fan interaction. Wagoner's testimonial for WSM emphasized the seediness of the Opry's location and the need for a family-friendly venue for fans: "We will have vastly improved parking facilities and better access to the fans, rather than meeting them in a dark alley. The entire complex is safe for the children and the whole family."[23] Wagoner focused on the alley between the Ryman and Lower Broad businesses, even though the auditorium was actually surrounded by retail businesses that drove a great deal of concentrated pedestrian traffic. In an oral history recorded the next year, Snow echoed Wagoner, claiming, "But the good point . . . is that we got out of that alley. We got out of that which actually is known as really the slums of the city, until they clean it up a little more."

Snow went on to mention the lack of dressing rooms, parking, and air conditioning, but the "slum" location of the Ryman was, for him, the first strike against the old Opry. His disdain for "that alley" revealed an urgent desire to leave downtown.[24]

Acuff, more than any other Opry star, spoke out against the downtown neighborhood in the weeks before the show's exit to Opryland. He too used the term "slum" but with a second layer of meaning: he used it to describe both the deteriorating urban neighborhood of Lower Broad and the degraded position that country music itself occupied in the broader Nashville culture. He linked how most middle-class white Nashvillians felt about inner city African Americans to how he believed they felt about Opry stars and their fans. He argued, of Opryland, "It's first class, and nothing is too good for country music. . . . People in Nashville don't want to come down here [to the Ryman]. They thought the Ryman was a good place for country music. A slum."[25] His comment connected the built environment and surrounding space of the Opry to its standing in the community and argued that the country fans deserved better facilities and more respect from the city of Nashville. Acuff's use of the word "slum" indicated his feeling that the city of Nashville still understood country people as a racialized minority, and Acuff saw the Opry's move to the suburbs as a key path to changing this conception.

Proponents of the move did not limit the range of perceived threats to physical ones; leading Opry figures also warned of the moral hazards of downtown Nashville's commercial amusements. In particular, Acuff frequently referenced the combination of drinking establishments, X-rated movie theaters, and "massage" parlors as not in keeping with the Opry's image and its fans' sensibilities. Acuff told an interviewer six months after the move, "So many of the undesirable types of establishments got up around us down there. It went from a beer joint to a drink joint to the rubbing parlors, and all the different things of sin."[26] Acuff owned property around the corner from the Ryman, so his interest in the condition of the neighborhood may not have been purely confined to the Opry's image or the fan experience, but even so, his pronouncements speak to the character he expected the Opry to exhibit. In contrast with his moralist position at this point in his career, Acuff had actually recorded off-color songs in the early stages of his career, including "When Lulu's Gone" and "Doin' It the Old Fashioned Way." Acuff refused to issue these under his own name, instead using the pseudonym The Bang Boys for his band.[27] The same recording session that produced these songs also featured his recording of the gospel tune "The Great Speckled Bird," which propelled Acuff's career and secured him a place on the Opry. This familiar country music paradox suffused the entire debate about the future of the Opry. Who was the Opry for? Who was its true audience? Was country music spiritual guidance for morally upstanding families or was it the gritty and colorful soundtrack of the down and out? The Opry's corporate steward, National Life and Accident, appeared to come down on the side of the former in the early 1970s, imagining the Opry as a program tied to the history of millions of middle-class families who could now be theme park visitors, not the soundtrack to a rural and working-class life.[28]

National Life chairman G. Daniel Brooks shared Acuff's disdain for morally questionable "cheap amusements" but also implicated a particular strand of country music as one such entertainment by using the phrase "honky-tonk." In justifying the decision to surround the Opry with a larger amusement park complex, Brooks invoked the taverns and souvenir shops of the blocks surrounding the Ryman when he proclaimed in 1969, "It is our plan to create a park of great beauty. We expect to give it the strictest maintenance, and the surrounding land will enable us to keep out the garish, honky-tonk commercialism that has sprung up around some of the other amusement areas around the nation." Brooks's decision to enfold the Opry within the new privatized and controlled park officially and literally enacted the charges many traditionalist critics had laid at the feet of the industry's leaders over the previous decade: that honky-tonk and its fans were left outside the gates of the new, more moderate country-pop Nashville Sound. Brooks defined the contemporary version of the Opry and country music as *not* the honky-tonk style of old.[29]

The National Life chairman's statement argued that Opryland belonged to middle-class families, *not* to potentially lower-class urban revelers. Like the downtown retailers who were afraid of their commercial districts' catering too heavily to a kind of cheap shopping and recreation experience, the Opry's protectors constructed a particular style of middle-class tourism as normal for fans of country music. Brooks (along with prominent de facto spokespersons such as Acuff) favored one particular space and recreational milieu (suburban, controlled, and predictable) over another (urban, unpredictable, more colorful), a position that was neither inevitable nor obvious for country music. Acuff's disdain for drinking joints, for instance, hardly squared with country music's lyrical content over the previous decades, which frequently presented social life in terms of a provocative cultural mix of the seamier side of life and a sterner moralism. This dynamic was often understood through a kind of hedonist Saturday night / penitent Sunday morning dualism. Historically, both sides had a place in country culture and worked together to create country music's unique appeal. In an oral history conducted in May 1974, country star and Opry announcer Grant Turner lamented the Opry's move and argued that much of the important colorful character of the Opry came from its wilder, more unpredictable surroundings; Turner mentioned street performers, peddlers, transients (eating chicken from shoeboxes on the steps of the downtown buildings), and even the massage parlors and prostitutes.[30] He mourned the Opry's loss of the surrounding mixed-class character and the various pleasures it offered, but his was a minority voice. Most of the rest of the Opry community embraced their new comfortable home in the suburbs as a fitting environment for the show's modern incarnation and its many fans. If the unseemly characteristics of downtown pushed the Opry away, the suburban space that gave way to Opryland also had its own unique pull.

Opryland U.S.A. and the Opry's New Suburban Home

The move from an inner city space deemed undesirable to a new suburban development may have seemed wholly intuitive for other industries in the late 1960s, but in abandoning the venerable Ryman, the Opry grappled with resistance to change and the fact that much of its appeal stemmed from the show's maintenance of tradition (even as fans and performers alike were very aware of the performative aspect of the Opry's traditional facades). Country music fans and performers had always been savvy about the theatrical aspects of the industry within its setting as a wholly commercial entertainment form.[31] But Opry leaders understood that the late nineteenth-century Ryman held a special place in the hearts of country music fans. When fans and critics referred to the Ryman as a "tabernacle" or "mother church," they invoked not just the auditorium's original function as a religious meeting place but also this sacred place in country music culture. Therefore, National Life and WSM intended to minimize the extent to which they discussed the Ryman and instead focus on the spectacular new facilities that they believed the Opry so richly deserved.[32] Opry manager Bud Wendell emphasized that the show would remain exactly the same: "What we're planning to do is simply lifting it out of the Opry House and putting it into more pleasant surroundings."[33] In fact, WSM and leading figures literally lifted a circular piece of the Ryman's stage out of the old Opry House and transported it to the new theater so that Opry performers could still sing on the sacred ground of the old place.[34]

This literal preservation of a piece of the old stage signaled an intention to maintain Opry traditions and values, but another more potent narrative about the preservation of tradition was developing as well. At the time of the move, Opry stars and fans both contributed to a more nuanced narrative justifying the move and reassuring skeptics that the Opry would continue to value tradition, memory, and family. These figures argued that, like any home, the true life of the place came from the people who lived there, and the show and its fans would not lose their unique downhome sensibility in a modern, expensive theme park complex such as Opryland U.S.A.

How would an old-timey show run like a seemingly disorganized barn dance translate to a comfortable, modern, climate-controlled, and spacious new theater? The question hovered over the debate about the move and the Opry's final performances in the Ryman. In order to answer this question, Opry stars combined sometimes pointed statements regarding their own modernity with often humorous illustrations of their unique but authentic country character. Their lines worked to emphasize that such character did not necessarily depend on the material space it inhabited. As Opry star Jean Shepard told the *Nashville Banner*, "The new place is gorgeous, but it makes you wonder if you can kick your shoes off out there. But you know Jean Shepard, I kick my shoes off wherever and whenever I feel like it."[35] Shepard dispelled the fear that behavior at Opryland would have to be more ordered and regulated. She instead suggested that the Opry's relaxed and intimate character would remain intact despite all the money that was poured into the convenience and technology of the place, and despite what skeptical critics might say.

Many stars emphasized that the new venue was unequivocally superior and that fans and performers alike would be more comfortable and happy at the new place. WSM circulated a set of testimonials from Opry stars in defense of leaving the Ryman that contained passionate support for the new Opryland complex. Minnie Pearl summed up the feeling well: "There is always a certain sadness connected with a move from an old place to a new. . . . The most important factor, as I see it, is the comfort of the fans. The fans are the Opry—the most important part of it—and they have certainly been uncomfortable in the old house. Now, they'll have comfortable seats, air conditioning, plenty of room, and a space to park, plus other advantages."[36] Pearl placed the most emphasis on fan comfort, and also leaned on the fans' own presumed experience with leaving an old home to shore up support, essentially saying, "you know this is true because you have had to do this in your own life." The bond between fans and performers was central to the new park: the fans had to be comfortable in order to play their role in co-constructing the authentic Opry experience.

Fan club newsletters in turn celebrated and supported the new complex. Newsletters from the time of the Opry's move indicate fan awareness of opposition to the new theater complex (most noticeably, that the technologically advanced and expensive environment of the new theater would change the Opry's intrinsically spontaneous downhome nature) but echoed Shepard in minimizing the change in location. They presented a narrative in which slightly dubious fans almost immediately realized that the spirit of the Opry would survive any change in venue. A Tex Ritter fan wrote, "Despite all the mechanization and new-theater respectability, Cousin Minnie's 'HowDEEEE' carried with it an unmistakable message—the Opry might have moved, but it will stay down-home."[37] Downhome, here, was clearly not tied to any geographic or structural space: the continuity of Pearl's distinctive greeting still fully signified downhome in a modern, suburban entertainment complex.

The president of a Loretta Lynn fan club paralleled this quick dismissal of any fear that the Opry had changed: "We had been a little anxious about whether the old mass-of-organized-confusion type setting would be banished with the move from the old Ryman. How delighted we were when the curtain went up that evening and there was the same old everybody-running-around, talking, and joking and just a general air of unorganized fun and brotherhood!" She went on to emphasize that the *people* mattered more than the material space of the home: "No, the Opry hasn't changed. The HOME of the Opry is the only change and believe us, it is only for the better!"[38] According to these fans, Minnie Pearl's possibly disruptive "HowDEEEE" and the general air of unruliness that were hallmarks of the Opry had seamlessly followed the program to its new, expensive environment. As long as the people were the same and nobody tried to put on any airs, the program would remain the same.

Country fans did raise the specter of respectability, mechanization, and money changing the Opry, but most quickly dispelled the notion. Other cultural critics who were not necessarily fans of the Opry, however, still weighed in, pointing out the more vulgar side of the transformation and expressing shock and dismay that the show would be happier in shiny new digs. The striking juxtaposition between the old auditorium and the new theme park complex sparked this commentary. Even as Opry stars and fans defensively celebrated the complex's many amenities as a long over-due recognition of country's enduring connection to millions of ordinary Americans, critics viewed the multi-million dollar commercial develop-ment as the perfect symbol of modern country music repudiating its hum-ble roots. For the most part, the criticism came from outside the industry, from critics often with their own agendas to push. For instance, *New York Times* architecture critic Ada Louise Huxtable scoffed at the notion that there could be a *new* Grand Ole Opry House, as she contrasted what she referred to as the "phony" Opryland Theater with the "real" Ryman. Garrison Keillor, writing in the *New Yorker,* pointed to the new complex's inaccessibility for a writer without a car and instead gleefully chose to listen to the first show at Opryland on the radio in his hotel room. Finally, and perhaps more damning, outlaw country gonzo journalist Paul Hemp-hill dismissively referred to "an antiseptic new air-conditioned Grand Ole Opry House amid a hokey Disneyland-type complex called Opryland, U.S.A."[39] The perspective on the move seems to have depended both on views of suburban theme parks (crass and kitschy or genuine family fun) and on views of "country folk" (simple rubes only at home in an old-time setting or competent modern Americans who also happen to possess a unique heritage). The Opry community came down firmly on the side of genuine family fun that could be shared by competent modern Americans who possess a unique heritage.

Despite the potential controversy, most Opry performers agreed that the show would remain the same, and that the move was both positive and necessary. In some cases, they responded to the criticism directly and made a bold case for the need to move forward, not look backward. Shortly after the Opry's debut at Opryland, Country Music Foundation writer Patricia Hall interviewed Opry star and pianist Del Wood about the new theater's character and atmosphere, suggesting perhaps that the show should never have moved.[40] Even while admitting that she had only once been to the Opry, Hall asserted that moving from the older Ryman to the new Opry-land was like "moving from a great old Victorian house into one of these new plastic apartments." To Hall's biting critique, couched in terms of contemporary architectural complaints, Wood promptly responded by pointing to the Ryman's cramped dressing rooms and inadequate restroom facilities, suggesting that, for the performers, access to improved facilities trumped the ramshackle charm of the old Victorian. Wood then further explained her willingness to leave the Ryman behind, in the process providing a cogent analysis of nostalgia for childhood homes: "If I could go back to my home and my grandmother and my daddy could be there, who are both now gone, and my mother, and we were all young again, oh, how wonderful it would be. But we can't do that. We must take what we have now, and what we have now is the family we have left, and this is true at that new Opry House."[41] Reminding Hall that country music must live in the present and not the past, Wood suggested that the feeling of home that the Opry provided would be just as authentic, if not more authentic, at the Opry House, even if it did remind Hall of "one of those plastic apartments." It was the *people* who made a home. By drawing the comparison with her own childhood home, Wood metaphorically aligned the Opry's geographic history with that of many of its fans, who had left their own childhood homes behind. National journalists also paralleled the Opry's move with the relocation many country people had made in the previous decades. One article, headlined "The Gran Ole Opry Leaves Old Homestead," personified the music and asserted that, with the Opry leaving the Ryman, "American music last night walked away from a childhood homeplace."[42]

While some critics believed the Opryland development to be too commercial and synthetic, leading Opry figures argued instead that country music had finally gained the level of national recognition and respect that it deserved, and that their new "home" at Opryland was both the proof of this and the best way to showcase its modernity. This sentiment found expression in a phrase commonly attributed to singer/songwriter Tom T. Hall and repeated by a number of Opry stars at the time of the move: "They're taking us out of the barn and into a home."[43] Hall's analogy presented the old Ryman auditorium as no longer modern enough to house the Opry, and the new complex at Opryland as a more appropriate and welcoming home for the program and its fans. In Hall's formulation, the barn was to be remembered and cherished, certainly, but only as a nostalgic totem of lifestyles often celebrated in country music's memory but no longer lived by the people of country music. The fact that so many Opry fans and country people no longer lived in rural spaces was actually a point of pride in this formulation—they too had gotten out of the barn and into a home.

Several of the Opry stars' testimonials collected by WSM at the time of the move echoed these sentiments. Fifteen-year Opry veteran Archie Campbell said, "But most important, amid all this change, one thing will stay the same—the people. . . . Up in Bull's Gap, where I come from, there's a saying: 'It ain't the house that makes a home, it's the people that live there.' We're just moving to a new home." Much as the Loretta Lynn fan club president took pains to emphasize that the home of the Opry would be the *only* thing to change, Campbell's use of "just" minimized the specifics of any particular home and prioritized the inhabitants instead. Country comedian Jerry Clower further tied the Opry's move to a larger cultural shift with a statement fully supporting moving forward, not looking backward: "My home is not like it used to be, my church is not like it used to be, my car is not like it used to be—in fact, I can't think of much that is."[44] Clower stressed that the world of country people had changed and argued that there was therefore no reason why the move to Opryland should seem all that striking. These Opry stars foregrounded their own modernity (against the stereotypical assumptions to the contrary), and their acute awareness of the changes in the world worked to reassure fans and cultural critics that the Opry would stay the Opry in the new suburban theme park complex. Still, like Clower's home, church, and car, it was understood that the Opry might not be *quite* like it used to be.

In 1973, President Richard Nixon tapped into and helped disseminate this discourse when he declared, in proclaiming October as National Country Music Month, "Now the term describes not just a locale but a state of mind and style of taste, as much beloved downtown as on the farm."[45] Nixon's description of country music referenced two seemingly spatial opposites but ultimately downplayed the importance of geography, instead emphasizing temperament and taste. This formulation mirrored the discourse employed by Opryland's defenders. Nixon's support for the ideology of the Opry reached its ultimate expression when he visited the *new* Opry House on its opening night, officially endorsing the location (the Ryman had never hosted such a prestigious Opry visitor). Nixon took the stage, played two songs on the piano, and bantered with Roy Acuff. The triumphant industry press coverage trumpeted Nixon's visit as further proof that country had arrived and been validated.[46] Despite moments of scattered apprehension about the move to Opryland, by the time of the actual move, the Opry community was publicly behind the new place and the theater's status as its new home.

In addition to housing the Opry itself, however, Opryland U.S.A. (the official name of the entire complex) purported to showcase all forms of homegrown American music, not just country music, and thus catered to a much broader audience at a time when the genre of country music was expanding to include chart-topping country-pop hybrids. Opryland also signaled this larger move away from strictly country music by incorporating *all* varieties of American music into the park's rides and shows. National Life looked to cash in on country's new national and international successes, as well as country's ability to position itself somewhere between

The new Opryland complex offered rides, live animals, musical productions, and pageantries of Americana. Courtesy of Brenda Colladay, Grand Ole Opry Museum, Nashville.

the pop and country charts and markets. The Opry itself remained home to many older acts and sounds that were not as commercially successful as the Nashville Sound country-pop hybrid, while maintaining an uneasy alliance with the more commercially successful country-pop stars.[47]

Following the model of Disneyland, Opryland's planners divided the park into thematically organized nodes. Since Opryland billed itself as a presentation of all forms of American music, the park's design pattern broke down based on five different musical genres. Opryland's programs reflected a new emphasis on contemporary pop sounds. Brochures and press releases highlighted the wide range of the country's musical heritage that the park intended to cover, including "Music of the American West," "American Jazz and Blues" (the New Orleans section), "American Music of Today" (contemporary pop music), and the "American Country Music" section, which housed the new Opry House.[48] The modern country section, however, was not the home of traditional country music.

In fact, Opryland's musical organization presented *traditional* country music as a relic (albeit a relic dear to its heart) of the past. The fifth genre of music, recognized with its own section of the park, was the "American Folk Music" area, which featured old-time folk performances in the Roy Acuff Music Hall. The folk music area was located in the "Hill Country" region, which the park presented as more of a historical reenactment space. WSM's description of the park section reinforced this distance from the contemporary world: "Appalachian mountain town artifacts set the scene in the Hill Country Area of the Park. There weren't any modern electric machines to handle the work in those days, so everything was done by hand. . . . The warm, friendly staff of Hill Country, dressed in their authentic costumes of the day, make this Area a delightful and rewarding experience for all."[49] Opryland positioned the hillbilly era of country music as part of the distant past, historically reenacted by modern performers, and in so doing continued the trend of country music's representing its newest incarnation as more modern and palatable (while still maintaining reverence for past incarnations). This completed the journey begun in the Opry's earliest days—country music productions gradually made more and more explicit the fact of their own distance from the country.[50] The park relegated rustic lifestyles to the past while still celebrating them nostalgically, and efforts to promote the park focused more on Opryland's wide range of offerings other than country music.

John Hartford's prophetic 1972 song about the Opry's departure from downtown, "Nobody Eats at Linebaugh's Anymore," captured this sense that the Opry was not the centerpiece of the Opryland development: "Somewhere in the suburbs the Opry plays tonight / but the people come around to take the rides."[51] Hartford had also released "Tear Down the Grand Ole Opry" the year before. This song also bemoaned the move away from the Ryman Auditorium, so much so that the narrator predicted that the Opry would simply be gone once it left the Ryman:

> I've been in love with the grand ole opry
> And I guess I have now for a good many years
> When I hear the grand ole opry
> It makes me sad that it's gonna disappear, gonna disappear.

The song was released in 1971, after plans had been announced for the new Opryland complex but before construction was completed. Presumably Hartford knew the Opry would continue in the new location, but the song equates taking it out of the Ryman with killing it completely. It is telling that Hartford was affiliated with bluegrass, as the other scattered critiques of the Opry's move to Opryland (in addition to those from national journalists and *New York Times* architecture critics) were also found in a bluegrass publication, *Pickin'*.[52] Bluegrass artists and commentators seemed to have either a greater personal investment in defending the Opry's traditional location, because of the subgenre's stronger associations with older instrumentation and songs, or less of an investment in defending the status quo when it came to WSM and the Opry, because of their distance from the commercial mainstream of country music. But theirs were minority voices in 1974, when the Opry finally walked away from the old homestead.

Country "Homes" Outside of the Country

The discourse surrounding the opening of Opryland succeeded because it resonated with an ongoing and collective rethinking of country music's socio-spatial place in the American imagination. The idea that country music could be more a state of mind than a specific set of genre conventions had been around since the late 1950s. In 1957, a *New York Times* reporter claimed, "Country music is not really a kind of music; it is a style, a way of playing. The one quality indispensable to a country music performer is 'down homeliness'—an amalgam of simple virtues of the kind that your sweet old Grandmother used to praise."[53] This idea, however, became much more resonant in the 1970s, as country music figures became increasingly militant about not being kept "down on the farm" or "out in the barn." The spirited defense of the new Opry theater resonated with ideas produced by and about country music in the early 1970s that relegated agrarian lifestyles and iconography to a fondly remembered past, while simultaneously suggesting that country figures could successfully retain their country values in modern homes and contexts. The beginning of the 1970s witnessed a series of country songs that reexamined country's humble roots, adopting a darker perspective toward the rigors of farm life and the despair of rural poverty, and emphasizing the importance of keeping the *memory* of country life alive without actually having to live there.

Even in the late 1960s, this ideology about country fans outside of rural spaces could be found in texts produced by the industry. In the Grammy-winning liner notes to his 1967 album *Suburban Attitudes in Country Verse*, John Loudermilk normalized country fans' middle-class consumption patterns and suburban residences while asserting that their country values had remained intact.[54] He argued that a subdivision of suburban homes could be the new location of country homes and opened his essay by suggesting, "If you don't believe it, just go out Interstate 65 to Exit 19, drive on through Brentwood, and between the shopping center and the country club you'll find an entire village of country houses. John D. Loudermilk's is the forty-eighth, three-bedroom brick on the right." Loudermilk boldly asserted that the new milieu for country homes was in a suburban housing tract. He used typical suburban hallmarks—the interstate, the shopping center, and the country club—to explicitly locate what turned out to be his own modest home, the forty-eighth in a row of other, similar homes. Unashamedly taking pride in his location, Loudermilk suggested, as did the defenders of the Opryland complex as a suitable new home for the Opry a few years later, the powerful portability of the "country home."[55]

The essay further used wordplay and inversion to take familiar elements of the country stereotype and use them to argue that country people were now middle-class consumers and not rustic throwbacks from a bygone era. In a tone typical of his essay, Loudermilk admonished an imagined visitor: "Talk about the weather, sports, flying saucers, anything but farming. If you ask him how's the crop doing, he'll tell you fine but they're about to drive the good wife out of her skull. (Their 'crop' being three young sons . . . who are country boys, too.) If a wagon pulls up outside, don't look for the horse. He's under the hood with the rest of his 249 brothers." This passage subverts key elements of the rural stereotype to provide different, more contemporary, meanings—a "crop" of children in a station wagon, horsepower as a measure of an automobile engine—allowing Loudermilk to argue against the outdated understanding of "country people" as farmers who still rely on horse-drawn wagons. Even though country music fans had been enmeshed in urban and suburban social worlds for decades, Loudermilk still felt the need to address the confining rural stereotype in 1967. His style of wordplay resonated directly with that produced by the CMA earlier in the decade to distance country music fans and performers from the hillbilly stereotype. As Tex Ritter joked to the Adcraft Club of Detroit in 1964, "The songwriter who once tended stock on his daddy's farm is now consulting his broker regarding another kind of stock."[56] These stereotypes were still the starting point from which these industry players hoped to move general understandings of "country folk."

Not only did the inversions of traditional stereotypes work to counter or undermine the stereotypes, but seen in another light, they charted a trajectory or transformation, from a time when the crop was rural goods to a time when it meant the suburban family's young boys. Loudermilk did not want to lose his country folks' ties to the rural past, and so he was able to project both ends of the trajectory into one piece of text, in essence arguing, Yes, we did use to live this way, and are proud of it, but now we can live a different kind of life.[57]

This strategy of emphasizing the rural roots of a modern way of life was useful for the essay's pointed conclusion. Loudermilk's text ultimately established that although the outward trappings of many rural-rooted people had changed, their core values had not, despite, as his album's title suggested, a shift to suburban attitudes (and spaces). In this formulation, what made them "country" was not living on the farm but retaining their traditional values—and it was these enduring values in the face of homogenization that made suburban country fans unique: "They believe kids ought to be thanked when they do good, and spanked when they don't. They know tears are just as normal as laughter and they're not ashamed to do either in public if they feel like it. Why, these corny country hill people have even been known to say family grace in a public restaurant. Yea, when you think about it, I guess country people *are* a different breed after all . . . especially nowadays." Here Loudermilk slyly returned to the stereotypical understanding of the "corny country hill people" only to trumpet their unwillingness to give up their core values. Loudermilk took this opportunity to highlight country people's distinctiveness, but in a positive light: nowadays, he seemed to be saying, most people do *not* think it acceptable to say family grace in a public restaurant. Loudermilk clearly celebrated this refusal to conform to more "modern" ways, and it was this reclamation of traditional rural values that made the essay's earlier wordplay and inversions so resonant.

The emphasis on traditional values tied in with another prevalent strand of country music culture: opposition to the counterculture. Country stars frequently and vociferously weighed in on the issue of the counterculture and the emblems of drugs, long hair, and crazy kids with which they and their fans were supposedly confronted. Singer Bill Anderson, in a 1973 speech at the Broadcast Executives' Luncheon, celebrated a fan who told him she liked the music because, "it was real, nothing phoney. She said, I can sing along with it if I want to, and I don't have to listen to some weird long-haired kid with weird, loud, music, telling me all about his drug experiences."[58] Roy Acuff declared to his biographer, "Country music reflects our good American way of life. It is down to earth, for the home—not to get all hepped up and smoke a lot of marijuana and go wild about."[59] Acuff's and Anderson's reactions against drug use was more visceral than moral but still made the point that country music clearly claimed to stand for respectability and what they saw as family values.

This explicit support for retaining an authentic country identity despite technological changes, new homes, geographic relocations, and drastic cultural shifts resonated with (but also shifted) a longstanding discourse within country music culture. As early as the 1940s, Opry figures comfortably straddled a line between the rustic past and the urban present. In the late 1950s and early 1960s, groups such as the Country Music Association more forcefully argued that country music fans no longer lived in the country or acted like country rubes but were in fact the regular working people of America's cities. But starting in the late 1960s, a new strand of this discourse developed emphasizing neither the city nor the country but instead focusing more strongly on the importance of keeping the country home alive in memory even while moving into a modern home and away from the actual country.

Country song lyrics from the turn of the decade also frequently addressed this tension. As in Loudermilk's essay, the references to country life did not elide the fact of the narrator's rural past; in fact, this past experience was still central to who they are today. In 1969, rising country star Dolly Parton released a song that turned on a fascinating duality about country living, "In the Good Old Days (When Times Were Bad)." Her song foregrounded the hard work involved in agrarian life (working from sunup to sundown, daddy's bleeding hands), and the economic peril that always loomed as a possibility (going to bed hungry, being unable to afford a doctor, where "anything at all is more than we had"). But the chorus suggested both that she wanted to keep the memories with her forever and at the same time never wanted to have to relive the experience: "No amount of money could buy from me the memories I have of then / no amount of money could pay me to go back and live through it again." Parton asserted that rural poverty made her who she is, and while she would never be able to forget it, she would also never go back to such conditions.[60]

In her most famous song, 1970's "Coal Miner's Daughter," Loretta Lynn celebrated her father's ability to provide a home for his children in even the direst poverty, but the song's final verse, like Parton's song, also firmly located this milieu in the past and in Lynn's memory. The song clearly detailed her humble upbringing and the rustic conditions of her childhood. But the song's narrator firmly positioned these conditions in the past, and in the final verse returned to her childhood home and found nothing but "memories":

> Well a lot of things have changed since way back then
> And it's so good to be back home again
> Not much left but the floor
> Nothing lives here anymore
> Except the memories of a coal miner's daughter.

Lynn revealed and celebrated her humble country roots but located her present self in the modern world. She emphasized the importance of humble roots but used the final verse to definitively situate that world in the past.[61]

The same year, Charley Pride released a song that lyrically drew on some of the same themes as Parton's "In the Good Old Days." Pride openly questioned the viability of living in the country with his 1970 number one single, "Wonder Could I Live There Any More." Like Loudermilk's essay and Parton's commentary on the "bad times," Pride emphasized and even celebrated the fact that his rural life was now a thing of the past. Like Parton's tune, the song deconstructed the romanticized mythology of country living by showing instead the combination of hard work and hard times associated with living "there." Each verse took a specific piece of an idealized rural past and questioned whether anyone would trade in the comforts of modern life for the hard work and economic uncertainty of the past. In the opening verse, the narrator invoked a pastoral image of an early morning rooster call but quickly shifted the focus to the number of chores that needed to be done in the course of "another hard work day." The chorus then suggested, quite happily, "It's nice to think about it / maybe even visit / but I wonder could I live there anymore." The song firmly located the narrator outside of the country and actually took a strong stance against the country as a viable site of anything but nostalgia—by suggesting that the country is only *maybe* nice to visit.

While ambivalence about "the country" certainly can be found in plenty of earlier songs, a number one single that so forcefully rejected the country life (finding pleasant feeling only in memories of the past) was unprecedented. Pride did not specifically juxtapose either the city or suburbs to this vision of the country but did reject the ideals of country life, at least for contemporary middle-class people. In Pride's vision of the rustic past, the family was too busy working just to keep their heads above water to have time for any meaningful contact. The distance Pride evoked was meant to be shared by a wide swath of country fans who similarly had left behind their childhood country homes of three-room houses filled with hard work and no time for leisure.

Not surprisingly, given the lyrical content, the song featured elements of the new Nashville Sound—the requisite background choral group supplemented Pride's vocals at the end of each verse and into the chorus, and the song's beat carried it forward without traditional country sound signatures like mournful steel guitar or fiddles. Pride celebrated his distance from country life by using a musical style, the Nashville Sound, associated with country's push to be recognized as a more modern and less rural form. In fact, Pride's descriptions of the hardships of rural life potentially paralleled the decision to leave the uncomfortable and hazardous Ryman Auditorium—one could easily imagine an Opry performer a few years removed from the auditorium penning an elegiac song called "Wonder Could I Perform There Anymore." The overarching argument went something like, "Why should you put up with inferior circumstance when you have achieved the means to provide yourself and your family with the best possible accommodations? Just so you can prove some kind of rural authenticity to an outsider?" This is why Loudermilk's essay was so profound in this historical moment—he reasserted that you could still be "country" in a modern suburban home.[62]

The same year that the Opry departed the Ryman, Tom T. Hall recorded a number one single, "Country Is," that further enshrined the notion that country was not a particular space, or set of spaces, but a state of mind. The song opened with conventional rural imagery by declaring that "country is" sitting on the back porch and listening to the whippoorwill. Two verses later, however, "country" had moved out of the country and become "living in the city/knowing your people/knowing your kind." As the song continued, country became not any place in particular but instead "what you make it . . . all in your mind." Finally, as in Loudermilk's liner notes, which referenced traditional parenting and the importance of honest emotions, Hall's speaker declared that "country is" all about values: "Working for a living, thinking your own thoughts/loving your town, teaching your children/finding out what's right and standing your own ground." As Hall said of country in the final verse, "it's all in your heart." This declaration fully resonated with the justifications and celebrations proffered by other Opry stars who endorsed the program's move out of the Ryman into the gleaming new theater inside the Opryland U.S.A. theme park complex.

In tandem with songs that deconstructed the mythology of an idyllic rural past, other songs recognized that the authenticity of country music was being questioned. A series of songs addressed the very nature of "country" and authoritatively provided an answer, tautological though it may have been. Loretta Lynn's "You're Lookin' at Country" and Lynn Anderson's "Listen to a Country Song" both forcefully addressed the listener and directed them to recognize authentic country. Lynn's song asserted her own country identity and went one step further to argue that there was not a drop of "city" in her: "You don't see no city when you look at me/cause country's all I am." Anderson directed her listener to hear a "country song," though her music was a far cry from what many traditionalist fans described as true country.

Jeannie C. Riley's 1970 song "Country Girl" told a different story. The song contrasted the "lonesome" big cities in which she spent too much time with the country home and family which she missed and wished she could return to (but does not). The repeated line "Oh Lord what I'd give to be a country girl again" seemed to suggest a possible return to the country but the nostalgic tone also foreclosed this possibility. Or, conversely, it allowed for a celebration of the country without having to actually live there. But unlike Loretta Lynn's self-description as "all country," Riley appeared to lament her inability to truly return to being a "country girl."

While country music has always been about the negotiation of rural performances from within an urban commercial world, the notion that the genre would lose its identity with far fewer fans living in rural spaces still hung over country music discourse in the 1970s. The resolution provided by country music fans, performers, journalists, and industry leaders was to suggest that the intrinsic country nature of its people would keep country values and traditions intact despite the migration from the country. This argument rested on an assertion that the old homes and home spaces were special because they were infused with all of the treasured qualities of their inhabitants anyway, and that country migrants would be able to do the same for the new spaces. Accordingly, the justifications for the Opry's move to Opryland aligned with these sentiments. Opry host Carolyn Holloran summarized this discursive resolution with her tautological statement on the move's impact several months after the fact: "It's true you can take the boy out of the country but you can't take the country out of the boy, and the same goes for Country music. Country music is wherever the soul of a Country music fan is!"[63] The statement deterritorializes country music, suggesting that it can be in any kind of space because country music fans can inhabit any kind of space.

Holloran's declaration harkened back as far as the early 1960s when the commercial success of the Nashville Sound spawned country-to-city rhetoric and the Sound's defenders claimed, "You can take the song out of the country, but you can't take the country out of the song." The statement could conceivably cut both ways for country-to-city migrants, who could not always fit in urban spaces and cultures (and surely did in instances where "city people" saw country people as irredeemably rustic and would not let them forget it). But Holloran in this moment unequivocally *celebrated* their inability to shake their "country" nature, taking it as a badge of pride.

As song lyrics and liner notes suggested, there was widespread ideological support for Holloran's comments. Rather than needing to stay in the country (or in older live music venues) to maintain its claim to authenticity, the genre had continually reworked what authentic country identity could mean in the first place and emphasized traditional *values* over everything else. Fan club writers praised the Opry's ability to maintain its unique charm in the sleek new theater, Charley Pride firmly located his rustic roots in the long gone past, and John Loudermilk reminded his readers that country folks' values trumped just about everything else. These concerns and desires both conditioned the move to Opryland U.S.A. and shaped the contours of the discourse used to defend, rationalize, and in some cases embrace the Opry's new home. Not coincidentally, in 1974, the emphasis on traditional values and an appropriate "home" coincided with the Opry's move away from the unpredictable space of downtown Nashville and stars' frequent declarations that the show should not be near the city's "slums." For the Grand Ole Opry, the new definition of "country homes" meant declaring suburban Nashville's new Opryland U.S.A. entertainment complex as a more appropriate home than the show's previous host, the decaying Ryman Auditorium on the precarious edge of respectability in downtown Nashville.

As EARLY as the 1950s, the beginnings of the Nashville Sound had led some traditionalist fans to publicly question whether the combination of massive migration from the country to the city and the synchronous changes in the production and sound of country music were not taking the genre too far from its roots and its original rural working-class fan base. These fans argued that country music belonged to rural working people and equated the new sonic and stylistic changes with the influence of upper-class *city* people who were interested in country music only for its commercial possibilities. In 1974, the Opry's move from downtown to the suburbs potentially represented yet another rejection of country music's past, though this time the perceived spatial markers of this corruption were not urban but suburban. In response, industry figures responded by arguing that the music was still country music and that their fans were still "ordinary people," despite the tony new zip code. As Music Row leaders did in rebutting the charges of excessive commercialism in the 1960s, the Opry's representatives painted the construction of Opryland as a much deserved result of country's popular and artistic success, and a newly appropriate setting for the more modern incarnations of country music and its fans. Given the Opry's deeper attachment to country music's rural roots (at least compared to Music Row and Nashville Sound artists), this ideological shift was more striking than it had been with the Nashville Sound proponents in the previous decade.

In responding to questions about the price and accessibility of the new park, Nashville mayor Beverly Briley told a reporter, "The music will still sell itself due to its tradition as music of the people. I don't think the move or increased cost will affect the Opry. I don't think that poorer people were ever the support of the Opry; so attendance will not change."[64] This comment was particularly jarring, given that various imagined incarnations of the "common folk" were almost always cited as the backbone of country music, in terms of both its performers and its fans. Briley simultaneously argued that country had been the music of "the people" while arguing that "poorer people" never comprised the Opry's fan base. His comment drew boundaries around the common default country fan identity, "the people," asserting that poorer folks did not belong. This chapter shows that the question of just who the common folk were (and where they lived), permeated debates about the current and future state of country music, and the construction of Opryland helped to make sense of Briley's language.

His tendentiously ambiguous use of the popular expression "the people," in tandem with the spatial understanding of country's new home in the suburbs, allowed for a generic invocation of common folk with implicit race and class identifications. While there was still much debate and division on the issue of whether Nashville's form of country music was "country" enough, the Opry's move to Opryland was part of a larger discursive argument made by the country music industry that the current, modern, middle-class instantiation could both remain true to the authentic spirit of country music and appeal to millions of mainstream Americans. In the early 1970s, a wide variety of individuals within the world of the Opry drew on a dominant American discourse that marginalized the urban poor and promoted the suburban conservative values of private property, geographic mobility facilitated by socioeconomic resources, and security from the perceived urban threats of crime and immorality. The spatial and rhetorical move played well in terms of branding the Opry and country music as more suburban, middle-class, and family-friendly, but for a genre that drew much of its appeal from the claim to be the "music of the people," the move also raised the question, *which* people? The next chapter shows that these questions would continue to circulate through additional developments in country music tourism: the return almost twenty years later of country music tourism to downtown and the honky-tonks and other entertainment options of Lower Broad.

"They're Not as Backward as They Used to Be"

Country Music's Commercial Success in the 1990s and the Transformation of Downtown Nashville

IN THE SPRING of 1974, even as the last Opry stars were still packing up their gear and loading their touring buses with a collection of souvenirs and memories that for some stretched back thirty years, observers were wondering what would happen to Lower Broadway without its world-renowned cornerstone and weekend night fixture. Eulogies were issued for Tootsie's Orchid Lounge, which had played a key role in the mythology of the Opry for well over a decade, and most industry observers believed, for better or worse, that the neighborhood would be bereft of country music fans and culture. But Tootsie's did not close its doors, and in fact the lounge and other establishments continued to offer live music throughout the rest of the decade and into the next. Visitors interested in country music heritage continued to make pilgrimages to the Ryman, and the bars of Lower Broad frequently landed on their itineraries.[1] Likewise, a varied mix of local residents kept the bars alive amid the other establishments on the block.

The 1970s Opry stars' mischaracterization of downtown was not likely consciously or willfully misleading. Still, it probably came as a surprise that country music remained a driving force behind the development and economic prosperity of the city's downtown. Nonetheless, country music heritage was not the only salient piece of history in the neighborhood. Three blocks east of the Ryman, a stretch of late nineteenth-century warehouses was beginning to attract interest from historic preservationists, architecture buffs, private investors, and local small business owners. This row comprised the largest intact stretch of this kind of Victorian architecture outside of the East Coast, and interest in these buildings sparked the first wave of revival on the southeastern edge of downtown in the late 1970s. The warehouses covered the entire length of the long block north of Broadway, between First and Second Avenues, and their historical value derived from the fact that the structures were all relatively intact and featured unique and untouched Italianate details on their facades. Furthermore, according to one report, the "streetscape has a strong sense of unity as if every building is locked arm in arm with its neighbor profoundly but silently testifying to the spirit and vigor of Nashville in the 1870s."[2] The same month that the Opry left, Farris Deep, director of the Metropolitan Planning Commission, told one of the city's civic groups that efforts were already underway to turn First and Second Avenues into a "renovated historically-oriented" entertainment area along the lines of the "Underground Atlanta" concept that had been successful in that city for a few years in the early 1970s.[3]

In 1975, Historic Nashville, Inc. (a Nashville nonprofit interested in preserving the city's architecture) partnered with the Metropolitan Historical Commission (MHC) to create the Market Street Festival. The festival focused on Second Avenue and was intended to promote interest in the area's architecture and bring more lucrative traffic to the downtown core.[4] The festival featured walking tours, cocktail hours, and gala events and was geared toward an affluent audience. The MHC and Historic Nashville also published pamphlets designed to orient visitors to the historically significant buildings in the area, and these materials fully encouraged tourist traffic. The area's transformation thus began with the emergence of Second Avenue as a destination for urban loft dwellers, historic preservationists, antique dealers, and art gallery patrons. This development provided a stark contrast with the heritage of live country music on Broadway, and an uneasy tension between the historic preservation movement and the honky-tonks and other remnants of country music heritage persisted for the next decade.

Spurred on by the efforts of preservationists and private investors on Second Avenue, the metropolitan government also contributed significantly to the transformation of the area. Throughout the 1980s, the MHC was a key player in the area's redevelopment through public-private financing schemes that provided small loans for cleanup and infrastructure support, which then encouraged larger private investments. By the late

1980s, municipal efforts had created two landmarks at either end of Lower Broad, the newly constructed Convention Center at the west end, and Riverfront Park, near the warehouses of First Avenue at the other end. Many municipal leaders and local business leaders promoted these two nodes as positive development for the neighborhood.[5] But the axis between these two poles ran straight down Lower Broad, which was seen by many as an unfortunate and dangerous stretch of real estate, what a 1986 *National Geographic* article referred to nastily as "a five block backwash of adult bookstores, pawn shops, hustlers and honky-tonks where your feet stick to the floor."[6] Key Nashville players were already at work to ensure that this perception of the area would not last.

Perhaps because of the association between honky-tonks and other unsavory elements on the block, government organizations and historic preservation groups in the early 1980s did not generally reference the Ryman and the historical legacy of country music in their visions for the area's future. Instead, civic efforts focused more on historic preservation and Second Avenue.[7] The initial impulse among those looking to redevelop the neighborhood was to deliberately keep country music and its fans over on Music Row or out at Opryland (instead of downtown), and the future these developers envisioned for Lower Broad and Second Avenue featured antique stores, art galleries, wine bars, and an approach to historic preservation that focused on late nineteenth-century buildings, not the tacky midcentury history in which country music had played a central role.[8] As the decade went on, interest in redeveloping the neighborhood followed both tracks, and Lower Broad became the frontline in the battle over who would define and represent the area. Creating tourist zones for country music fans that did not overlap with other areas of Nashville's economic interests functioned to segregate these fans and their dollars from other parts of the city. There was a long history of cultural divide within Nashville between the country music industry and its fans and the city's self-styled elite. This divide persisted into debates over what Lower Broad and the other components of a revitalized downtown Nashville should look like.

Down but Not Out: Lower Broad after the Departure of the Opry

Ever after the Opry's departure, the surrounding honky-tonk bars nonetheless continued to offer live country music shows for residents and tourists alike who were drawn to these venues by their association with country music's midcentury heritage. Of these, Tootsie's Orchid Lounge was the most notable and thus the most frequently referenced in discussions about whether the block would retain its heritage. When the Opry left the neighborhood in 1974, much of the regret expressed publicly stemmed from the prospect of losing Tootsie's. But despite some legal troubles and brief closings, Tootsie's persevered, its endurance powered in part by its legendary attachment to the Ryman and the Opry and country music tourists' desire to see the famous watering hole where many legends imbibed, socialized, and, according to the mythology, wrote out their hit songs on cocktail napkins.[9]

In the late 1980s, the honky-tonks had to stake out a space between drunk and disorderly patrons, whom they did consider detrimental to their business, and the new establishments catering to an affluent audience, who tended to treat all honky-tonk customers as "undesirables." The bar owners believed the newer businesses had champions in the city government who had their sights set on running all the honky-tonks and their clientele off Lower Broad. In order to keep the space somewhat regulated and monitored, the bar owners wanted the police to step up patrols to keep unruly customers out of their establishments, and to keep sidewalks and the surrounding blocks safe and visually appealing. It was difficult, however, for these bar owners to pull this off without becoming the proverbial baby thrown out with the bath water.

In the summer of 1988, Lower Broad bar owners asked the police to more intensively patrol the street. The police department complied with their request, making more drunk and disorderly arrests and stepping up a visual presence on a nightly basis. But in the summer and fall of 1989, the police and municipal liquor boards turned the tables on these bars, withholding liquor licenses and citing them for serving over-intoxicated individuals. The bar owners theorized that it was part of the city's effort to "clean up" Lower Broad to pave the way for more high-end development.[10] The bars fought back, accusing the city government of targeting them because their "rough-and-tumble" clientele and atmosphere did not match the city's vision of a more respectable future for Lower Broad. The owner of the Turf, Kathleen Moore, boldly claimed that Ed Stolman (owner of the newly restored Merchant's Restaurant) and Mayor Bill Boner "want that street."[11] The owner of the Rhinestone Cowboy, who had complained that the Metropolitan Beer Board had repeatedly deferred his beer permit renewal, claimed, "We cater to tourists, and when they get down to Lower Broad, they finally find country music. They've fancied up the Merchants, but just try to find country music in there. We lose this, it's lost forever."[12]

The bar owner was referring not just to his business and livelihood but to the practice of live country music played in downscale bars for an audience of ordinary folks.

The renovation of the Merchant's Hotel, completed in 1988, was one of the first highly visible "success" stories for the area around Lower Broad and the groups working to promote its redevelopment. The new Merchant's Restaurant took over a spot that used to house Linebaugh's restaurant, a 1950s-era landmark and frequent destination for Opry goers before and after shows. The symbolism of Ed Stolman's boutique hotel development taking over a space formerly associated with the Opry was not missed. A 1991 article in the *Nashville Tennessean* used the demise of the midcentury Lower Broad landmark to illustrate the changes: "Like the song says, no one eats at Linebaugh's anymore. They can't. Linebaugh's bit the dust and became a parking lot for Merchant's Restaurant, where haute couture and Perrier and yuppies hold court."[13] The song was John Hartford's tune from 1972, written after Opryland opened but before the Opry actually left the Ryman. Hartford foresaw the hole that the Opry's departure would leave on Lower Broad. The article used the reference to pit a piece of Opry-era country music lore against yuppie trends and markers of urban affluence. As with most of the debates about what should happen to Lower Broad, the specter of the Opry loomed large. By the summer of 1990, the Merchant's bar hosted live country music events but emphasized their offerings were smoother and more pop-friendly than the competing honky-tonks across and down the street.[14] The title of one article, "Tootsie's Was Never Like This," carried a clear connotation: the new development heralded by the Merchant's renovation was a sharp and potentially unwelcome contrast with the block's past watering holes.

The local business owners who catered to country music and its fans argued that they were preserving the authenticity of what actually made Nashville both famous and prosperous. They argued that the true heritage of downtown Nashville was the bars and live music for the common folks. Advocates for the honky-tonks celebrated the music's lack of pretension, the performers' humility, and a kind of working-class sociability that would be eliminated by an influx of high-end establishments. Supporters of the honky-tonks and their culture framed their arguments in terms of the marketability of the city's heritage as well. With the Opry gone and the Ryman holding on only as a museum and not a live performance venue, the honky-tonks were the last vestige of live country music in downtown Nashville.

In 1990, a local artist staged a public art installation that playfully addressed this tension. Olin Calk created seven larger-than-life sculptures of cowboys poised to draw their guns as if engaging in a high-noon-style duel. The sculptures were made from discarded and found metal and plastic objects, and while their somewhat cartoonish faces and poses provoked laughter and amusement among the tourists and other visitors who posed for photographs beside them, the art also had a political bent. Calk intentionally placed the statues in a vacant lot across the street from the Merchant's Hotel. Calk named the artwork *Showdown on Broadway,* and local media quickly picked up on the piece's crystallization of the simmering tensions over Stolman's efforts to eradicate country music from the block. A public-private partnership of local merchants and city officials purchased the sculptures for six thousand dollars (Calk had higher offers from private collectors who wanted to move the sculptures elsewhere) and worked with the owners of the empty lot to keep the artwork on Broadway indefinitely.[15] Although there were many proponents of Stolman's push for respectability within the metropolitan government, those who wished to preserve at least some significant piece of country music heritage also began to make their voices clearly heard. Ann Reynolds, for instance, director of the MHC, told a journalist that the organization hoped to keep Lower Broad a "fern-free" zone (using what was common code for yuppie bars in the early 1990s) and claimed that the honky-tonks should always have a permanent place on the block.[16] This shift within the MHC and other metropolitan organizations ultimately led to an approach that accepted both sides of the divide in order to make the neighborhood one of Nashville's prime entertainment destinations.

In the early 1990s, a collection of groups had the idea to more formally link downtown Nashville's three prime nightlife destination areas—Printer's Alley, Second Avenue, and Lower Broad—under one umbrella concept of "the District." The Broadway Committee, an ad hoc group consisting of the mayor's office, the Metropolitan Development and Housing Agency (MDHA), the MHC, the Metropolitan Arts Commission, and Historic Nashville, came up with the idea as a way to promote visitor traffic across the neighborhood, and the group relied on MDHA grants along with federal tax incentives and intense marketing and politicking to promote investment in the district.[17] Key players realized that the different components of the neighborhood could feed off of and lend support to each other, although the question of what role Lower Broad would play and what the future would hold for the bar owners was still up in the air. Eventually, though, the organizations behind the District chose to support all kinds of development while minimizing tensions among the different factions, and opted for a marketing approach that emphasized the unique appeal of being able to experience *all* kinds of food, drink, and culture in one centralized neighborhood. As one promotional pamphlet put it, "Where else can you peruse an art gallery, kick up your heels and dance, sing along with a bluegrass band, dine on a rolling train, buy an antique mandolin, quaff suds at a brewery, hear an Irish folk song, and eat anything from spaghetti to sushi, chitlins to chateaubriand? Nowhere but The DISTRICT—where everything old is new again."[18] This promotional text intentionally included markers of rural milieus as well as emblems of urban sophistication, mandolins and bluegrass as well as sushi and chateaubriand, and attempted to resolve the question of which heritage the neighborhood should embrace by including them all.

Nashville's government played a key role in the transformation of Lower Broad and the surrounding blocks. As part of the planning for the District and cleanup of Lower Broad, for instance, the MDHA purchased and renovated key properties, including one on the corner of Fourth and Broadway that had previously housed the Swinger's World adult bookstore.[19] When, in 1987, Robert Matthews formed an investment group in tandem with Opryland U.S.A. and Central Parking, the group persuaded the MDHA to declare the space between Fifth and Second on the east and west, and Commerce and Broadway on the north and south, part of the Capitol Mall Redevelopment Plan, a redevelopment district that the agency had already approved. This declaration meant the government could use eminent domain to take land from property owners who would not work with it in developing the space.[20] The investment group formed by Matthews, Opryland, and Central Parking was formally named the Ryman Group, and, as its name suggests, a refurbished Ryman Auditorium was at the heart of the group's vision for a forward-looking, mixed-use space that combined modern architecture with the renovated auditorium. The Ryman was to be the "hook" on which the rest of the development hung, keeping live music a priority for the area's development, but the potential use of eminent domain scared many of the bar owners on Lower Broad. Metropolitan government officials were on board from the beginning, but the owners of the plots on the north side of Broadway felt threatened. They too wanted the area improved but were skeptical of what would actually happen, and thus were hesitant to take action to renovate their properties, worried that they might be evicted regardless.[21]

The Ryman Center project was originally conceptualized as a continuous three-block development, with three corner office towers, a hotel, one giant anchor tenant, and numerous retail and entertainment options on the lower floors. The development was promoted by Matthews and his partners, including Opryland, and endorsed by local government, media, and business owners.[22] Opryland's participation was significant because this was the first time a highly visible player in the country music industry had committed to investing in the area around the Ryman again. The development would have left the Ryman Auditorium intact but would have significantly transformed the immediate landscape around the historic auditorium by surrounding it with larger office and hotel towers.

By January 1992, as debates over the future of the avenue simmered, the Ryman Group, with the help of the MDHA, had put together a parcel of land across the street from the Ryman. The group found an owner in BellSouth, who purchased the property in order to build the company's state headquarters.[23] While the office tower development did not fully match the ambitious initial plans for the Ryman Center, which would have been a more capacious development to include a massive office tower along with a hotel and other retail options, the plans to build the BellSouth office tower were enough to jumpstart development on the southern edge of downtown, where the perceived decline of Lower Broad had scared off large investors for over a decade. Matthews himself talked up the importance of redeveloping downtown and pointed to the value of the new office tower's two thousand employees as well as the symbolic importance of investing in the downtown space.[24] Even though the office tower did not open until 1995, the decision to build the headquarters across the street from the Ryman and a half-block up from Lower Broad influenced other investment and development plans over the next three years.

Urban gentrification in the late 1980s in other U.S. cities generally consisted of affluent groups' taking over the spaces of economically marginalized people through a combination of factors, including the increased value of urban property driving up prices, and investors' funneling capital into commercial and retail enterprises that appealed to higher-end consumers.[25] The difficulty in Nashville was that the most obvious local engine of economic revitalization, country music, carried with it the stigma of lower-class disorder and ill-repute that urban redevelopment was generally supposed to replace. When local country fans and honky-tonk bar owners complained about the invasion of "fern bars" and "sushi bars," they were invoking a larger narrative about urban gentrification and arguing that, because of Nashville's unique heritage, the outcome in Nashville could and should be different. They believed that redevelopment and a return of investment capital to the downtown area could actually be driven by country music, once stigmatized as hillbilly music and seen as entirely out of place in the city. Despite strands of opposition from certain players in the neighborhood, the country music bars survived, and in many ways, because of their persistent "ground-up" occupation of the space, local preservation groups, investors, government officials, and downtown business owners eventually realized that country music and cultural and structural connections with Opryland and Music Row were necessary to achieve the desired levels of reinvestment and development. But even as developers and property owners on Lower Broad debated the role country music should play in the area's redevelopment, the genre itself was beginning to experience a titanic shift in style, image, and popularity.

Garth Brooks and the Meteoric Rise of Country Music Sales

Country music sales plummeted in the 1980s, but a wave of "neo-traditionalists" in the middle of the decade sparked a first wave of revival. When Randy Travis's release of *Storms of Life* in 1986 sold a shocking 3 million records, industry figures suddenly realized that the pendulum was swinging back toward the traditional sounds. Across the industry, people understood there was a market for this throwback style that combined 1950s honky-tonk, western swing, and folk.[26] The early 1990s saw the rise of numerous young artists who nodded to country music tradition and this revival, but whose work was more a synergy of country, rock, folk, and pop. While country's early 1990s boom was often portrayed by media commentators as happening essentially overnight, there had of course been many country stars who had found extensive commercial success, in the United States and abroad. In the 1960s, Nashville Sound stars such as Glen Campbell, Porter Wagoner, and Johnny Cash had national network television shows, and country stars played large halls in New York City and Los Angeles, as well as headlining in Las Vegas. In the late 1970s and early 1980s, even more explicitly crossover country artists such as Kenny Rogers, John Denver, and Dolly Parton topped the pop charts.[27]

Between 1989 and 1993, however, country music's share of the overall commercial music market in the United States doubled, and the number of country radio stations increased dramatically.[28] In 1990, 39 country albums "went gold" (selling 500,000 copies) or platinum (1 million copies);

in 1995, the number was 135. By 1996, there were 2,600 country radio stations, more than double that of the next most popular format (in part, presumably, because Top 40 stations still refused to play country).[29] This wave of success did not come from older stars with name recognition; in fact, older stars had difficulty finding spots on country radio stations that had not adopted the "classic country" format. Instead, this wave of commercial success was led by a crop of new artists who produced a complicated hybrid of traditional country imagery and sounds, contemporary production values, and sometimes overt nods to the rock and folk stars of the 1970s. These artists depended heavily on a new cable network devoted to country music, Country Music Television (the network was owned by Gaylord Entertainment Company, owners since 1983 of the Opry, Opryland, and the Ryman Auditorium), whose MTV-style music videos fundamentally transformed the way in which country music was consumed by its audiences.[30] Between 1989 and 1996, country record sales more than quadrupled, driven in no small part by the phenomenal sales of Garth Brooks.

Brooks started out as one of a crop of impressive rising young stars but quickly left them all behind, becoming one of the biggest sellers in the history of commercial pop music in the United States. By the mid-1990s, he had sold 60 million albums, making him second only to the Beatles in total record sales in America.[31] Despite Brooks's fairly open embrace of elements of rock and pop, his highly stylized stage shows, and his unashamed interest in self-promotion, early industry media coverage of his rise still stuck to a traditional narrative and description of his country "roots." One article referred to Brooks as having come "from a simple, well-founded upbringing in a small country town. He stepped out of Yukon, Oklahoma last year with a sound Music City was looking for." Much like the 1950s discourse that positioned country artists as "stumbling out of the backwoods" or "emerging from the fields," the article subtly suggested that Brooks had only in the moment of becoming a country star emerged from his natural home community. The article mentioned Brooks's time spent working in the oil fields but downplayed his college education and marketing degree.[32]

There is a long history of this kind of spatial discourse being used to describe country musicians' entering the national stage. In the early 1990s, though, the discourse flipped the traditional roles. In the 1950s, national discussions about country music blithely portrayed commercial stars as having stumbled out of the hills or backwoods, while the industry's own promotional material, by contrast, worked to show that the artists had both urban and rural roots. In the early 1990s, country music conversations more often emphasized the unadulterated country nature of its stars, while national media commentators generally highlighted the seeming artifice of urbanites and suburbanites pretending to be everyday country folk. National media coverage questioned the new music's ties to the genre's past and focused on how it was being smartly marketed to a suburban audience turned off by other forms of pop music.[33] Bruce Feiler, for instance, described Brooks as, "a man from Oklahoma who had little in common with the social pedigree of Sarah or the rural charm of Minnie, yet whose suburban, all-American background would become the perfect symbol for the new middle-class ascendancy in the South."[34]

In January 1992, Brooks aired an NBC television special that highlighted the most performative and hyper-stylized aspects of his live concerts. Critics emphasized the production values and analyzed Brooks not necessarily as a country musician but as a modern television star. A *New York Times* article on him opened with a description of his stage costume—"his cowboy hat held a headset microphone; on the back of his cowboy shirt was its wireless transmitter"—to emphasize the high-tech approach to his stage show.[35] Ken Tucker's review of the special highlighted the star's expert showmanship abilities and dismissed the scenes of a philosophical Brooks strolling through the Tennessee countryside as unbelievable nonsense.[36] But Brooks's dominant milieu was not the rural countryside, which really only served as an inspiration to the massive media production that Brooks was selling and listeners were buying. His epic stage shows, hyper-mediated celebrations of excess, were the selling point, and this approach was duplicated by other pieces of country music television production in the early 1990s.

In perhaps one of the most bizarre examples of a traditional country music icon adapting to the new marketing environment, *Hee Haw,* the oldest-running country music television show, responded to changes in country's demographics by attempting a makeover for the 1992 season aimed at new audiences. There was a significant shift in tone and visual style accompanying the larger shift in music video production, and the self-consciously cartoonish vision of farm life presented by *Hee Haw* did not fit this new vision. For the start of the 1992 season (filmed in the fall of 1991), the show's famous cornfield set was chucked in favor of city-street and shopping mall sets (appealing to both the urban and the suburban milieus), several older members of the cast were replaced by younger performers, and the stage for the musical performances was transformed into a turquoise and pink neon nightclub set.[37] The makeover did not work, and the show was finally cancelled because of low ratings only a few months after the transformation. It turned out that neither incarnation of the program could resonate with the new demographics of country music fans.

That same season a weekly country music and variety show debuted on NBC. *Hot Country Nights,* like the new *Hee Haw,* eschewed any trace of rural iconography, and presented country artists and comedians on a stage designed to look more like that of an awards show gala.[38] Ken Tucker of *Entertainment Weekly* described the program through a spatial perspective: "The crucial difference between *Hot Country Nights* and earlier country TV shows is that *Hot* assumes there's nothing intrinsically rural or exotic about country music." Tucker went on to position the new program against a lengthy tradition of televised country programs that were heavily invested in rural imagery: "Earlier attempts to put country music on TV—*Ozark Jubilee* in the late '50s, variety shows starring Jimmy Dean and Johnny Cash in the '60s, and, most stereotypically, *Hee Haw*—presented country as the work of grinning rubes whose preferred seating arrangement was atop a bale of hay."[39] The Garth Brooks live concerts and *Hot Country Nights* put contemporary country music front and center on television across the nation, the genre's most visible presence in that medium since the early 1970s. Along with the music videos of CMT and the new look for *Hee Haw,* these primetime specials' emphasis on nightlife resonated with Gaylord Entertainment's next plan for country music's presence on Lower Broad, a television production facility, live music venue, and dance club all rolled into one, the Wildhorse Saloon.

The Return of "Big Country": Gaylord's Transformation of Lower Broad

Responding to changes in both the urban landscape of Lower Broad and the demographics of country music, the Opry's stewards envisioned a return to the downtown scene the program had abandoned nearly two decades before. After Bell South announced its plans and began construction on a giant office tower in the neighborhood, the next commitment of private capital came directly from the Gaylord Entertainment Company. In the spring of 1993, the company announced a threefold plan to contribute to the revitalization of downtown Nashville and connect their suburban theme park and music entertainment complex to the cultural activities happening downtown in the District. The three planks were a substantial country music dance hall/live music/television production facility at Second and Broad; an $8 million renovation of the Ryman, which would transform the auditorium into a functioning live music venue once again; and the opening of water taxi service connecting Opryland to Lower Broad via the Cumberland River.[40] The dance hall, called in an Old-West fashion the Wildhorse Saloon, occupied two nineteenth-century buildings on Second Avenue and was home to stages for live music, a dance club that could hold 1,600 people, facilities for televising live performances, and a restaurant and several bars.[41] The name of the venue invoked a stylish "urban cowboy" milieu more so than the hillbilly iconography of the Opry's past, suggesting that the saloon could and would appeal to a younger crowd of partygoers.

Gaylord used the synergy among the three new additions to downtown's entertainment landscape to connect their suburban theme park complex to the entertainment action on Lower Broad. Whereas earlier in the decade commentators had speculated that Gaylord would not want to prop up a potentially competing tourist destination, the company eventually made the decision that the connection between the spaces could benefit both, and that there were enough profits to be made in each. Gaylord believed that tourists staying in the hotels and campgrounds out by Opryland were possibly driving downtown to check out the scene there, and it might as well be grabbing some of those tourist dollars in the process. Furthermore, if the tourists had not already planned a trip to downtown on their itinerary, Gaylord could use the force of its entertainment properties (including the newly developed cable television networks) to "sell" downtown Nashville to the public.[42] On the heels of Gaylord's announcements, plans for a publicly funded arena and event center one block from the Ryman were revealed in 1993, and the Country Music Foundation also declared its plan to move the Country Music Hall of Fame downtown (one block south of Broadway and the honky-tonks) in 1994. A vision of an entertainment district with country music at its heart was clearly taking shape, but not everyone was happy about this outcome.

Gaylord's expansion into downtown Nashville led some local business owners to declare that tacky tourists would infiltrate the area. These business owners believed that Music Row and Opryland were already overrun with tacky tourists and did not want the same thing to happen to Second Avenue and Lower Broad. On the eve of the Wildhorse Saloon's opening and the start of water taxi service from Opryland to downtown, some local merchants worried that this influx of new tourists would ruin the character of downtown. One local reporter declared, "But for loyal patrons of longtime Second Avenue establishments, the boom threatens to turn downtown into a parking nightmare and a series of trashy tourist traps not far removed from Music Row's souvenir shops."[43] The word "trashy" was not incidental and tied tacky country music tourism to the perception that the visiting fans would be lower on the socioeconomic scale. The daytime manager of Windows on the Cumberland was quoted as saying, "Now, it's going to become one big tourist trap. There'll be dark socks and plaid shorts everywhere." Another employee of an oyster bar claimed, "I'm afraid this avenue will become the next Music Row, and I have no doubt that Gaylord Entertainment has that specific agenda in mind." This observer painted Gaylord as a corporate behemoth looking to take as many tourist dollars as possible from the tacky dark-socked country music fans, at the expense of the integrity and cachet of one of Nashville's more prestigious neighborhoods.[44]

As in previous decades, country music's promoters were upfront about their marketing strategies and what they deemed to be a necessary corrective to the existing stereotypes that still dogged the genre. Several spokespersons for Nashville's marketing departments addressed the backwoods specter that continued to hang over the genre. One financial analyst praised Gaylord's savvy synergy of Nashville tourist spaces with their theme park and national cable network ventures: "Entertainment people in New York are finally discovering that country music is not just for people with more children than teeth." This comment suggests a false history in which country music was *only now* being respected as a commercial phenomenon while degrading traditional country folk at the same time.[45] Joe Mansfield, original architect of Garth Brooks's marketing campaign and marketing and sales vice president at Capital Records Nashville in the early 1990s, claimed, "Just because an artist wears a cowboy hat doesn't mean he's only going to be bought by hayseed people wearing bib overalls."[46] The statement could have just as easily been uttered by a CMA official in the association's 1960s campaign to persuade radio ad buyers of the viability of the country music audience. This continuity speaks to both the enduring persistence of country stereotypes and the savvy marketing rhetoric of country music industry figures.

In contrast with how the city reacted to attempts to claim municipal funding for the expansion of Music Row Boulevard in the early 1970s, the city's full support of the renovation of Lower Broad and the construction of a unified and themed entertainment district built around country music in the early 1990s demonstrated how far the industry had evolved, how much the relationship between the city and the industry had been transformed, and how much of a place country music occupied in the cultural imagination of Nashville. In the 1990s, Nashville leaders finally and wholly recognized the importance of country music to the region's overall economy, even if some local business owners had complaints about the nature of the tourists coming downtown. It was not until the early 1990s that the local Chamber of Commerce finally realized the intense marketing potential of country music for the city, and looked to officially partner with the industry to promote country music tourism.[47]

As country music became astoundingly successful, the momentum from Gaylord's expansion in the neighborhood pushed even more large-scale development, on the part of both private investors and Nashville's metropolitan government. After debating for years about how to fund it, Mayor Phil Bredesen finally saw his dream of building an arena downtown realized in 1993 when plans were announced for the construction of a publicly funded twenty thousand seat arena on the corner of Fifth and Broadway, across the street diagonally from Tootsie's and the Ryman. The arena was funded by the city government, facilitated by Bredesen's ability to pass an increased property tax, and was designed with both music and sporting events in mind.

The city actually tapped one of country music's most popular stars, Vince Gill, to be on the jury that chose the winning design (along with four architects and a former NBA star, to represent the sporting world's interests). In the winning design, the main concourse floor featured a guitar fretwork mosaic, a small horn-shaped rehearsal hall was built adjacent to the main building, and an asymmetrical seating bowl with a focus on a stage at one end was implemented to maximize seating and viewing experiences for concerts, instead of a center court focus for sporting events.[48]

The genre exploded commercially in the early 1990s, but many traditional observers bemoaned (not for the first time) the fact that the new material had strayed too far from country's roots. These critiques of glossy commercialism and the abandonment of country's past overlapped with criticism of the state of country music, whether it was on the radio, at the Opry, or on recorded albums. Not surprisingly, a strand of "alternative" country emerged to contest popular country's sole claim to the mantle of country music.

"Alternative" Country in the Shadow of the Opry

By the summer of 1994, the Ryman had reopened, Gaylord had opened the Wildhorse Saloon, and plans were on the books for both a new arena and a new Country Music Hall of Fame building in the two blocks south of the Ryman. These developments appeared to have the potential to run the small bar owners out of business and off Lower Broad, much to the chagrin of many fans of the neighborhood's honky-tonk heritage. In the summer of 1994, however, two live bands started plying their trade at two different bars, three doors down from each other on the north side of Lower Broad, both of which had back exits that opened onto the alley that ran beside the Ryman. These bands drew on 1950s-era country music styles, and eschewed hillbilly or cowboy trappings in favor of thrift store suits and fedoras. They quickly gained a popular following and drew appreciative crowds of, among others, hip young Nashville urbanites. BR5-49 (whose band name was a *Hee Haw* reference) performed at Robert's Western World, and Greg Garing's band performed at Tootsie's. The momentum of the two acts gave hope to those who had gloomily predicted the gentrification of the block and its musical offerings.[49]

BR5-49, in particular, created a sound that quickly resonated with large crowds of both Nashville residents and national journalists. Before they had even signed with a label or released a recording, a front-page article in *Billboard* claimed the band had made Lower Broad the "hippest place in Music City."[50] The band covered country songs from the 1930s through the early 1960s, and focused on western swing, honky-tonk, and rockabilly. The band's appeal was rooted, as many observers noted, in the stark contrast they provided to the homogenized country dance songs of the 1990s. As one country publication described BR5-49's success, "They've attracted attention because of a growing feeling that something intangible—yet important to country music—had been tossed aside at some uncertain point in the past few years."[51] Chuck Mead, the band's guitarist and one of the lead vocalists, outlined his own understanding of the spatial dimensions of pop versus "authentic" country music in the mid-1990s: "We were drawn to Lower Broadway because of the real honky tonks—the real spirit of country music. We're not interested in Music Row or Opryland, which is so fake and plastic. People go to Lower Broad because they feel it's the actual continuation of history rather than a preconceived production concept."[52] Mead dismissed both Music Row and Opryland, even though those two sites certainly had substantial claims as pieces of country music history,

Today the Ryman Auditorium is sandwiched between the thriving honky-tonks of Lower Broad and the corporate office buildings of downtown Nashville.

and instead considered them part of a "production concept." For Mead, these emblems of mainstream commercial music had become prepackaged experiences, but the aura of Lower Broad was more organically tied to the genre's heritage. Even though the story was often told that Mead and his band awakened Lower Broad, or brought the honky-tonk spirit back, Mead himself argued that that spirit was there before BR5-49 and was in fact what brought them to Lower Broad in the first place. Defenders of Robert's Western World and the other "authentic" honky-tonks claimed that gentrification on Lower Broad was replacing true country music and true fans in order to appeal to tourists who were not country music fans, and supportive media coverage of BR-549 contrasted the band's authenticity with the "kitschy renewal" on Lower Broad.[53]

By the summer of 1996, the emerging popularity of these live bands led Bloodshot Records, an independent label based in Chicago, to release a compilation album of songs by artists who appreciated older country music styles but blended this traditional bent with rock and an unruliness not found in the squeaky-clean, homogenized sound produced in the studios of Music Row. Bloodshot itself had been formed in 1994 and was a self-proclaimed alternative to mainstream country music; the label in its early years claimed the mantle of "insurgent country." *No Depression* magazine was established in 1995 by co-editors Grant Alden and Peter Blackstock to chronicle what the publication referred to as "radio-free country music," which encompassed more punk-influenced bands such as those on Bloodshot as well as folk and roots-based artists who operated in the milieu of country music but could not or did not want to find a home on the country radio stations controlled by major country labels. The term "No Depression" was first applied to the genre in the early 1990s, when the Midwestern band Uncle Tupelo covered the classic Carter Family tune of the same name, and the phrase suggested a blend of rock and punk with classical country music. Uncle Tupelo's work and that of other likeminded bands challenged the reigning Music Row orthodoxy of attractive singers, pop production, and glossy celebrity lifestyles.[54] The appeal of these artists also sprung from the fact that they sang songs that more vividly evoked specific experiences of rural, exurban, small-town, and working-class life.

The title of the Bloodshot compilation, *Nashville: The Other Side of the Alley,* explicitly used the spatial connection between the Lower Broad honky-tonks and the Ryman Auditorium, which was still a potent symbolic marker of the country music "industry" in Nashville. The reference to the "other side" suggested that country music fans were not looking beyond the Opry or what the Opry seemed to stand for in this formulation, popular and commercial country music in general. This proclamation suggested that there existed a whole other exciting world of "true" country music at Tootsie's and Robert's Western World, mere steps away from the old auditorium that stood as a powerful symbol of the Opry and the institutions of country music. The liner notes for *The Other Side of the Alley* emphasized this divide. The essay suggested a contrast between the "weeds" of the alternative country bands on the compilation, who defiantly sprouted up through the sidewalks, and the "unnaturally manicured environment" of those who would try to repress and sanitize this kind of music. The essay's skeptical reference to downtown development (with the phrase "new paint and neon-lit chrome") suggested that something authentic was being glossed over and lost.[55] Even as the album was released in the summer of 1996, a new arena was being constructed on the corner of Fifth and Broadway, practically right across the street from Tootsie's. No one knew for sure who or what the arena would bring to lower downtown, but many were certain that the developers behind the construction would not want ratty or tacky bars that played rough-around-the-edges country music for sometimes rowdy working-class customers.

Still, the neighborhood was not completely sanitized, homogenized, or cleaned up. In the summer of 1996, adult establishments still operated on the block, sandwiched among the honky-tonks and new businesses, and local media coverage emphasized that tourists were frequently discouraged by the crowds of ruffians hanging out outside some of these establishments. For example, one property owner, Inez Silverfield, held six properties on which she did not have to make any renovations because she was "grandfathered" out of the current metropolitan codes.[56] Her properties became a lightning rod for other business owners, who were worried both about the potentially dangerous structural problems with her buildings as well as the dubious moral character of her tenants' patrons. But not all business owners on Broadway agreed that Silverfield had to go. While some were concerned that she did not renovate and upgrade her businesses or keep them up to code, other owners were more concerned that Silverfield's properties would be purchased by corporate entertainment chain developers or higher-end investors. One property owner declared, "I'm a lot more concerned about upscale yuppie fern bars coming in here than I am worried about the winos."[57] Once again, "yuppie fern bars" were contrasted with the authentic grit of the honky-tonks. In fact, one of Silverfield's properties was not an adult establishment but Robert's Western World, the home for BR-549, who had brought positive attention and publicity to the city and Lower Broad specifically.

After the opening of the Wildhorse and the reopening of the Ryman, Gaylord Entertainment's transformation of their tourist offerings continued at the end of the decade. In 1997, Gaylord shuttered the amusement park portion of the Opryland U.S.A. complex and decided to partner with a shopping mall development firm to turn the space into Opry Mills, a large project that combined shopping with some live music and other entertainment options (such as movie theaters and a bowling alley), to create what their promotional machine referred to as "shoppertainment."[58] Opry Mills shifted the focus of Gaylord's suburban property to convention-goers staying at the hotel (now the largest non-casino hotel in the country and a top destination for national conferences and conventions) and regional shoppers, and in turn shifted some of the focus for country music tourism back downtown. In the fall of 1998, Gaylord also experimented with broadcasting the Opry from the renovated Ryman. The event was a success, and in January 1999, the program was again performed in the old venue. Since then, the Opry has broadcast all of its winter shows from the Ryman. The same blocks that had been deemed unfit for the families of the Opry audience a few decades earlier were now home to late-night revelers, tourists on the hunt for souvenir bargains, and country music heritage enthusiasts seeking out traces of the old tunes.

The connotations of urban space had changed, the specifics of this particular neighborhood had changed, and the demographics and culture of country music had changed. Country music's presence in the Nashville region, whether it was productions recorded in studios on Music Row and other areas around the city, consumption driven by fans who flocked to downtown's live music nightlife district, or visitors who combined a trip to the Opry House theater in the suburban location with shopping at the new Opry Mills mall, all helped to produce a resonant identity for country music at the end of the twentieth century not tied to any *one* particular space.

By the final decade of the century, country music was more popular than ever before, and was a presence in the social lives of more Americans than ever before, but the question remained, what made it country? With more and more country songs compared to pop music, and more country stars openly affiliating their music with singer/songwriters and rock, one answer was that Nashville itself had become a marker of geographic difference that could stand in for genre difference. This development built on descriptions of the Nashville Sound in the 1970s, which had focused on studio settings and the relaxed session musicians who made a Nashville Sound record "country." If it was harder to tell the difference between a country song and a pop song, the fact that it was recorded in Nashville and its performers lived or had significant roots there could provide the song with authentic "country" credentials.

Observers defined Nashville in terms of a kind of middle ground that avoided the ugly excesses of both the rich and poor of larger cities like Los Angeles and New York. *New York Times* author Peter Applebome charted this middle ground for Nashville by first comparing the relaxed vibe in Nashville, even among the music executives, with the "edgy overdrive of Doberman-style gatekeepers and power lunches at Spago or the Four Seasons" in Los Angeles and New York.[59] He also, however, quoted a producer's justification for leaving Los Angeles and moving to Nashville: "Between crime, riots, gangs, earthquakes, and fires, it's like Blade Runner out there." The producer invoked an urban dystopia at the other end of the spectrum from the power lunchers at Los Angeles's toniest haunts, setting Nashville up as a peaceful counterpoint that had neither extreme. In Nashville, the producer continued, "you don't see graffiti every time you open your eyes, and you don't hear helicopters over your house all the time."[60] This reassuring middle space between the racialized urban criminal elements and the power-hungry and impersonal coastal elites was a powerful element in the reservoir of cultural and political associations attached to country music.

Alan Jackson's "Gone Country," which came out in 1994, captured this line of thinking. Even though the song has often been read as a satire and critique of opportunists cashing in (literally) on country's cresting popularity, the verse that described the Los Angeles pop star moving to Nashville to raise his family could have easily been pulled straight from the approving media coverage of this exact phenomenon:

> He commutes to L.A., but he's got a house in the Valley
> But the bills are piling up and the pop scene just ain't on the rally
> And he says, honey, I'm a serious composer, schooled in voice and
> 　　composition
> But with the crime and the smog these days, this ain't no place for
> 　　children.

The "crime and smog" were common enough critiques of Los Angeles, and worked in this verse to make Nashville seem like a clean and safe place to raise one's family. Even as Jackson was potentially chiding California pop stars for jumping on the country bandwagon, he provided an explanation for their exodus from the coast that no one in Nashville would dispute.

Jackson's tune, released after the tremendous wave of commercial success of the early 1990s had crested, also featured a description of an aging Vegas lounge singer who sees herself as a "simple girl" and therefore able to fit into the Nashville scene, and a folk singer who recognizes the affinities between Nashville's country music and the stuff of Bob Dylan. The song worked as both a satire of artists from other genres who try to put on the mantle of country, and a celebration of the wide appeal and inclusivity of the genre, depending on your perspective. A key couplet astutely portrayed how northern perceptions of Nashville and country music had changed: "I hear down there it's changed, you see / Well, they're not as backward as they used to be." Whether the narrator believed this change of heart or not might be ambiguous, but the lyric still invoked the older stereotypes and argued for the presence of a more modern incarnation for country music. There was really nothing to indicate that the narrator himself did not agree with this sentiment, potentially lamenting the earlier stereo-types but celebrating the fact that they no longer held much water and that folks from across the nation were willing to embrace the Nashville musical culture. The consolidation of various pieces of the industry in one easily recognized location helped to maintain country music's generic stability even as musically, country music began to sound more and more like other genres.

Conclusion

IT WOULD be hard to argue that the vision many critics of Lower Broad's development had in the mid-1990s, of corporate chains destroying the local flavor and culture which made the block unique, actually transpired. As tourism-driven urban entertainment and nightlife districts go, Nashville's Lower Broad is generally regarded as a home to top-notch musicians playing country music in relatively authentic settings.[1] Robert Moore, the owner of Robert's Western World, known around the world in the 1990s as the home to BR5-49, had an idea for what Lower Broad and downtown Nashville could become. According to Nashville chronicler Laurence Leamer, Moore "had this dream of turning Lower Broad into a hillbilly Bourbon Street, where folks would come and listen to real country music, not some gussied-up tourist version played in soulless rooms, but the real thing played in real places."[2] Of course, the "real thing" is impossible to define and will always be a contested term, but anecdotal evidence suggests that this vision has been realized. A stroll down Broadway today reveals something very similar to this vision, and Robert's Western World reigns supreme as one of the most popular honky-tonks on the block.

The authenticity of the neighborhood got an important stamp of approval and enhanced degree of historical prestige at the turn of the twenty-first century when the Country Music Hall of Fame chose to move its museum to a site a stone's throw from Tootsie's and Robert's. In 2002, the Country Music Foundation moved its hall of fame and museum from a barnlike structure built on Music Row in the 1960s to a modern building one block south of Lower Broad. The new site was carefully chosen to be close to the Ryman Auditorium as well as Tootsie's and the other

honky-tonks, and also sat across the street from the new arena. When the
first home for the hall opened in 1967, the Opry and other Lower Broad
venues operated downtown, but neither municipal or music industry leaders could fully envision country music tourism taking over the downtown
space in such a wholesale way. In fact, in only a few short years, the Opry
itself would shutter the Ryman and skip town for the hills of suburbia.
When the hall of fame did finally make its way downtown, however, not
only had the Ryman reopened, and the Opry returned after a twenty-five
year hiatus, but the Lower Broad neighborhood had become one of the
premier urban nightlife and entertainment districts in the nation. The
hall of fame added an extra layer of tourist interest and historical prestige
but also provided a crucial space that could tie together the various sites
of country music tourism. The hall became a jumping-off point for tours
of both the Ryman Auditorium and historic studios on Music Row, as
well as promoting tours of and tickets to the suburban Opry House at the
Opry Mills shopping and hotel complex. This successful synergy between
Nashville's city and suburbs, between Music Row and the Opry, was a long
time coming.

In 2001, Fan Fair, the Country Music Association's annual event giving
fans the opportunity to attend shows, meet stars, and obtain autographs,
joined the downtown bandwagon. In 1982, as yet another part of the exodus from downtown, the fair had moved from the Municipal Auditorium
to the Tennessee State Fairgrounds three miles south, where it stayed for
nearly two decades. But declining attendance numbers and the proposed
demolition of the fairgrounds caused the CMA to seek another location.
As a result of aggressive outreach from Mayor Bill Purcell, who thought
Fan Fair would be another great boon for the downtown economy, the
CMA saw the density of downtown and Lower Broad as a perfect opportunity to organize the fair around different kinds of live music venues,
some free and open even to those without tickets, and other session sites
within blocks of the convention center and other country music tourist
attractions.

Even though the space of downtown was dense, the geography of the
event was still more far-flung than it had been at the fairgrounds. There,
every event was essentially held in one central place, but downtown there
were more opportunities over a wider network of venues, including the
new football stadium across the river, to see live shows and attend the festival's famous autograph sessions and star-studded panels. The new layout
required journeying among multiple sites, which drew some grumbles

from older fans who complained that the fair involved more hiking up and down the hills of Nashville's riverfront neighborhood.[3] Nonetheless, the first Fan Fair downtown was a resounding success, shattering attendance records and starting a new tradition in downtown Nashville.[4] In 2005, the city's weekly cultural publication, the *Nashville Scene,* heartily endorsed moving Fan Fair downtown and referred to the fairgrounds, negatively, as "rural as all get out."[5] The dismissive use of "rural" was undoubtedly striking but, in the long view, made a certain kind of sense. While there could not have been anything more "country" in the earlier decades of the genre's history than a state fairground, by the turn of the century, the fair was "too rural" and the most natural space for the country music industry's biggest fan event was a neighborhood downtown. In 2004, the CMA even changed the event's name from Fan Fair to the CMA Music Festival, further distancing the festival from its rural connotations.

Fan Fair had started in 1972 and was intended to resolve tensions between the CMA and country music fans over fan participation in an annual disc jockey convention.[6] Although many fan club presidents were unhappy with the move at the time, the fair quickly became a popular attraction, as fans relished the chance to meet their favorite performers up-close and personal, and the format—several days of concerts, panels, sessions, and meet and greets—turned out to be innovative and popular. Fan Fair was a critical site for promoting the accessibility and fan-friendly nature of country stars, and has been a crucial part of the notion that country stars are more down to earth, sincere, and approachable than those of other popular musical genres. In 1996, Garth Brooks spent a stupefying twenty-three hours signing autographs, a now legendary (but apparently not apocryphal) feat in country music circles. As some observers suggested at the end of the century that country music had come perilously close to sounding too much like other genres, this particular characteristic of country stars and their fans, the personal bond and easy rapport between them, helped to keep country music distinctive.[7] Therefore, the organizers gave serious consideration to the ramifications of the spatial associations of downtown before undertaking the move. But by the early 2000s, downtown and Lower Broad were central components of country music's public presentation and the tourist economy of both the country music industry and the city of Nashville.

COUNTRY MUSIC has come a long ways since the 1920s and Jimmie Rodgers, the Carter Family, and the early "barn dance" variety programs.

One of the principal through lines sewing disparate pieces together has been the notion of traditional values and a stance toward rural life that does not denigrate or dismiss, that preserves rural values in some fashion. Country music's unprecedented success in the 1990s prompted journalists to make some of the same points I have made throughout this book about keeping rural roots alive while combining them with a modern urban or suburban sensibility. In the early 1990s, as a wave of new country stars stormed the nation's record stores, radio stations, and television programs, a *New York Times* reporter claimed, "The new country stars are the suburban cowboys: they're in touch with country's roots, but they're adapting these traditions to address the urbanized realities of the present."[8] The author recognized the importance of maintaining a connection with country music's traditions but not necessarily becoming beholden to them in the present day. Even in this regard, however, it was not country's earliest "hillbilly" roots to which the reporter approvingly turned but instead to the more mythic and less pointedly rural cowboy figure. The reality is that, since its inception, and even when it was still unashamedly hillbilly music, country music has often addressed the "urbanized realities of the present," and in fact has provided a soundtrack for millions of rural southerners' passage into urbanization since at least the 1920s. Another journalist wrote of Garth Brooks that "Mr. Brooks speaks to a suburbia that wants a hint of rural roots—he has more of a twang in his countryish songs, less in his folky ballads—but distrusts both small-town isolation and big-city chaos."[9] While the suggestion of a suburban perspective with just a hint of rural roots might have seemed novel to some observers in the early 1990s, this book has shown that this idea had been evolving over many decades. My analysis shows how these descriptions came to make sense through the course of a long period of development, beginning as early as the 1950s and extending across industry marketing strategies, song lyrics, album liner notes, and declarations from stars and fans alike. The acceptance of this idea has been central to the genre's continuing evolution as the music of the people. Today, as always, the question remains, which people? Who are they, and where do they live, work, and play?

The suggestion that Brooks distrusted both small-town isolation and big-city chaos also resonates with another theme that has been woven throughout country music's spatial evolution: the importance of Nashville to the genre's identity. The blending of spatial categories, the suburban reality with the rural spirit, and even the de-emphasis of geographic particularity in country lyrics and iconography, has actually helped to shape a genre and an industry with a very specific place attachment. No other genre of popular music in America has such a clear identification with one particular place, and this attachment has been crucial to maintaining the genre's distinctiveness. Country music has retained its distinctive identity in part because of its place associations with an urban space that does not have the often negative connotations of such larger cities as New York and Los Angeles, but that can provide vibrant urban neighborhoods, rustic country settings, and suburban comfort and convenience. Country may have "come to town" metaphorically, but the industry's transformation significantly shaped the history and development of one particular town. Today Nashville's economy still thrives in no small part because of other ventures, such as publishing, universities, health care, and churches, but more than ever, it is known for the guitars, fiddles, and twang of its international stars.

Notes

Introduction

1. Rufus Jarman, "Country Music Goes to Town," *Nation's Business*, February 1953, 51.

2. "National Country Music Month," *CMA Close-Up*, November 1973, 12.

3. Bruce Feiler, *Dreaming Out Loud: Garth Brooks, Wynonna Judd, Wade Hayes, and the Changing Face of Nashville* (New York: Avon Books, 1998), 103–22.

4. James Gregory, "The Southern Diaspora and the Urban Dispossessed: Demonstrating the Census Public Use Microdata Samples," *Journal of American History* 82 (June 1995): 111–34. Gregory shows that the number of southern-born persons living elsewhere in the United States rose from 2.7 million in 1920 to nearly 10 million in 1960. See Jeffrey J. Lange, *Smile When You Call Me a Hillbilly: Country Music's Struggle for Respectability, 1939–1954* (Athens: University of Georgia Press, 2004), 14–15, on the shift within the South from a rural majority to almost 50 percent urban residents between 1940 and 1950. See also Jack Temple Kirby, *Rural Worlds Lost: The American South, 1920–1960* (Baton Rouge: Louisiana State University Press, 1987).

5. Louis M. Kyriakoudes has argued that the Opry gave audiences a way to cling to and express their affection for a rural past even while participating in modernization: "The program's musicians often addressed the ambivalence rural southerners held towards modernization, alternately praising and damning the changes sweeping the countryside. In doing so, the Opry performers stood at the forefront of a larger trend of creating a new southern music that had roots in the region's rural past but spoke to the concerns and anxieties of a present undergoing rapid change." Kyriakoudes, "The Grand Ole Opry and the Urban South," *Southern Cultures* 10 (2004): 75. See also Richard Peterson, *Creating Country Music: Fabricating Authenticity* (Chicago: University of Chicago Press, 1997).

6. Scholars of spatial identity have identified a tantalizing duality in the hillbilly or rustic figure. Rural space and its inhabitants have been considered both a revered repository of the values that modernity has trampled, and simultaneously a hopelessly backward milieu that reinforces the superiority of this same modernity. Raymond Williams has even argued that the framing of a stark rural/urban dichotomy is one of the central ways we have come to understand modern society. Williams, *The Country and the City* (New York: Oxford University Press, 1973), 289. In this vein, Alexander Sebastian Dent argues that "the rural makes the city conceivable, by stipulating the bygone days in terms of which the present may be celebrated or indicted." Dent, *River of Tears: Country Music, Memory, and Modernity in Brazil* (Durham, N.C.: Duke University Press, 2009), 1.

7. Anthony Harkins, *Hillbilly: A Cultural History of an American Icon* (New York: Oxford University Press, 2004).

8. Carolyn Holloran, "A Touch of Sadness: Impressions of the Last Night at the Ryman," *Country Song Roundup*, September 1974, 32.

9. "Amusement Week," *Nashville Banner*, March 2, 1974.

1. "Nothing but Realism"

1. Charles K. Wolfe, *A Good-Natured Riot: The Birth of the Grand Ole Opry* (Nashville: The Country Music Foundation Press and Vanderbilt University Press, 1999), 21–22. The story comes from George Hay's own memoir, but Wolfe argues, based on an analysis of program listings and early Opry culture, that there is no reason to doubt its general accuracy. Hay, *A Story of the Grand Ole Opry* (Nashville: N.p., 1953).

2. Richard Peterson refers to the early Opry as a kind of "rustic variety show," influenced more by vaudeville than an actual agrarian barn dance. Peterson, *Creating Country Music: Fabricating Authenticity* (Chicago: University of Chicago Press, 1997), 70.

3. National Life's later self-promotion efforts shifted the focus to the "industrial classes" and noted their innovative use of industrial insurance policies to open up a new market in the first decade of the twentieth century. Bill Carey, *Fortunes, Fiddles and Fried Chicken: A Nashville Business History* (Franklin, TN: Hillsboro Press, 2000), 66–67; Powell Stamper, *National Life Story: A History of the National Life and Accident Insurance Company of Nashville, Tennessee* (New York: Appleton-Century-Crofts, 1968).

4. Craig Havighurst, *Air Castle of the South: WSM and the Making of Music City* (Urbana: University of Illinois Press), 2007.

5. Barbara Ching has similarly understood the use of "hillbilly Shakespeare" to describe Hank Williams. She refers to a "mixture of praise and condescension," and argues that the moniker "insisted upon a contrast between European high art and

inbred American low life, between the sublime and the ridiculous." Ching, *Wrong's What I Do Best: Hard Country Music and Contemporary Culture* (New York: Oxford University Press, 2001), 53.

6. Kyriakoudes, "The Grand Ole Opry and the Urban South," *Southern Cultures* 10 (2004): 75.

7. Wolfe has shown that the marketing strategy took time to develop. Photographs of the Opry cast in 1928 show them in suits and dresses while in 1933, the cast is dressed in overalls in a cornfield. *A Good-Natured Riot*, 15.

8. Richard Peterson and Paul DiMaggio, "The Early Opry: Its Hillbilly Image in Fact and Fancy," *Journal of Country Music* 4 (Summer 1973): 39–51.

9. Peterson, *Creating Country Music*, 75; Wolfe, *A Good-Natured Riot*, 53–55. See also Hay, *A Story*, 2. Opry star Uncle Dave Macon grew up in Nashville, and his father owned a hotel, but he played a rustic figure on stage, often performing old minstrel songs that he had learned from vaudeville performers who had stayed at the family's hotel while traveling through Nashville. Tony Russell, *Country Music Originals: The Legends and the Lost* (New York: Oxford University Press, 2007), 12. Sam McGee had been a farmer but in the early 1920s gave it up and opened a blacksmith shop. He met Macon in Franklin in the mid-1920s and began playing with him. Ibid., 32. See also Havighurst, *Air Castle of the South*, 74. Dr. Bate and another Opry performer, Herman Crook (a cigar maker by day), both performed on the Opry but did not want full-time musical careers, which would have taken them away from their families and home. Peterson and DiMaggio, "The Early Opry," 43–44.

10. William R. McDaniel and Harold Seligman, *Grand Ole Opry* (New York: Greenberg, 1952), 45–46.

11. Wolfe, *A Good-Natured Riot*, 37; Bill Malone, *Don't Get above Your Raisin': Country Music and the Southern Working Class* (Urbana: University of Illinois Press, 2002), 40.

12. Michael Ann Williams and Larry Morrissey have shown that the Renfro Valley Barn Dance actually changed location from Cincinnati to a rural area of Kentucky in the late 1930s. The organizers even gave the auditorium where the show was performed and broadcast the appearance of a barn. Although the structure had been built specifically for the radio program, Renfro Valley promotional material claimed the program was "the only barn dance in America broadcast from a real barn," most likely a pointed contrast with the Grand Ole Opry and its urban location. Williams and Morrissey, "Constructions of Tradition: Vernacular Architecture, Country Music, and Auto-Ethnography," in *People, Power, Places: Perspectives in Vernacular Architecture*, ed. Sally Ann McMurry and Annmarie Adams (Knoxville: University of Tennessee Press, 2000), 161–75.

13. Jeffrey Lange, *Smile When You Call Me a Hillbilly: Country Music's Struggle for Respectability, 1939–1954* (Athens: University of Georgia Press, 2004), 190.

14. Ibid., 253.

15. Ibid., 89–91.

16. The Opry only tentatively accepted electric instrumentation, however, creating a tension between popular national and western performers and the traditional stewards of the Opry and hillbilly music. Ernest Tubb, one of the most popular country singers in the 1940s, featured electric guitar on his recordings beginning in 1941, and "Walking the Floor over You" became his ticket to the Opry. Facing resistance from the Opry's managers, Tubbs told a disapproving Judge Hay, "Judge, this is how I make my records." Hay relented, and the Opry saw electric instrumentation for the first time in 1943, the same year the show moved into the Ryman Auditorium. Lange, *Smile When You Call Me a Hillbilly*, 85.

17. Bob Wills, the most visible western swing star, declared, "Please don't anybody confuse us with none of them hillbilly outfits." But he always maintained his *southern* allegiance, if not his hillbilly identification, in song lyrics and in his retention of certain instrumentation like the fiddle. "Strictly by Ear," *Time*, February 11, 1946, 48–50. *Time* magazine declared that Wills's innovation was bringing "ranchhouse music nearer to the city."

18. Lange, *Smile When You Call Me a Hillbilly*, 67–70. See also "Hillbilly Music Is Big Favorite with Baltimore Patrons," *Billboard*, July 3, 1943, 62.

19. See Diane Pecknold, *The Selling Sound: The Rise of the Country Music Industry* (Durham, N.C.: Duke University Press, 2007), 54–57, on the structural shifts, and "Gold in Them Thar Hillbillies: B'way Pubs Hungry for Corn as Rural Rhythms Skyrocket in Disk and Music Sales," *Billboard*, August 21, 1943, 12, for awareness of the importance of the licensing struggle in the trade press.

20. John Rumble, "Fred Rose and the Development of the Nashville Music Industry, 1942–1954" (Ph.D. diss., Vanderbilt University, 1980).

21. Lange, *Smile When You Call Me a Hillbilly*, 188–90.

22. Many southern civic and business leaders agreed that they needed to modernize their economies, and municipalities across the South embarked on aggressive campaigns to bring industry and much needed capital to their communities. This civic embrace of modernity also led to support for New Deal–era programs such as the Tennessee Valley Authority and Rural Electrification Administration, which conservative, pro-business southern officials and industrialists supported as necessary for luring industry. The acceptance of the increased role of the federal government and the welcome of northern capital and business did not match the national narrative of the Benighted South, and in fact did not appear in national cultural discussions of the South until well after World War II. David Carlton, "Smokestack-Chasing and Its Discontents: Southern Development Strategy in the Twentieth Century," in *The American South in the Twentieth Century*, ed. Craig S. Pascoe, Karen Trahan Leathem, and Andy Ambrose (Athens: University of Georgia Press, 2005), 106–26. See also Norman Carlisle, "Is Dixie Leaving the North Behind?" *Coronet*, July 1952, 38–42.

23. *Polk's Nashville (Davidson County, Tenn.) City Directory* (St. Louis: R. L. Polk, 1943). See also Convention and Tourist Bureau, Chamber of Commerce, "You'll Enjoy Nashville, Tennessee," 1953, Nashville Area Chamber of Commerce Publications and Reports, Special Collections Division, Nashville Public Library. This publication mentions the Opry and Ryman as one among many of Nashville's possible attractions. The explicit invocation of and contrast with the rest of the South within the nickname "Athens of the South" was intentional, and consistent with Nashville's self-promotion and presentation throughout the century.

24. *Polk's Nashville (Davidson County, Tenn.) City Directory* (St. Louis: R. L. Polk, 1953), 15.

25. *Polk's Nashville*, 1943, 13.

26. Anthony Harkins has deftly demonstrated the shift over time in the characterization of hillbilly, arguing that the emergence and success of hillbilly music from the 1920s through the 1940s played a large role in tempering the menace of the earlier figure by substituting instead a genial, harmless, more nostalgic avatar of America's agrarian past. Harkins, *Hillbilly: A Cultural History of an American Icon* (New York: Oxford University Press, 2004), 105. See also George B. Tindall, "The Benighted South: Origins of a Modern Image," *Virginia Quarterly Review* 40 (Spring 1964): 281–94, and Malone, *Don't Get above Your Raisin'*, 17–18.

27. "Nashville—The Heart of American Folk Music," in *Nashville Real Estate Board 1953 Yearbook* (Nashville: Real Estate Board, 1953), 56, suggested the boost to the local economy that the Opry and the industry could provide, and pointed out that hillbilly music was big business for the city of Nashville because people who came to see the Opry also spent significant sums of money at restaurants, shops, and motels.

28. After World War II, like many American cities, Nashville became increasingly car-dependent; vehicle registrations in Davidson County jumped from under 50,000 in 1938 to 150,000 in 1960, while the number of yearly revenue passengers on Nashville's mass transit declined from 60 million in 1945 to 18 million in 1959. See Wilbur Smith and Associates, *Nashville Metropolitan Area Transportation Study*, report prepared by the Tennessee Department of Highways in cooperation with the U.S. Department of Commerce, Bureau of Public Roads, and city of Nashville and Davidson County (New Haven, Conn., 1961), 2–3.

29. See Wilbur Smith and Associates, *Nashville Metropolitan Area Transportation Study*, 21, and *Polk's Nashville*, 1953. See also "Eddy Arnold: The Tennessee Plowboy," *Country Song Roundup*, March 1955, 8–9.

30. Ronnie Pugh, *Ernest Tubb: The Texas Troubadour* (Durham, N.C.: Duke University Press, 1996).

31. Havighurst, *Air Castle of the South*, 121–22.

32. The City Council created the Nashville Housing Authority in 1938, one of the earliest in the country. Despite strong opposition from anti–New Deal

conservatives, advocates of public housing supported this organization as the best way to prevent the spread of slums and blight. When, a decade later federal urban renewal legislation was passed, the Nashville Housing Authority was well positioned to take early advantage of federal dollars for the razing of "blighted" housing and the construction of new roads, green spaces, and retail/office/housing mixtures. Robert G. Spinney, *World War II in Nashville: Transformation of the Homefront* (Knoxville: University of Tennessee Press, 1998), 100–102.

33. *Polk's Nashville,* 1943.

34. Tubb's Record Shop first opened at 720 Commerce Street in 1947 and then moved to 417 Broadway in August 1951. Pugh, *Ernest Tubb,* 122.

35. "Over the Cracker Barrel," *Pickin' and Singin' News,* August 1953, 3.

36. WSM's own survey, in the early 1950s, found that 88 percent of Opry attendees came to Nashville solely to see the show and that the average visitor traveled 485 miles. The leading states, in order of Opry attendance, were Alabama, Illinois, Tennessee, Indiana, Missouri, Georgia, and Kentucky. Tennessee ranked only third despite its residents' obviously having the shortest distance to travel. Nashville newspapers rarely mentioned the Opry until the 1950s, and generally the Opry only appeared in the listings of the featured performers in the nightly schedules for Nashville's three main radio stations (which did not even use the word "Opry"). WSM itself spent little money on print advertising within Nashville. McDaniel and Seligman, *Grand Ole Opry,* 3–5. See also "Response Is Good to 'Audition' Issue of Pickin' and Singin' News; Artists, Fans Give Encouragement," *Pickin' and Singin' News,* May 23, 1953, 6, for the same poll results.

37. As *Billboard's* premier country writer explained in 1949, "A paramount factor in maintaining the steady climb of folk music, when all other branches of the music business are declining over the postwar years, has been the consistency of the farmers' incomes. As the federal program for subsidy payments to farmers has and will continue, rustic music has had a strong basis upon which to base its expansion in all fields." Johnny Sippel, "Rustic Rhythm Reaps \$\$ Reward," *Billboard,* October 22, 1949, 97.

38. See "Hillbilly Bash in Carnegie Perks Stem Interest," *Billboard,* September 27, 1947, 1, for an example of an article that refers to the music as "country music" but the performers and their style as "hillbilly" and "cornbilly." Half a decade later, on the occasion of Jimmy Rodgers's death, *Billboard* still used the moniker "hillbilly" to describe the culture if not the music; see "Jimmie Rodgers: Hillbilly World to Honor His Memory," *Billboard,* May 16, 1953, 16. *Variety* continued to refer to the music and its practitioners in derogatory slang well into the 1950s as well. See "Cornseed Crooners Reap B.O. Bonanza as City Slickers Lap Cider-Jug Tunes," *Variety,* June 27, 1951, 1, and "Jazz Plays Second Fiddle to Corn as Hillbillies Make Abroad," *Variety,* November 25, 1953, 1.

39. Maurice Zolotow, "Hillbilly Boom," *Saturday Evening Post,* February 12, 1944, 36. See also Joe Carlton, "Today's Platter Pilgrimages Show Folk Fellahs Plenty

Hep," *Billboard*, February 16, 1946, 20: "Back in 1940 it was a simple task to pack a load of portable recording equipment into a truck, hook on a cowcatcher, and head for the watermelon patches of Carolina and Georgia."

40. See also, "Country Music Is Big Business, and Nashville Is Its Detroit," *Newsweek*, August 11, 1952, 84, for the persistence of the spatializing metaphor to describe the discovery of "true" country talent: "They travel, listen to local radio stations, and ferret out talent—from the plains of Texas, the bayous of Louisiana, or the mountains of Tennessee and North Carolina." Nowhere in this list of musical origin spaces (plains, bayous, and mountains) is there room for the discovery of talent in the *urban* South.

41. This suggestion that Satherley had gone to places where there were no passable roads resonated with another common space-phrase, "deep into the woods," found in a 1947 *Billboard* article: "Educational process started by h.b.'s [hillbillies] and handlers has already reached deep into the woods and has chilled many folksters from signing royalty waivers, blanket disk-pub papers." "Hillbillies Are Hepping to Dollar Sign, Dotted Line and Biz of 'Yours Is Mine,'" *Billboard*, January 18, 1947, 13.

42. Nat S. Green, "King Korn Klondike: Hillbilly Troupes Roll up Dizzy Box Office Scores in One-Day and Repeat Stands," *Billboard*, March 6, 1943, 1.

43. Kyle Crichton, "Thar's GOLD in Them Hillbillies," *Collier's*, April 30, 1938, 24–27.

44. Zolotow, "Hillbilly Boom," 36.

45. Doron K. Antrim, "Whoop-and-Holler Opera," *Collier's*, January 26, 1946, 18.

46. Bill Davidson, "Thar's Gold in Them Thar Hillbilly Tunes," *Collier's*, July 28, 1951, 34. See also Zolotow, "Hillbilly Boom," 36: "But, above all, sincerity, even if it is awkward unpolished sincerity, is the criterion used to judge the performer."

47. Carlton, "Today's Platter Pilgrimages," 20. Carlton's reference to "the boys from the hills" was also typical of the time, most importantly in the spatial map that it drew, on which the musicians and singers originated from a separate geographical place from everyone else in the industry. See Hal Webman, "Gold in Them Hillbills! Folk Grosses Give Bookers New ($) Look," *Billboard*, December 27, 1947, 3, for another article that marveled at the commercial capacity of folk or hillbilly music by using an oft repeated titular metaphor of "gold in the hills." See also "Gold in Them Thar Hillbillies," *Billboard*, August 21, 1943, 12: "Unprecedented success of hillbilly music is prompting Broadway music publishers to don their overalls for a whirl at the corn field." "Field" here takes on a double meaning, as both an agricultural space and the business or genre designation of hillbilly music.

48. See also "September Records," *Time*, September 2, 1940, 45, for a description of the variety of hillbilly performers as "blues singers, hillbilly fiddlers, guitar-strummers, jug-players, washboard-slappers."

49. Rufus Jarman, "Country Music Goes to Town," *Nation's Business*, February 1953, 51. See also Broadcast Music, Inc. (BMI), *Meet the Artist* (New York: BMI, 1957), A-1, which portrays Roy Acuff as a "natural" singer: "Although he is unable to

read a note of music, those who know rate him the most enduring and successful of all singers of folk songs. Roy is an authentic folk artist, a man who came by his talent 'natural,' as the folks in Coon Run would say." See also Eddy Arnold's biographical sketch in the same publication: "Eddy and his Tennessee Playboys give their songs the warm sincerity and earnest appeal of the simple farm country from which they all come. Their artistry has helped a great deal to lift folk music out of the fields and hills and valleys into urban areas across the entire nation." Ibid., A-10.

50. Elizabeth Schlappi, *Roy Acuff, the Smoky Mountain Boy* (Gretna, La.: Pelican, 1978), 153–56.

51. Ibid. See also "Dunbar Cave Re-opening Further Proof That Acuff Makes His Money Work for Him after He Makes It before Nation-Wide Microphones," *Pickin' and Singin' News,* Audition Issue, May 1953, 5, for a celebratory discussion of Acuff's riches and unparalleled popularity around the nation.

52. "Text of Reece Address," *Nashville Banner,* August 31, 1948.

53. Zolotow, "Hillbilly Boom," 37. See also "Reece and Acuff Draw 7,500 at Memphis Rally," *Nashville Banner,* October 25, 1948, for a summary of Acuff's political career that mentions Acuff's indignation without mentioning Cooper's slight.

54. Leslie T. Hart, "Thousands Hear Reece, Acuff End Campaign," *Nashville Banner,* November 2, 1948.

55. Ibid.

56. Don Eddy, "Hillbilly Heaven," *American Magazine,* March 1952, 122.

57. Red O'Donnell, "Merry, Rollicking Minnie Pearl Gathers Many Interesting Experiences While Mimicking the Country Ladies . . . and Making Them Like It," *Pickin' and Singin' News,* May 1953, 7. See also Martha Fergerson, "Cousin Minnie Pearl Taught Youngsters the Simple Way," *Pickin' and Singin' News,* December 30, 1954, 3, and BMI, *Meet the Artist,* P-4.

58. Eddy, "Hillbilly Heaven," 121.

59. "WSM's Grand Ole Opry Prince Albert Show," November 12, 1949, 12, Papers of WSM, Country Music Hall of Fame and Library, Nashville.

60. Ibid., 10. The transcription was from the WSM script and does not necessarily represent the actual sounds produced by Pearl and Brasfield. Pearl also used a conversation with her "Uncle Nabob" to further present rustic misunderstandings of international travel: "Uncle Nabob got the idea I was gonna join up with one o' them burlesque shows because I'd told him we had to take off on a runway and come in on a strip!" (9). The network portion of the Opry program was the only portion for which there was a script and rehearsal, providing a rare written record. See also Hank Williams, *Live at the Opry* (Mercury Nashville, 1999), for recorded examples of Pearl's stage humor.

61. "WSM's Grand Ole Opry Prince Albert Show."

62. Around 1945, after appearing with Lawrence Welk and his orchestra, Foley earned the nickname "Sweet Singer of Songs of the Hills and Plains." Lange, *Smile When You Call Me a Hillbilly,* 215.

63. Eddy, "Hillbilly Heaven," 29.

64. Davidson, "Thar's Gold," 34. See also "Country Music Is Big Business," 82–85, whose author acknowledged that the genre's practitioners prefer the term "country music" but then repeatedly used "hillbilly" anyway.

65. Jarman, "Country Music," 51.

66. Eddy, "Hillbilly Heaven," 119.

67. Jarman, "Country Music," 44. See also Rufus Jarman's earlier article on Nashville in the *Saturday Evening Post:* "Proud of its forebears, its schools and its gracious way of life, Nashville styles itself the Athens of the South. Yet this is the city where a monument was erected to a horse thief, where some citizens have to be warned not to ride escalators barefoot." Jarman, "The Cities of America: Nashville," *Saturday Evening Post,* October 27, 1951, 22. See also Antrim, "Whoop-and-Holler Opera," 18: "Lines form at the ticket windows in the morning, and the customers, many of them in overalls, pack their own food and drinks."

68. Eddy, "Hillbilly Heaven," 28.

69. Ibid.

70. Ibid., 34.

71. Hay, *A Story.*

72. Davidson, "Thar's Gold," 42.

73. Carlisle, "Is Dixie Leaving," 38–42. See also BMI, *Meet the Artist,* wherein almost all the biographies of country stars reference their youths on farms.

74. The journal referred to the impressive "impact of the rural pickers and singers." This phrase mirrored rustic-specific descriptions of the genre produced by national publications. "Amazing Advance of Country Music Stirs Entertainment World: Music People Turn More and More to 'Country Style,'" *Pickin' and Singin' News,* October 10, 1953, 1. See also Pecknold, *Selling Sound,* 114–16, for an extended analysis of the journal's confused stance toward the "hillbilly" moniker.

2. "Country Comes to Town"

1. Michael Kosser, *How Nashville Became Music City U.S.A.: 50 Years of Music Row* (Milwaukee: Hal Leonard, 2006), 9.

2. "Music City, U.S.A. . . . The New Frontier of Sound," *Music Reporter,* June 29, 1963; "Nashville's Music Row," *Billboard's World of Country Music 1967–68* (Cincinnati: Billboard Publications, 1967), 44.

3. Joli Jensen, *The Nashville Sound: Authenticity, Commercialization, and Country Music* (Nashville: The Country Music Foundation Press and Vanderbilt University Press, 1998), 73. See also "Pop and Nets Grab Country Talent," *Country Music Reporter,* March 16, 1957, 8.

4. Jeffrey Lange, *Smile When You Call Me a Hillbilly: Country Music's Struggle for Respectability, 1939–1954* (Athens: University of Georgia Press, 2004), 200–201.

5. Michael Streissguth, *Voices of the Country: Interviews with Classic Country Performers* (New York: Routledge, 2004), 103–7.

6. Streissguth, *Voices of the Country,* 30; Joel Whitburn, *Joel Whitburn's Country Annual, 1944–1997* (Menomonee Falls, Wis.: Record Research, 1998).

7. Michael Freda, *Eddy Arnold Discography, 1944–1996* (Westport, Conn.: Greenwood Press, 1997).

8. Jensen, *The Nashville Sound,* 41–43.

9. Michael Bertrand, *Race, Rock, and Elvis* (Urbana: University of Illinois Press, 2000).

10. See Lange, *Smile When You Call Me a Hillbilly,* 210–11, on the industry's consolidation in Nashville facilitating a move in the direction of country-pop, and Diane Pecknold, *The Selling Sound: The Rise of the Country Music Industry* (Durham, N.C.: Duke University Press, 2007), 90–94, on the importance of rockabilly to the rock-and-roll boom and the way in which that connection actually gave Nashville the clout to bring more recording and publishing operations to town.

11. See "Hillbilly on a Pedestal," *Newsweek,* May 14, 1956, 82, for a description of Presley as a hillbilly singer.

12. See "Country Music Is Here to Stay," *Music Reporter,* November 17, 1958, 1, for the belief that country artists had failed miserably in their attempts to join the rock bandwagon. See also "Music Biz Now R&B Punchy: Even Hillbillies Are Doing It," *Variety,* February 9, 1955, 51.

13. Joli Jensen has found a rock-almost-killed-country narrative in a series of oral histories conducted in the 1970s, but this was perhaps more a function of the workings of collective memory than the actual reality at the time. Jensen, *The Nashville Sound,* 38–40. Rather than seeing rock and roll as a clear-cut enemy, for instance, *Country Music Reporter,* a new trade journal based in Nashville (and with an unashamed emphasis on the country music industry), argued that rock and roll was closer in spirit to country music than any other genre, and that rock and roll's success was actually *good* for country. The magazine's staff editorialized, "Rock 'n roll is considered Pop, yet it comes about as close as any type of music has ever come to being based upon the same principle upon which C&W is based." The article further suggested that what the two genres shared was also what led both to such high levels of success: "That principle is raw simplicity in musical technique, with no inhibitions, a strong beat, and lots of 'heart.' It is this same principle which is responsible for C&W music's 'catching on' and its skyrocket-climb into the popularity picture." The journal did not demonize rock and roll but instead understood that country music was back on the rise, in part *because* of the changes rock brought to the pop music landscape. "Music Trade Paper Snobbery for Birds: Sales Show Difference," *Country Music Reporter,* August 3, 1957, 1. See also "Will Rock 'N Roll Merge with Ballad Form in '58," *Music Reporter,* December 9, 1957, 1, for further discussion of the fruitful relationship between rock and country.

14. "Columbia Modernizes CW," *Country Music Reporter,* December 22, 1956, 1. The article's opening line summarized the change that was underway: "A modernized approach to country music is being followed by Columbia Records in the

conviction that the country music of a few years ago with its repetitious style of performance cannot compete to advantage with listeners exposed to other entertainment." The article then detailed the comprehensive study undertaken by Columbia to discover exactly who constituted the country audience and how best to maximize its potential.

15. McCandlish Phillips, "Country Stylist: Connie B. Gay Discusses Lucrative Formula," *New York Times,* September 8, 1957, emphasis added.

16. Harold Bradley, interview by Douglas Green. January 17, 1974, Country Music Foundation Oral History Collection, Country Music Foundation Library and Media Center, Nashville.

17. See Jensen, *The Nashville Sound,* 76–83, for an extended discussion of the instrumentation of the Nashville Sound.

18. "Floyd Cramer Interview," in *Country Musicians,* ed. Judie Eremo (Cupertino, Cal.: Grove, 1987), 30.

19. For the success of Husky's "Gone," see Robert Price, "Ken Nelson: Bakersfield Bonanza," *Journal of Country Music* 19 (1998): 32–35. Price quotes Husky himself as saying later, "I'll swear by it: It's the one that started the trend. The first one that had an echo chamber, and the first one that put background (vocals) on music the ways songs before had used strings. It was the Nashville Sound, the one that started it all." See also Charles Portis, "That New Sound from Nashville," *Saturday Evening Post,* February 12, 1966, 31, for a quote from Buddy Killen claiming that "Gone" was the first song to feature the Nashville Sound.

20. See Owen Bradley's quote, "I believe in continual evolution of styles. Now we've cut out the fiddle and steel guitar and added choruses to country music," in "Owen Bradley Seeking the New; Views the Old," *Billboard Music Week,* August 7, 1961, 4, as well as Paul Hemphill, *The Nashville Sound: Bright Lights and Country Music* (New York: Ballantine, 1970), 57–58. For descriptions of the Sound as strings and background vocals taking the place of fiddles and steel guitars, see Bill Malone, *Don't Get above Your Raisin': Country Music and the Southern Working Class* (Urbana: University of Illinois Press, 2002), 80, and John Lomax III, *Nashville: Music City, USA* (New York: Harry N. Abrams, 1985), 90.

21. By 1963 nearly one half of all music recordings in America came from Nashville, and most of that from the studios on Music Row. See "A Big New Sound Blows out of Nashville," *Broadcasting,* January 28, 1963, 67. For articles that refer to "Record Row" rather than Music Row, see Elton Whisenhunt, "Nashville Scene," *Billboard,* September 18, 1965, 44, and "Neal Wilburn Readies Studio in Nashville," *Billboard,* October 2, 1965, 20.

22. "Nashville Booms as Music Mecca," *Music Reporter,* November 17, 1958, 1.

23. "A Big New Sound," 78. For other descriptions that invoke an ambiguous "feel" of the music, see "World of Music Finds New Frontier in 'Magical Nashville Sound,'" *Music Reporter,* June 23, 1962, 2, and "The Nashville Sound," *Time,* November 27, 1964, 76–79.

24. Hemphill, *The Nashville Sound*, 50. In 1974, journalist John Egerton described the Sound with an all-encompassing but still vague enough definition: "An indefinable quality that derives from unexcelled recording studios, superb backup musicians, a cadre of highly professional songwriters and producers and publishers, and an atmosphere that is relaxed and unhurried." Egerton, *The Americanization of Dixie: The Southernization of America* (New York: Harper and Row, 1974), 204. See also a Chet Atkins quote—"In New York when they have a recording session, an arranger brings in a part for every instrument. It's all there, but it's only one man's ideas. In Nashville we get together and everybody down to the janitor throws in his two cents worth. As a result we get a mixture of ideas and a better sound"—in Chester Campbell, "The Tin Pan Valley Boom," *Nashville Magazine,* November 1963, 8. Joli Jensen has impressively argued that country commentators used the distinction between New York's cold urban professionalism and Nashville's relaxed, downhome warmth to soften (or attempt to soften) the transition from rural-oriented, seemingly spontaneous live performances at the Opry to slicker, more explicitly commercial recordings in the studios on Music Row, in other words, to make Music Row more downhome. Referring to a 1961 *McCall's* article that explicitly spelled out the differences between a Music Row studio and one in New York, Jensen writes of the article's argument, "It implies that the Nashville studio offers a recording experience that is personal rather than professional, more rural than urban, more down home than uptown, oral not written. In other words, it symbolically identifies Music Row as much like the already authenticated symbolic origins of country music—the Opry, front porch, and honky-tonk." Jensen, *The Nashville Sound*, 82.

25. See Pecknold, *The Selling Sound*, 135–41, on the founding and organization of the CMA. See also Harry Stone, "The Country Music Association," in *Country Music Who's Who 1960,* ed. Thurston Moore (Cincinnati: Cardinal Enterprises, 1960), 79. Stone foregrounded the commercial nature of country music and argued that it was thus perfectly natural that the industry had a trade organization "for the purpose of improving it, marketing it, and publicizing it."

26. Stone, "Country Music Association," 79–81.

27. Pecknold, *The Selling Sound*, 135–36.

28. Diane Pecknold, "The Selling Sound of Country Music: Class, Culture, and Early Radio Marketing Strategy of the Country Music Association," in *Country Music Annual 2002,* ed. Charles Wolfe and James Akenson (Lexington: University Press of Kentucky, 2002), 62.

29. Pecknold, *The Selling Sound*, 138.

30. "Our Respects to . . . Connie Barriot Gay," *Broadcasting,* February 2, 1959, 81.

31. Diane Pecknold has shown the effect the hearings and the proclamations they contained had on the industry's self-image, and that much of the CMA's initial public relations work stemmed from hearings and expert testimony which characterized hillbilly music as trashy and lamentably forced on an innocent public. Pecknold, *The Selling Sound*, 107–11.

32. "CMA Committee Works on Second Sponsor Mailing," *Music Reporter,* October 31, 1960, 40.

33. Phillips, "Country Stylist." See also "Hillbilly on a Pedestal" for a description of "hillbilly" singer Elvis Presley at a fancy Las Vegas show as "somewhat like a jug of corn liquor at a champagne party." Even *Broadcasting*'s seminal 1963 article recognizing Nashville as an established commercial music center still relied on older ideas about the music similar to the ones described in chapter 1. "A Big New Sound," 78.

34. "Sincerity No. 1 'Must' for C&W Show, Says CMA," *Music Reporter,* October 31, 1960, 26. See also a September 1965 news release for a new country station, "Country Music Comes to Town: 24 Hours a Day on WJRZ Radio," which quotes Joe Allison: "When you mention country music, people immediately picture an illiterate, overall-clad hill billy picking away on a one string guitar and plucking a washtub bass fiddle. This is not the case at all." Papers of Joe Allison, Country Music Hall of Fame and Library, Nashville. See also "Country Music Goes Uptown in Classy Carnegie Hall Show," *CMA Close-Up,* December 1961, 2: "The Grand Ole Opry troupe opened the door to a brand-new culture to some of the 'big city folk' who expected barefooted hillbillies with barnyard manners."

35. See Dal Stallard, "The KCKN Country Music Story," *CMA Close-Up,* June 1961, 3, and Charles Bernard, "The Madison Avenue Report," *CMA Close-Up,* July 1961, 3, for articles that stress the connection between taking country music seriously and without caricature in order to connect with the adult record-buying market.

36. Joe Allison, "The Sound of Country Music," presentation for the Sales-Marketing Executives of Chicago, June 7, 1965, 5. See also a presentation of the same title for the Adcraft Club of Detroit, April 17, 1964, 4—"The singer who once gathered the eggs and milked the cow has become a big butter and egg man from Nashville. . . . The songwriter who once tended stock on his daddy's farm . . . is now consulting his broker regarding another kind of stock. . . . The Nashville musician knows that Dow Jones is not old Farmer Jones' city cousin. . . . And the disc jockey knows that Capital Gains does not mean beating the other pickers to the end of a cotton row"—for an example of an argument rooted in rich wordplay that positioned the modern country performers explicitly in the city and not on the farm. Papers of the Country Music Association, Country Music Hall of Fame and Library, Nashville.

37. "CMA Committee Works on Second Sponsor," 40.

38. Phrases such as "countrypolitan" and "town and country" also circulated and caught fire to describe the new direction (out of the country!) of country music. The phrase "countrypolitan" indicated both the sense of where country was going (urban-friendly pop with broad geographic reach) and where it was assumed to have been (at the opposite end of the spectrum from cosmopolitan, an art form limited by its regional and provincial ties). The phrase derived its cachet from its shock value: "country" as cosmopolitan was incongruous enough to generate attention but also plausible enough in the 1950s to register as something real.

39. For use of the "coming to town" rhetoric, see "Editor's Report: Country Music Goes to Town," *Sponsor*, August 8, 1966, 10; "Seems Like Country Music's Gone to Town: Some Reflection on Today's Country Music," *Country News and Views: Past and Present in Country Music*, January 1967, 13–14; Mrs. W. L. Tallman, "Letter," *Music City News*, April 1967, 3; Paul Dickson, "Singing to Silent America," *Nation*, February 23, 1970, 213; "There's New Life in an Old Radio Art Form: Country Radio Has Come to Town in a Big Way," *Broadcasting*, September 18, 1972, 30–44; and Biff Collie, "Inside Nashville," *Radio and Records*, January 17, 1975, 30.

40. See Richard Peterson, *Creating Country Music: Fabricating Authenticity* (Chicago: University of Chicago Press, 1997), 12–25, on the centrality of Atlanta to the birth of commercial country music in the 1920s; Charles Wolfe, A *Good-Natured Riot: The Birth of the Grand Ole Opry* (Nashville: The Country Music Foundation Press, 1999), 166–70, for a description of Ralph Peer's first Nashville recordings for Victor in the late 1920s; and Patrick Huber, *Linthead Stomp: The Creation of Country Music in the Piedmont South* (Chapel Hill: University of North Carolina Press, 2008), for the important contributions to country music's development made by textile mill workers in North Carolina's Piedmont.

41. Slim Whitman, *Country Songs, City Hits* (Imperial, LP-9268).

42. In 1963, there were 97 all-country stations; only two years later there were 208. "Growing Sound of Country Music," *Broadcasting*, October 18, 1965, 72. By 1971 there were 525, and by 1974 this number had grown to 856, representing a full 20 percent of all the AM stations in America. George O. Carney, "From Down Home to Uptown: The Diffusion of Country-Music Radio Stations in the United States," *Journal of Geography* 76 (March 1977): 107. See also "CMA Radio Survey Shows Upsurge in Fulltime C&W," *CMA Close-Up*, May 1963, 1. This study puts the number at 115 in May 1963.

43. An anonymous writer, addressing the CMA several years later, framed the transition as a switch from country to uptown: "Comments are made that the orchestras backing many of the modern Country singers, the mod clothes instead of the western cuts and boots, and even the songs themselves, are no longer Country, but an up town sound that is causing Country Music to no longer be the American art form for which it is so well known." "Country Music—Is It Losing Its Identity?" *CMA Close-Up*, September 1973, 8.

44. James Kennison, "Letter," *Music City News*, October 1965, 2.

45. See Pecknold, *The Selling Sound*, 169–77, for a more detailed analysis of the tension between fans and the CMA over who the music "belonged" to, the urban middle class or the rural working class.

46. Lynn Nickless, "Letter," *Music City News*, November 1964, 2.

47. "Eddy Arnold," *Country Music World*, September 1972, 28–31.

48. "Interview with Dave Dudley," *Country Song Roundup*, January 1973, 14.

49. Phillips, "Country Stylist," 17.

50. Other institutional factors were at work as well—WSM's first annual disc jockey festival in 1953, for instance, brought together various players from around the country to Nashville. See Peterson, *Creating Country Music,* 200–201. See also "Capitol Bldg. Proves Faith in Music City," *Music Reporter,* November 3, 1962, 1, for an early assertion of the connection between investment in the neighborhood and investment in the industry's future.

51. Dixie Deen, "Country Music Hall of Fame Opens," *Music City News,* April 1967, 4; *Polk's Nashville City Directory* (Detroit: R. L. Polk, 1967), 60.

52. Jack Hurst, "Industry Sings Blues over Road," *Nashville Tennessean,* April 11, 1970.

53. Betty Hofer, "Inside Music City," *Country Song Roundup 1968 Annual* (Derby, Conn.: Charlton, 1967), 68.

54. "Music City's Booming Land Rush," *Music Reporter,* June 29, 1963.

55. Jack Hurst, "Song Writer Tom T Hall Joins Opry," *Nashville Tennessean,* January 10, 1971.

56. According to the 1960 census, census tract 11, the section of Edgehill bordering Music Row was 90 percent black. Tract 12, which contained Music Row, was 95 percent white. The racial dividing line is even better understood by comparing block-by-block statistics for 1960. Between Sixteenth and Villa Place, the blocks were about half nonwhite, whereas between Villa Place and Fifteenth Avenue, they were almost 100 percent nonwhite. Presumably, the Sixteenth Avenue edge of the blocks contained the white households and the Villa Place side the black homes. Bureau of the Census, U.S. Department of Commerce, *1960 Census of Population and Housing: Block Statistics, Nashville-Davidson, Tenn. Urbanized Area* (Washington, D.C.: Government Printing Office, 1961), 6. Sixteenth Avenue was the census tract dividing line throughout the period, and by 1970 the tract east of Sixteenth was 91.4 percent black and the tract on the Music Row side was 2.5 percent black.

57. "Music City Expands with New Buildings," *Music City News,* November 1968, 3. See also "Long Complex in Step with Urban Development," *Music City News,* January 1968, 29, and Frank Sutherland, "Nine New Buildings Slated in Music Row Plans," *Nashville Tennessean,* October 16, 1968, 1.

58. Don Doyle, *Nashville since the 1920s* (Knoxville: University of Tennessee Press, 1985), 125.

59. See also Robert Battle, "Nashville: Residential Building Booms as Population Expands," *National Real Estate Investor,* December 1961, 22.

60. Final Project Report, Part 1 of Application for Loan and Grant, University Center Urban Renewal Area-One, Tenn R-51, August 4, 1967, binder 15, p. 3, Metropolitan Clerk's Office, Nashville; Minutes of the Board of Trust, October 19–20, 1956, November 1–2, 1957, Special Collections, Jean and Alexander Heard Library, Vanderbilt University, Nashville.

61. "Background Statement," in Final Project Report, binder 15, pp. 3, 11.

62. "University Center Project Affects Total Community," *Nashville Tennessean,* August 6, 1967; "Council Sees, Buys a Bargain in Renewal," *Nashville Tennessean,* August 15, 1967.

63. Wayne Whitt, "Wrong Way on 1-Way Street?" *Nashville Tennessean,* December 20, 1970. For descriptions of the traffic concerns that the boulevard was intended to solve, see "Project Area Report," in Final Project Report, binder 15, p. 11.

64. In 1960, the blocks between Division and Grand, and Sixteenth and Eighteenth Avenues (the heart of Music Row), contained 278 housing units, 208 of which were classified as sound, 50 were deteriorating (37 of these had all plumbing facilities and none of the deteriorating structures were without flush toilets), and only 20 of which were dilapidated, according to the 1960 census definition. Only 12 of the 278 total units were occupied by nonwhites. In the whole census tract, only 70 of the 1,088 units were dilapidated. Bureau of the Census, U.S. Department of Commerce, *1960 Census of Population and Housing: Block Statistics, Nashville-Davidson, Tenn. Urbanized Area* (Washington, D.C.: Government Printing Office, 1961), 6.

65. See Larry Daughtrey, "College Area Work to Start," *Nashville Tennessean,* July 12, 1967, which mentions the project and the boulevard without referencing country music or Music Row.

66. Planning documents emphasize the importance of Vanderbilt's wishes: "Vanderbilt University decided to expand its existing campus; this decision has served as a major basis for the overall planning of University Center." "Report on Planning Proposals," in Final Project Report, binder 15, p. 6. See also Pat Welch, "HUD Defends Funding VU Area Project," *Nashville Tennessean,* August 11, 1971: "Edmunds said the project was cut in half, however, because ambitious plans to rehabilitate the area around Peabody and Scarritt college campuses, put in a 'Music City Boulevard' and expand the Hillsboro Village shopping center cost almost twice as much as the $7 million HUD had allocated."

67. Robert Kollar, "C. of C., Metro Officials Differ on Boulevard," *Nashville Tennessean,* September 17, 1970.

68. Frank Ritter, "Boulevard $$ Down Drain?" *Nashville Tennessean,* September 20, 1970.

69. The 1963 merger of the city of Nashville and surrounding Davidson County led to the formation of a Metropolitan Council. Doyle, *Nashville since the 1920s,* 215.

70. Dick Battle, "Council Discusses Urban Renewal at Tonight's Meeting," *Nashville Banner,* October 20, 1970.

71. "Music Row Promise Ought to Be Honored," *Nashville Tennessean,* September 18, 1970.

72. "Fulton Vows Boulevard Fund Help," *Nashville Tennessean,* April 18, 1970.

73. Christine Kreyling, "Reading the Row," in *Reading Country Music: Steel Guitars, Opry Stars, and Honky-Tonk Bars,* ed. Cecilia Tichi (Durham, N.C.: Duke University Press, 1998), 307–21.

74. Wayne Whitt, "Council Votes against Music Row Boulevard," *Nashville Tennessean,* October 21, 1970.

75. Robert Kollar, "Row's Rah-Rah Spirit Fades: Cool to New Music Mall Pitch," *Nashville Tennessean,* December 15, 1970.

76. Wayne Whitt, "Slums Creeping up around Music Row," *Nashville Tennessean,* December 22, 1970; Wayne Whitt, "Boulevard to Halt at Music Row," *Nashville Tennessean,* December 21, 1970; Kenneth Jost, "Will Music City Move On?" *Nashville Tennessean,* January 10, 1971.

77. "A Tale of Two Cities," *Nashville Tennessean,* December 23, 1970.

78. Jack-Warren Ostrode, "California Country—'Suburb' of Nashville," *Country Music Who's Who* (Nashville: Record World, 1970), pt. 3, 27.

3. "You Sound Like Us but You Look Like Them"

1. Tennessee Governor Frank Clement in 1956, and U.S. Representative Richard Fulton in 1964, both invoked country as "the music of the people," and Presidents Richard Nixon and Gerald Ford hyperbolically described the music's appeal in their official proclamations of National Country Music Week in the early 1970s. "Governor Ready to Fight for BMI before Congress," *Country Music Reporter,* November 24, 1956, 1; Rep. Richard Fulton, "What Country Music Means to Me," *Music City News,* November 1964, 28; "President Proclaims Country Music Month," *Music City News,* November 1972, 2. Gerald Ford's 1974 proclamation making October National Country Music Month provided a typically sweeping summation of country's appeal: "It is a music which can be happy or sad, fast or slow, but it is always about life. The words of country music songs talk about life how it is really lived. Country Music is life with a melody." Ford, Proclamation 4326, Country Music Month, October 1974, www.presidency.ucsb.edu. For early examples of the assertion that country is the "music of the people," see "Crying, Dying or Going Away," *Pickin' and Singin' News,* August 1953, 2, and "Jack Stapp, 'Maker of Stars,' Engineers Country Music's Greatest Talent Display," *Pickin' and Singin' News,* June 12, 1954, 3.

2. W. D. Kilpatrick, manager of the Grand Ole Opry, to "Music Vendor," November 8, 1958, WSM Radio and TV, box 1, folder 3, Special Collections, Jane and Alexander Heard Library, Vanderbilt University, Nashville.

3. "New York City Writers Want to Know What Makes Music City So Great, Q & A with Teddy Bart," *Music City News,* October 1964, 3.

4. Jon Swope, letter to the editor, *Music City News,* November 1965, 2. The ellipses appear in the original.

5. Don Doyle, *Nashville since the 1920s* (Knoxville: University of Tennessee Press, 1985), 228.

6. Ibid., 235. See also Benjamin Houston, *The Nashville Way: Racial Etiquette and the Struggle for Social Justice in a Southern City* (Athens: University of Georgia

Press, 2012), for a more nuanced and critical treatment of Nashville's claims to racial moderation.

7. The National Council of Churches (whose office was only blocks from Bradley's studio) produced a 1957 report to appraise various groups interested in integrating Nashville schools on the basic situation in Nashville: which groups were opposed, to what degree were they opposed, how violent they would be in their opposition, and which groups or individuals to whom they would be able to turn for support. Will Campbell, "Memorandum," box 3, folder A105, NAACP Records, Manuscript Room, Library of Congress. In 1957, Nashville African Americans boycotted a Louis Armstrong show at the Ryman Auditorium because of segregated seating policies. The auditorium instituted segregated seating after a bombing at an Armstrong concert in Knoxville two weeks before. The community boycott succeeded; only a few hundred blacks attended on the lower level while whites were crammed into the balcony.

8. The Council of Churches report pointed out that "Nashville is probably the only city in the South with at least a veneer of Deep South tradition that has within it a group of 600 people who have placed themselves on public record . . . as offering support to the school board in bringing about a peaceful transition from segregated to desegregated schools." Campbell, "Memorandum," p. 2. The *Nashville Tennessean* actively supported integration and the *Banner*, while opposed to integration by federal declaration, also opposed violent and extralegal opposition on the part of segregationists. In the early 1970s, however, tensions flared over school busing. See Richard A. Pride and J. David Woodard, *The Burden of Busing: The Politics of Desegregation in Nashville, Tennessee* (Knoxville: University of Tennessee Press, 1985).

9. "Lawbreaker Comes to Nashville for One of His Tirades," *Nashville Globe and Independent*, August 9, 1957; "Kasper and Co. 'On the Run': Lawless Element Hears from Real Leaders of the City," *Nashville Globe and Independent*, August 16, 1957. See also the *Globe and Independent*'s generally optimistic (but cautionary) editorial "They Whom We Trust," August 16, 1957: "This is because white parents, well disposed toward their officials and other fine leaders, are showing that they also do not intend to be misled by any publicity-seeking hotheads of their race."

10. Doyle, *Nashville since the 1920s*, 242.

11. "Negroes Fight Back in the South," *New York Amsterdam News*, February 20, 1960.

12. Doyle, *Nashville since the 1920s*, 246.

13. Bobby L. Lovett, *The Civil Rights Movement in Tennessee: A Narrative History* (Knoxville: University of Tennessee Press, 2005), 137–40; "Violence in Nashville," *Daily Defender*, April 27, 1960. See also Carawan, *Nashville Sit-In Story*, and David Halberstam, "A Good City Gone Ugly," *The Reporter*, March 31, 1960, 17–19.

14. Various memoirs and histories of the movement devote substantial space to the Nashville sit-ins, but the only mention of country music as a defining feature of the city comes from John Lewis: "Nashville at that time was an odd mix of racial

progressiveness on the one hand and conflict and intolerance on the other. . . . [It had] established itself as a national center for music, religious publishing, and higher education. . . . Compared to other cities in the South, it was a truly progressive place in terms of race." John Lewis, with Michael D'Orso, *Walking with the Wind: A Memoir of the Movement* (New York: Simon and Schuster, 1998), 80–81. Even in this quotation, Lewis does not single out country music specifically as a force within Nashville but sees the city as a national center for music. See, for example, Jeffrey Turner, *Sitting In and Speaking Out: Student Movements in the American South, 1960–1970* (Athens: University of Georgia Press, 2010); Taylor Branch, *Pillar of Fire: America in the King Years, 1963–65* (New York: Simon and Schuster, 1998); Howell Raines, *My Soul Is Rested: The Story of the Civil Rights Movement in the Deep South* (New York: Penguin, 1977); Robert Weisbrot, *Freedom Bound: A History of America's Civil Rights Movement* (New York: Norton, 1990); and Andrew Young, *An Easy Burden: The Civil Rights Movement and the Transformation of America* (New York: HarperCollins, 1996).

15. W. O. Smith, *Sideman: The Long Gig of W. O. Smith, A Memoir* (Nashville: Rutledge Hill Press, 1991).

16. Advertisements from the black *Nashville Commentator* show Sixteenth Avenue businesses advertising to black customers in the late 1950s and early 1960s, including Buford's TV Sales and Service at 1028 Sixteenth Avenue South in 1957, and Belmont Meat and Grocery at 1019 Sixteenth Avenue South in 1961 (two and a half blocks from Bradley's studio). "Your South Nashville's Shoppers Guide," *Nashville Commentator*, August 10, 1957; *Nashville Commentator*, November 16, 1957; *Nashville Commentator*, April 1, 1961.

17. "Letter from Lee Berman," *Voice of the Movement*, August 11, 1961, Papers of the Student Nonviolent Coordinating Committee, reel 40, Special Collections Division, Nashville Public Library. See also "Picket Clash Trial Delayed," *Nashville Tennessean*, August 8, 1961, and "Store Picket Case Dropped," *Nashville Tennessean*, August 11, 1961.

18. Tennessee State Advisory Committee to the U.S. Commission on Civil Rights, "Housing and Urban Renewal in the Nashville-Davidson Country Metropolitan Area," February 1967, box 6, folder F121, NAACP Records: "The Negro in Nashville has been told that he has a right to be proud of his community. Nashville was the first city in the old Confederacy to have an ordinance-based human relations commission." The report further asserted that while black freedom was protected by law, opportunities were still limited and restricted, even though the city was more moderate. In early 1962, the NAACP celebrated gains made in employment with the phone companies, Ford Motor Company, the city government, and downtown department stores. Mayor Ben West arranged meetings with black activists, and civil service department heads and the Nashville chamber of commerce established an employer-employee committee to deal with "human relations," arguing that the use of "Negro manpower" was necessary for the region's economic development.

NAACP Newsletter, Nashville Branch, January 27, 1962, box 3, folder C170, NAACP Records. See also "Committee Recommends Open Housing Ordinance for Nashville," *Nashville Commentator,* April 15, 1967.

19. Mansfield Douglass III, "To the Metropolitan Commission on Human Relation (Sub-Committee on Housing)," December 5, 1966, box 6, folder F121, NAACP Records. The Edgehill project was first given federal approval in early 1962, approved by the Nashville Metropolitan Planning Commission in October 1963, and approved by the Metropolitan Council in October 1965. "Millions Slated on Urban Renewal," *Nashville Banner,* April 30, 1962; "Metro Commission Approves Edgehill," *Nashville Banner,* October 24, 1963; and Rob Elder, "Edgehill Given 2nd Approval after Hearing," *Nashville Tennessean,* October 29, 1965.

20. Ben West, Mayor's Report, no. 14, "Urban Renewal," tape 312–61, Metropolitan Archives Sound Files, Nashville. See Guilford Dudley III, "Nashville Faces a Classic Urban Crisis," *Nashville Magazine,* October 1968, 30, for an example of boosterism which argues that urban renewal in Nashville was more humane than elsewhere.

21. See Frank Ritter, "NHA Urged to Stop Charging Rent in Ghetto 'Slum Property,'" *Nashville Tennessean,* June 24, 1968; "NHA 'Slums' Spark Protest," *Nashville Tennessean,* July 1, 1968; and "Rats Fail to Startle NHA Slum Tenants," *Nashville Tennessean,* July 8, 1968.

22. Summary of the Meeting, Tennessee State Advisory Committee to the U.S. Commission on Civil Rights, December 1966, box 6, folder F121, NAACP Records. See also W. A. Reed, Jr., "Edgehill Group Seeks U.S. Aid," *Nashville Tennessean,* September 19, 1966, and Elder, "Edgehill Given 2nd Approval."

23. A 1972 article from *The Real Dirt,* the newsletter of the People's Rights Party (an interracial organization fighting for the rights of working people in Nashville), indicted the country music industry, associating its key figures with the ruling elites of Nashville (in particular, the leaders of Vanderbilt University), and linking the two institutions' respective attempts to take over and convert land that could have been better used to house lower- and middle-income Nashville residents. The article employed familiar pieces of country iconography to needle the industry and associate it with the land-hungry rich, using phrases like "The Grand Ole Land Grab" and "Grand Ole Uproot" to describe their attempts to bring urban renewal to Music Row. This characterization missed the fact that the Opry and Music Row were not always aligned, however. Record Group 101, Changing Status—Town and Gown, Centennial History Collection, Special Collections, Jean and Alexander Heard Library, Vanderbilt University, Nashville.

24. "Notes from Edgehill Urban Renewal Meeting," September 11, 1966, 4, box 6, folder F121, NAACP Records.

25. Elder, "Edgehill Given 2nd Approval."

26. "Metro Mayor Hails C&W Industry; Appoints Tradesmen Ambassadors," *CMA Close-Up,* November 1963, 3; "The Day Music City Came of Age," *Music City*

News, March 1964, 1; "CMA Ground Breaking Huge Success," *CMA Close-Up,* March 1966, 1. In early 1967, *Music City News* changed their cover page subtitle to "The Sound of a City Heard around the World" to emphasize the journal's world-wide readership and country's international popularity. The phrase further tied the music to Nashville. Neither the journal's title nor its content, however, exclusively focused on country music; in fact, by this point a sizable chunk of the journal focused on gospel music and Nashville's role in that industry. By the mid-1960s, Nashville had become a major recording center for other genres besides country, including black and white gospel artists, and while the journal acknowledged this diversity, the separateness of gospel and its culture from that of country music was simultaneously emphasized.

27. "This Is Your Guide to Nashville . . . Music City U.S.A.," in *The Country Music Who's Who, 1966 Edition,* ed. Thurston Moore (Denver: Heather Publications, 1965), pt. 7, 30.

28. "Curfew at 7 p.m. after A&I Siege," *Nashville Banner,* April 6, 1968; "Guard Seals, Patrols North Nashville Area," *Nashville Tennessean,* April 5, 1968.

29. Jerry Thompson, "Guard, Police Disperse Crowd after Advance," *Nashville Tennessean,* April 7, 1968; Jerry Thompson, "City Calmer; Guard, Police Still Patrol," *Nashville Tennessean,* April 9, 1968.

30. Tom Gillem, "Curfew Closes Opry Program," *Nashville Tennessean,* April 7, 1968.

31. Harris Martin, "Curfew Cuts Country Capers . . . But the Roy Acuff Show Goes On," *Music City News,* May 1968, 32.

32. Suzanne E. Smith, *Dancing in the Street: Motown and the Cultural Politics of Detroit* (Cambridge, Mass.: Harvard University Press, 1999).

33. A few country songs later provided more nuanced treatment, and, after King had been enshrined as an acceptable national leader, two songs specifically mentioned him. Tommy Cash's "Six Whites Horses" focused on King's assassination, and Bill Anderson's "Where Have All Our Heroes Gone" listed King along with Jesse Owens.

34. Commentators often noted Nashvillians' indifference to country music and understood this fact as a peculiar trait of the city, which was in fact the second busiest recording center in the country. They noted that there were no clubs where country performers played live, no all-country radio stations within the Nashville city limits, and no autograph-seekers hounding country stars when they were out on the town. WSM surveys found that the "typical 'Opry' fan is a 29-year-old city dweller and that he and three other people in his party traveled an average of 480 miles to see the show." In this sense, the country music industry thought of its "in town" fans as tourists, not residents. See "A Big New Sound Blows out of Nashville," *Broadcasting,* January 28, 1963, 67–82, and Joseph Sweat, "Keep Opry out of the Space Age," *Billboard's World of Country Music 1966–67* (Cincinnati: Billboard Publications, 1966), 80. See also Smith, *Dancing in the Street,* 156–62, for a rich description

of the ways in which the Motown sound as well as its performers developed out of Detroit's public housing, public schools, and music clubs. Detroit also had the first radio station in the nation built, owned, and operated by African Americans, WCHB, which began broadcasting in 1956.

35. Donal Henahan, "Grand Ole Nashville Sounds: They're Achangin'," *New York Times,* October 22, 1967.

36. Diane Pecknold, ed., *Hidden in the Mix: The African American Presence in Country Music* (Durham, N.C.: Duke University Press, 2013).

37. Pam Foster, *My Country, Too: The Other Black Music* (Nashville: My Country, 2000); Ray Charles and David Ritz, *Brother Ray: Ray Charles' Own Story* (New York: Dial Press, 1978), 222; "A Negro Hillbilly? It's Charley Pride!" *Chicago Defender,* April 2, 1966; Hazel Garland, "Video Vignettes," *New Pittsburgh Courier,* November 16, 1974.

38. David C. Morton, with Charles K. Wolfe, *DeFord Bailey: A Black Star in Early Country Music* (Knoxville: University of Tennessee Press, 1991), 17. The generic separation between hillbilly and blues records in the 1920s and 1930s was often constructed by white record label executives and producers. Karl Hagstrom Miller, *Segregating Sound: Inventing Folk and Pop Music in the Age of Jim Crow* (Durham, N.C.: Duke University Press, 2010).

39. George Hay, *A Story of the Grand Ole Opry* (Nashville: N.p., 1953), 10. Bailey's biographer argues that he had never actually forgiven WSM, and Bailey avoided the Opry for decades. Morton, *DeFord Bailey,* 129.

40. Gayle Wald has shown the links between gospel and country performers and cultures, and how these often correlated with those of white and black fans and performers. Red Foley was one popular country star who included gospel songs on his records and claimed to love having black fans, and gospel performers such as Clara Ward frequently mentioned their respect for Foley as well. Wald, *Shout, Sister, Shout! The Untold Story of Rock-and-Roll Trailblazer Sister Rosetta Tharpe* (Boston: Beacon Press, 2007). See also Bob Rolontz, "Sacred Songs Close Kin to C&W Music," *Billboard,* December 5, 1953, 42, for further discussion of Foley's central place at the intersection of the two genres.

41. Charles Hughes, "You're My Soul Song: How Southern Soul Changed Country Music," in Pecknold, ed., *Hidden in the Mix,* 283–305.

42. Of the string of hits James released between 1969 and 1972, several were penned by black writers Brook Benton and Ivory Joe Hunter ("Endlessly" and "It's Just a Matter of Time" by Benton in 1970, and "Since I Met You, Baby" in 1969 and 1971's "Empty Arms" by Hunter). Foster, *My Country, Too,* 36, 105.

43. Diane Pecknold, "Making Country Modern: The Legacy of *Modern Sounds in Country and Western Music,*" in Pecknold, ed., *Hidden in the Mix,* 82–99.

44. Bill C. Malone, *Country Music U.S.A.: A Fifty-Year History* (Austin: University of Texas Press, 1968).

45. "Charley Pride Album Proves He's 'Country,'" *Music City News*, November 1966, 10.

46. Bill Williams, "Country Music Now Interracial," *Billboard*, August 17, 1968, 1. See Arnold Shaw, "Country Music and the Negro," *Billboard's World of Country Music 1967–68* (Cincinnati: Billboard Publications, 1967), 82, for an article that more directly acknowledged African American influence on country music and questioned why there were not more black country stars.

47. "Charlie Pride Says, 'I Just Gotta Talk to 'Em,'" *Country Song Roundup*, December 1967, 42.

48. See, for example, "He Sings . . . Music of the People," *Afro-American*, February 19, 1966; "A Negro Hillbilly?"; "Country Charley Pride Struck It Rich during Intermission," *Afro-American*, August 12, 1967; "Blue-Eyed Soul, Brown-Eyed Hillbilly: Tan Singer Shows It Works Both Ways," *Afro-American*, October 14, 1967; Hazel Garland, "Video Vignettes," *New Pittsburgh Courier*, June 28, 1969; "Country Singer Bags Gold Disk," *Afro-American*, February 21, 1970; and "Charley Pride Awarded Gold Record for Album," *New Pittsburgh Courier*, February 28, 1970.

49. "Charley Pride: First Negro Country Music Singer on Major Label," *Music City News*, February 1966, 11. See also Bob Battle, "Pride Tells What's Right with America," *Nashville Banner*, September 24, 1974, for an explanation of Pride's interest in country music that highlights African American Opry listeners.

50. Shaw, "Country Music and the Negro."

51. Virginia A. Alderman, "Charley Pride: Just Keeps on Breaking Records," *Country Song Roundup*, May 1972, 11.

52. Charley Pride frequently appeared on the Opry, Linda Martell made a guest appearance in September 1969, and Stoney Edwards performed in 1971. See Johnny Shealy, Grand Ole Opry Performance Log, 1961–2006, Special Collections Division, Nashville Public Library.

53. McClinton later told an interviewer that he was unhappy with the album and the producers' attempts to make him sound less "black" and more generically country: "I couldn't stand to listen to the playback and the reason why it sounded like that was because Jim Malloy was paranoid. He thought that the next black country singer had to be even countrier than Charley Pride. . . . In fact, he would come down out of the control room and say, 'You sound black on that word.' And I'd say, 'Well, look at me, 'cause I am!'" McClinton argued that he should be able to sing in his own "natural" style, but the producers disagreed. Even after Charley Pride's success there was still hesitation on the part of Music Row executives to fully support a black country star, and in fact very few black country stars followed in Pride's footsteps. Rob Bowman, "O. B. McClinton: Country Music, That's My Thing," *Journal of Country Music* 14 (1992): 23–29.

54. John Grissim, *Country Music: White Man's Blues* (New York: Paperback Library, 1970), 41. See also "'I'm a Country Singer Who's Black' Comments

O. B. McClinton, C&W Star," *Music City News,* May 1972, 12, for a discussion of McClinton that uses the same construction, a country singer "who happens to be black."

55. "Amusement Week," *Nashville Banner,* March 2, 1974. John Egerton provided a converse understanding, suggesting that because Pride did not sing soul or blues he was not really black: "Pride's blackness is a pigment of the imagination—his style is pure country, not blues or soul." Egerton, *The Americanization of Dixie: The Southernization of America* (New York: Harper and Row, 1974), 205.

56. See also LaWayne Satterfield, "O. B. Doesn't Mind Being 'The Other One,'" *Music City News,* October 1973, 3-C, for an article that foregrounds the fact that country fans often mistook McClinton for Pride, and for McClinton's own nonplussed response.

57. Charles Portis, "That New Sound from Nashville," *Saturday Evening Post,* February 12, 1966, 30. Anthony Harkins has located this sort of dualism in the discourse surrounding "hillbilly music" of the 1930s and 1940s, finding that hillbillies and their music were recognized as a particularly white kind of "other" music: "Although 'hillbilly,' both as a label for a musical genre and for its performers, clearly denoted 'whiteness,' therefore, it constituted a strangely mixed cultural and racial category, simultaneously distinct from and akin to African American and other nonwhite images." Harkins, *Hillbilly: A Cultural History of an American Icon* (New York: Oxford University Press, 2004). Another example Harkins provides is Bluebird Records's decision in the mid-1930s to create the category "Hill Billy and Race Records," lumping them together while marking their discreteness. Harkins refers to this as a "synchronous racial merging and dividing." See also Claude Hall, "R&B Stations Open Airplay Gates to 'Blue-Eyed Soulists,'" *Billboard,* October 9, 1965, 1, for an early discussion of the frequency with which R&B stations were "integrating" their playlists and the concept of "white" soul, which implicitly marked the default signifier of soul as black.

58. The institutional switch from rhythm and blues to soul fully solidified around 1968 or 1969 (*Billboard* changed its R&B charts to soul in 1969), but as early as 1965, *Billboard* articles commented on the "soul" of R&B singers and the concept of "blue-eyed soul" to describe white soul singers appeared as early as 1965 as well. In late 1965, *Billboard* song reviews frequently used "soulful" to describe R&B songs but not country songs. *Soul Train* began in 1968, locally in Chicago, and then went national in 1971. *Soul Beat* started publication in 1964. *Time,* also in the summer of 1968, explicitly argued that "soul" was a product of the black experience: "It emanates from the rumble of gospel chords and the plaintive cry of the blues. It is compounded of raw emotion, pulsing rhythm, and spare, earthy lyrics—all suffused with the sensual, somewhat melancholy vibrations of the Negro idiom. Always the Negro idiom." "Lady Soul: Singing It Like It Is," *Time,* June 28, 1968, 62–66. Beginning around this time, too, many books on black music and the black experience used "soul" in their titles.

59. Darrell Rowlett, "Shrine of the Hillbilly Blues," *Country Song Roundup*, December 1970, 6.

60. Although I do not substantially address issues of gender in this analysis, the phrase "white *man's* blues" certainly reveals its salience as does the fact that much of country music culture was structured around an assumed masculine center. For decades independent female voices were fairly anomalous and marked as such, though this began to change by the late 1960s and early 1970s with the careers of stars such as Loretta Lynn, Tanya Tucker, and Tammy Wynette. See Kristine M. McCusker and Diane Pecknold, eds., *A Boy Named Sue: Gender and Country Music* (Jackson: University Press of Mississippi, 2004), for rich analyses of the gendered aspects of country music culture.

61. "Interview with Penny DeHaven," *Country Song Roundup*, January 1972, 6.

62. Perhaps it was a measure of how central racial politics were to country's conservatism that self-styled rebels such as Johnny Cash and Merle Haggard used race as a way to measure their distance from Nashville's country music establishment. Cash, intentionally or not, contested Tandy Rice's claim that country stars did not affiliate with the folk and civil rights movements by bringing a variety of politically progressive performers on to his national television show, including Bob Dylan himself. Cash's program, which aired for two years beginning in the summer of 1969, featured a variety of musical guests including African American stars Ray Charles and Stevie Wonder, and rock and folk figures such as Neil Young and Joni Mitchell. Michael Streissguth, *Johnny Cash: The Biography* (Cambridge, Mass.: Da Capo Press, 2006), 168–69; Leigh Edwards, *Johnny Cash and the Paradox of American Identity* (Bloomington: Indiana University Press, 2009), 21. Haggard publicly refuted George Wallace's exclusionary racial politics and tried to get his own record label to release a song Haggard had written about interracial romance. Peter La Chapelle, *Proud to Be an Okie: Cultural Politics, Country Music, and Migration to Southern California* (Berkeley: University of California Press, 2007), 205–6.

63. As Matthew Frye Jacobsen has astutely pointed out, white ethnics'"inchoate sense of social grievance required only the right vocabulary to come alive." Jacobsen, *Roots Too: The White Ethnic Revival in Post–Civil Rights America* (Cambridge, Mass.: Harvard University Press, 2006), 20. In this analysis, the channeled social grievance was sparked in large part by the language and accomplishments of the civil rights movement. For European descendants and hyphenate Americans, Jacobsen intriguingly argues that during this period they *strategically* passed off their whiteness as "not-quite-white."

64. Thomas Sugrue and John Skrentny, "The White Ethnic Strategy," in *Rightward Bound: Making America Conservative in the 1970s*, ed. Bruce Schulman and Julian Zelizer (Cambridge, Mass.: Harvard University Press, 2008), 171–92. See also Michael Novak, *The Rise of the Unmeltable Ethnics: Politics and Culture in the Seventies* (New York: Macmillan, 1973), and Perry Weed, *The White Ethnic Movement and Ethnic Politics* (New York: Praeger, 1973).

65. Dan Carter, *The Politics of Rage: George Wallace, the Origins of the New Conservatism, and the Transformation of American Politics* (New York: Simon and Schuster, 1995), 136–38.

66. Thomas Byrne Edsall and Mary D. Edsall, *Chain Reaction: The Impact of Race, Rights, and Taxes on American Politics* (New York: Norton, 1991), 77.

67. Michael Kazin, *The Populist Persuasion: An American History* (Ithaca, N.Y.: Cornell University Press, 1995), 234.

68. Ibid., 230.

69. Joe McGinnis, *The Selling of the President, 1968* (New York: Trident Press, 1969), 122. Loretta Lynn, the Wilburn Brothers, Hank Snow, Marty Robbins, and many others officially supported Wallace and recorded "My Friend George" spots for country radio stations. "'Name' Artists Come to the Aid of the Party," *Billboard,* November 16, 1968, 30. The Nixon campaign did eventually get longtime Republicans such as Roy Acuff and Tex Ritter to perform its song and endorse the campaign. Paul Hemphill also singled out Acuff and Ritter as Nixon supporters and suggested that the rest of the industry supported Wallace. Hemphill, *The Nashville Sound: Bright Lights and Country Music* (New York: Ballantine, 1970), 90. For the industry's widespread support for Wallace, see also Bill C. Malone, *Don't Get above Your Raisin': Country Music and the Southern Working Class* (Urbana: University of Illinois Press, 2002), 239.

70. Harkins, *Hillbilly,* 184–202.

71. Hemphill, *The Nashville Sound,* 35.

72. Grissim, *Country Music,* 24.

73. "Model Cities Issues Still Unresolved," *Nashville Banner,* October 15, 1970.

74. "President Proclaims Country Music Month," *Music City News,* November 1972, 2.

75. Sharon Sweeting, "President's Report," Tex Ritter Fan Club (Snohomish, WA, January 1974), Fan Club Newsletters Collection, Country Music Hall of Fame, Nashville. Journalist John Egerton followed suit, writing in 1974 that country music "is about the everyday experiences of ordinary people, about love and faith, playing and praying, working and drinking, living and dying." Egerton, *The Americanization of Dixie,* 205.

4. "Country Music Is Wherever the Soul of a Country Music Fan Is"

1. As a 1970 article pointed out, "After all, the authenticity and charm of the Opry lies in its unique setting as well as its music." "History of the Grand Ole Opry House," *Country Music Who's Who, 1970* (Nashville: Record World, 1970), pt. 6, 36. See also Paul Dickson, "Singing to Silent America," *Nation,* February 23, 1970, 213, for a reference to the auditorium as the "mother church" of country music, and John Egerton, *The Americanization of Dixie: The Southernization of America* (New York: Harper and Row, 1974), 207, for a reference to the Ryman as country's "ancient holy temple."

2. Chamber of Commerce promotional publications emphasized Nashville's distinction as "Music City, U.S.A.," pointed visitors toward the Opry House downtown and the Hall of Fame on Music Row, and included a separate listing of "Music City U.S.A. Points of Interest." Nashville Area Chamber of Commerce Publications and Reports, folder 8, Special Collections Division, Nashville Public Library.

3. Paul Hemphill, *The Nashville Sound: Bright Lights and Country Music* (New York: Ballantine, 1970).

4. Ibid., 15–20.

5. Alison Isenberg, *Downtown America: A History of the Place and the People Who Made It* (Chicago: University of Chicago Press, 2004), 167, 174.

6. Stephen Macek, *Urban Nightmares: The Media, the Right, and the Moral Panic over the City* (Minneapolis: University of Minnesota Press, 2006). See also Eric Avila's chapter on science fiction and noir films of the 1940s and 1950s for analysis of an early incarnation of this trend. Avila, *Popular Culture in the Age of White Flight: Fear and Fantasy in Suburban Los Angeles* (Berkeley: University of California Press, 2004).

7. For a discussion of the neighborhood's decline and descriptions of its future as a "second-rate retail area," see John Pugh, "The Future of Lower Broad," *Nashville!* February 1974, 52–62.

8. Chester D. Campbell, "Reshaping a City," *Nashville Magazine,* April 1967, 39, Rhodes Johnston, "Downtown Renewal Tops Final Hurdles," *Nashville Tennessean,* July 26, 1968. On the explosion of suburban shopping centers in the region, see Kathy Sawyer, "Rich Nashville Area Offers Strong Lure for Retailers," *Nashville Tennessean,* June 2, 1968.

9. Nashville Housing Authority, *Central Loop General Neighborhood Renewal Plan* (New York: Clarke and Rapuano, 1963), 26.

10. "WSM Studies Future 'Opryland' Complex," *Music City News,* November 1968, 21.

11. "Interview with Irving Waugh," *Radio and Records,* January 27, 1978, 42–46. See also Everett Corbin, "Waugh Divulges New Grand Ole Opry Site as WSM Fest Gets Underway," *Music City News,* November 1969, 2, and LaWayne Satterfield, "Opryland U.S.A. Gets Go-Ahead," *Music City News,* October 1969, 11.

12. As Kevin Archer has shown with the case of Disney World (where the Disney Company was much more effective in this regard than at Disneyland), acquiring larger and larger tracts of land meant consolidating profits as well as taking over space that could have been used by competitors. Kevin Archer, "The Limits to the Imagineered City: Sociospatial Polarization in Orlando," *Economic Geography* 73 (July 1997): 322–36.

13. Roy Acuff, "Introduction," in Jack Hurst, *Nashville's Grand Ole Opry* (New York: Harry N. Abrams, 1975), 12.

14. Hurst, *Nashville's Grand Ole Opry,* 335.

15. Ibid, 5.

16. In 1970, 4,877 white individuals lived in the park's census tract while 2 African

American residents lived there (Davidson County, home to both suburban Opryland and the downtown Ryman, was 20 percent black in 1970). The percentage of
owner-occupied units near Opryland was 84 percent, and the median asking home
price was $21,300, which was ahead of the countywide median of $18,100 but not
even in the top ten census tracts countywide in that category. Mostly home to families, two thirds of families in the tract had incomes at least three times the poverty
level, and only 4.8 percent lived below the poverty line. Nearly 40 percent of the
population was under eighteen. U.S. Bureau of the Census, *1970 Census of Population
and Housing: Census Tracts: Nashville-Davidson, Tenn. SMSA [Standard Metropolitan
Statistical Area]* (Washington, D.C.: Government Printing Office, 1972), P-4, P-12,
P-20, P-28.

   17. Caleb Pirtle III, *The Grandest Day: A Journey through Opryland, U.S.A., the
Home of American Music* (Nashville: Opryland U.S.A., 1979), 23–24.

   18. "Opryland U.S.A. Sets America to Music in a 110-Acre Entertainment Park,"
Opryland U.S.A. news release, May 1972, Papers of Opryland U.S.A., Country
Music Hall of Fame and Library, Nashville.

   19. Don Doyle, *Nashville since the 1920s* (Knoxville: University of Tennessee
Press, 1985), 252–55. For descriptions of the violence perpetrated by white onlookers
against African American picketers of an H. G. Hills grocery store at Sixteenth and
Grand (in the heart of Music Row) in the summer of 1961, see Student Nonviolent
Coordinating Committee Papers, 1959–1972, reel 40, Civil Rights Collection of the
Nashville Room, Nashville Public Library.

   20. Avila, *Popular Culture in the Age of White Flight*, 1–4.

   21. Bill Hance, "Ryman Opened Eighty-Two Years Ago with a Prayer, Closes
on Amen," *Nashville Banner*, March 16, 1974.

   22. Alison Isenberg has shown that one of the principal concerns for downtown
retailers as early as the 1950s was encroachment by the "ring of blight" that was
generally thought to surround most American city centers and that was almost
always referred to as the "slums." Business and government officials were worried
that what they deemed less desirable commercial establishments would emerge
downtown because of its proximity to these residential slums. See Isenberg, *Downtown America*, 189.

   23. "Opry Member Quotes," courtesy of Brenda Colladay, Grand Ole Opry
Museum, Nashville. The space between the Ryman and Tootsie's Orchid Lounge
was, in fact, an alley, but one that was heavily trafficked on Opry nights. Wagoner's suggestion that they only encountered fans in a "dark alley" suggested a more
desolate urban space than the one Opry goers actually experienced. See also Hank
Snow's WSM testimonial from the same collection: "There is naturally a certain
amount of sentiment attached to the old building, but the change will be good. The
old Opry house is in a slum area, the parking is bad, and it's not a safe or fireproof
building."

   24. Hank Snow, interviewed by Douglas Green, September 22, 1975, Country

Music Foundation Oral History Collection, Country Music Foundation Library and Media Center, Nashville.

25. Jeannette Smyth, "The Grand Ole Opry Ain't Po' No Mo'," *Washington Post,* March 18, 1974.

26. Gerry Wood, "King of the Hillbilly Singers," *Nashville!* October 1974, 69. For other examples of Roy Acuff's referencing drinking and prostitution as the prime reasons to relocate the Opry from downtown, see Acuff, with William Neely, *Roy Acuff's Nashville: The Life and Good Times of Country Music* (New York: Putnam, 1983), 197; Acuff, "Introduction," 12; and Doug Green, "Roy Acuff," *Country Music World,* January 1973, 17. City directories indicate that most of these establishments cropped up *after* the land for Opryland had already been purchased and plans to move set in motion, though the properties changed hands mostly between 1966 and 1968. Acuff himself sold his museum on Lower Broad (for $110,000; he had bought it in 1964 for $30,000)—two years after the move—to an owner who converted it into an adult movie theater. Historic Nashville, Inc., "Downtown Survey," box 8, property no. 188, Special Collections Division, Nashville Public Library.

27. Elizabeth Schlappi, *Roy Acuff, the Smoky Mountain Boy* (Gretna, La.: Pelican, 1978), 28.

28. At the time of the move, Acuff stated his assessment directly: "It's the only music today that's right down to the American way of life. It's for families." Smyth, "The Grand Ole Opry." A fact sheet distributed by National Life "for use by Opry talent in answering questions during personal appearances" emphasized that "pews were chosen for seating because that is the seating in the old House *and* because they allow families to sit together in close contact." "Facts Sheet on New Grand Ole Opry House," courtesy of Brenda Colladay, Grand Ole Opry Museum. See also G. Daniel Brooks, National Life and Accident Insurance Company, news release, October 13, 1969, 2, courtesy of Brenda Colladay, Grand Ole Opry Museum, for the principal importance of the new park's being "family-oriented."

29. G. Daniel Brooks, National Life and Accident Insurance Company, news release, 5.

30. Grant Turner, interviewed by Douglas Green, May 13, 1974, Country Music Foundation Oral History Collection.

31. Richard Peterson, *Creating Country Music: Fabricating Authenticity* (Chicago: University of Chicago Press, 1997); Diane Pecknold, *The Selling Sound: The Rise of the Country Music Industry* (Durham, N.C.: Duke University Press, 2007).

32. In a memorandum dated March 12, 1973, Opryland's director of marketing, Ray Canady, advised, "Very little time should be devoted to explaining or excusing the Ryman. We must get away from discussing buildings and spend more time on the Opry itself. We need to look ahead, not backwards." "Move Into New Grand Ole Opry House," memorandum, courtesy of Brenda Colladay, Grand Ole Opry Museum.

33. "Opryland Begun; Show Is Unchanged," *Music City News,* August 1970, 1.

34. Joli Jensen, *The Nashville Sound: Authenticity, Commercialization, and Country Music* (Nashville: The Country Music Foundation Press and Vanderbilt University Press, 1998), 76.

35. Hance, "Ryman Opened Eighty-Two Years Ago."

36. "Opry Member Quotes."

37. Jim Cooper, "Minnie Says Howdy to New Ole Opry: Spirit of Tex and Others Present," *Tex Ritter Official Fan Club*, June 1974, Fan Newsletter Archive, Country Music Hall of Fame.

38. Kay Johnson and Loretta Loudilla, "President's Letter," *Loretta Lynn International Fan Club* (Wild Horse, Col.), March 1974, 4, Fan Newsletter Archive, Country Music Hall of Fame Fan.

39. Ada Louise Huxtable, "Only the Phony Is Real," *New York Times*, May 13, 1973; Garrison Keillor, "At the Opry," *New Yorker*, May 6, 1974, 46–70; Paul Hemphill, *The Good Old Boys* (New York: Simon and Schuster, 1974), 135. See also Roy Reed, "Grand Ole Opry Is Yielding to Change," *New York Times*, May 29, 1970, for a less harsh but still pointed summary of the implications of Opryland: "And now, as if to add one more flutter of acceleration to the headlong Americanization of the South, the Opry is getting ready to abandon familiar old Ryman Auditorium in the grit and Victorian decay of downtown Nashville and move to a fancy suburban home that would look as natural in Los Angeles as in the hills of Tennessee."

40. Del Wood, interview by Patricia Hall, March 4, 1976, Country Music Foundation Oral History Collection. Similar in spirit, Joseph Sweat's 1966 article in *Billboard* suggested that part of the Opry's appeal was actually "standing in a long ticket line, sitting on hard church pews, enduring another summer night in air-conditionless Ryman Auditorium." Sweat made this provocative claim despite the fact that polls of Opry visitors continually showed that the uncomfortable seats and lack of air-conditioning were seen as the main drawbacks of the Opry. Sweat, "Keep 'Opry' out of the Space Age," in *Billboard's World of Country Music 1966–67* (Cincinnati: Billboard Publications, 1966), 80.

41. Wood, interview, Country Music Foundation Oral History Collection.

42. "The Gran Ole Opry Leaves Old Homestead," *San Francisco Chronicle*, March 16, 1974.

43. Hance, "Ryman Opened Eighty-Two Years Ago"; Carolyn Holloran, "A Touch of Sadness: Impressions of the Last Night at the Ryman," *Country Song Roundup*, September 1974, 32.

44. "Opry Member Quotes." For a ringing endorsement of the new facilities, see also "Music City Hotline," *Music City News*, May 1974, 6.

45. "National Country Music Month," *CMA Close-Up*, November 1973, 12.

46. C. D. Jaco, "A Change of Address, a Change of Image for Country Music's Mecca," *Chicago Tribune*, March 10, 1974; Smyth, "The Grand Ole Opry"; LaWayne Satterfield, "Opry Has New Home," *Music City News*, April 1974, 6. Satterfield declared that the first show in the new place proved that "the beautiful feeling

so evident in the old Ryman Auditorium could be just as wonderfully warm in a strange new building."

47. "Opryland Sets America to Music: But It's Only a Little Bit Country," *Music City News,* April 1972, 30. See "'Grand Ole Opry' Preserves Country Music Heritage," in *Billboard's World of Country Music 1964–65* (Cincinnati: Billboard Publications, 1964), 38, for an argument as early as the mid-1960s that the Opry was a repository for musical styles that no longer fit the contemporary country mold.

48. "Opryland U.S.A. Sets America to Music."

49. *Our Shield,* special Opryland issue, courtesy of Brenda Colladay, Grand Ole Opry Museum.

50. See Robert Krishef, *The Grand Ole Opry* (Minneapolis: Lerner Publications, 1978), 64: "If the Grand Ole Opry house does not have quite the same 'down-home' feeling that the Ryman had, neither are the fans all down-home folks any more. They are generally more sophisticated, and they like many different kinds of country music."

51. Hartford's song also declared the "park shuts up at bedtime / there's nowheres else to go," seeming to mark a contrast with the Ryman location, which was surrounded by other nightlife to keep the experience going.

52. "Interview with the Hagers," *Country Song Roundup,* January 1974, 27; Bill Knowlton, "Cryin' the Ryman Blues," *Pickin',* May 1974, 10–12; Doug Tuchman, "Editorial," *Pickin',* August 1974, 2.

53. McCandlish Phillips, "Country Stylist: Connie B. Gay Discusses Lucrative Formula," *New York Times,* September 8, 1957.

54. Tom T. Hall's 1973 song "Subdivision Blues" would appear to offer a contrary view on country people in the suburbs, but is in fact more of a sardonic commentary on the flaws of the suburbs than an evaluation of whether country folk can fit in there.

55. John Loudermilk, "Country People ARE a Different Breed," *Suburban Attitudes in Country Verse,* RCA Victor LSP 3807, 1967.

56. "The Sound of Country Music," presented for the Adcraft Club of Detroit, April 17, 1964, 4, Papers of the Country Music Association, Country Music Hall of Fame and Library, Nashville.

57. As a dissenting voice, Paul Hemphill, in his paean to the vanishing breed of unique southern characters, *The Good Old Boys,* also recognized the suburbanization of country folk but, unlike Loudermilk, did not see anything positive about the development and did not think that country folk could retain their authentic identity in suburban locales. "The good old boys are out in the suburbs now, living in identical houses and shopping at the K-Mart and listening to Glen Campbell (Roy Acuff and Ernest Tubb are too tacky now) and hiding their racism behind code words. They have forfeited their style and their spirit, traded it all in on a color TV and Styrofoam beams for the den, and I find them about as exciting as reformed alcoholics." Hemphill, *The Good Old Boys,* 13.

58. "Country Music—Is it Losing Its Identity?" *CMA Close-Up,* September 1973, 8.

59. Schlappi, *Roy Acuff,* 66.

60. Rachel Rubin has found that country musicians based in Bakersfield, California, often provided a nuanced variation on this theme. On the one hand, they openly claimed to be happy that the "old days" were behind them. Rose Maddox said that her brother Fred started playing guitar because he "hated picking cotton," Buck Owens told interviewers that he hated the "old days" so much that he didn't remember much about them, and Merle Haggard covered Parton's "In the Good Old Days." Rubin also points out, however, that these same musicians were defensive if outsiders denigrated southern people and ways of life, and Haggard, for instance, could approvingly say of someone like Bob Wills that he brought a little of "home" with him. Rubin, "Sing Me Back Home: Nostalgia, Bakersfield, and Modern Country Music," in *American Popular Music: New Approaches to the Twentieth Century,* ed. Rachel Rubin and Jeffery Melnick (Amherst: University of Massachusetts Press, 2001), 93–110.

61. A 1970 advertisement for Columbia's country catalog employed a photo of a typical New York street scene, looking grim and forlorn, with the tag line, "As urban areas get larger and more crowded, our great country artists become more important. Singers like Stonewall Jackson, Barbara Fairchild, and The Chuck Wagon Gang remind us of where we're from. Their music is theirs and ours. . . . Their music brings the country into your home. Wherever you live." Columbia Records, "Country Music for the Whole Country," advertisement, *Music City News,* October 1970, 14-C.

62. For a more simplistic journalistic explanation of the appeal of suburbia that fails to apprehend the ability to feel some form of nostalgia for the country while still not choosing to live there, see "Suburbia Regnant," *Time,* July 6, 1970, 6: "Few modern Americans feel much nostalgia for the farm or the small town, and most now find the once glittering big cities tarnished with decay."

63. Holloran, "A Touch of Sadness," 32.

64. Jaco, "A Change of Address."

5. "They're Not as Backward as They Used to Be"

1. Nashville travel and guidebooks published in the late 1970s and early to mid-1980s heartily recommended visiting live music venues in both Printer's Alley (a nightlife district three blocks north of Broadway) and on Lower Broad. These publications geared toward tourists repeatedly emphasized the appeal of the downtown honky-tonks and the history of country music's legacy in this space. Thomas Davis, ed., *Around Nashville* (Nashville: Beta Publications, 1977); Janell Glasgow and Ed Shea, *The Good Times Guide to Nashville* (Nashville: Aurora Publishers, 1978).

2. Metropolitan Planning Commission, *Recycling Nashville's Waterfront* (Nashville: Robinson Neil Bass and Associates, 1975).

3. Allen Green, "'Lower Broadway' Future Eyed," *Nashville Banner*, March 7, 1974.

4. Metropolitan Historical Commission, *Market Street Fall Festival* (Nashville: Metropolitan Historical Commission, 1976). See also Metropolitan Historical Commission, *Preservation Comes to Nashville*, courtesy of Tim Walker, Metropolitan Historical Commission (in author's possession).

5. Metropolitan Development Task Force, *Nashville Center City Plan* (Nashville: Metropolitan Development and Housing Agency, 1985).

6. The *National Geographic* passage was quoted in Michelle Williams, "What Others Think about Us," *Nashville*, January 1987, 71. See also Michael Wimberley, "Officials Hope to Change Face of Lower Broad," *Nashville Banner*, January 31, 1987, and Alan Bostick, "Police Deny Extra Patrols Linked to Center Opening," *Nashville Tennessean*, January 31, 1987, for discussions of the municipal government's desire to clean up this stretch of Lower Broad.

7. Metropolitan Development and Housing Agency, Annual Report, 1983–85, Nashville Room, Nashville Public Library; Metropolitan Development and Housing Agency, *1983—A Master Plan for Exterior Development in the Central Business District*, (Nashville: Metropolitan Development and Housing Agency, 1983).

8. Margaret Dick, "Nashville Waits and Watches for a Miracle on Second Avenue," *Advantage*, November 1979, 36–40. One architect said there needed to be private investment and estimated a figure of $15 million, but said nobody wanted to do it because "everyone thinks Nashville is too hillbilly" (36). One property owner on Second Avenue, Barbara Kurland, "doubts the typical Music City tourist will be attracted to the area no matter what's done. 'Most are just Opryland-country music-fast food-souvenir trinket types'" (39).

9. Beth Stein, "Tootsie's in Limbo Yet Again," *Nashville Banner*, December 18, 1992.

10. Ellen Dahnke, "Tootsie's Beer Permit Yanked for Thirty Days," *Nashville Tennessean*, November 29, 1989.

11. Mayor Bill Boner was also known for being so committed to cleaning up this particular neighborhood that he would show up at night himself and point out to the police individuals he believed were too intoxicated and should be arrested. Cynthia Floyd, "Boner, Chief Defend Broadway Cleanup," *Nashville Tennessean*, September 20, 1989; "Firms Applaud Boner's Cleanup Efforts," *Nashville Banner*, September 21, 1989.

12. Cynthia Floyd, "Crackdown Threatens Honky Tonk Heritage: Owner," *Nashville Tennessean*, November 15, 1989.

13. Sylvia Slaughter, "Lure of Lower Broad," *Nashville Tennessean*, July 20, 1991. The article also refers to Broadway as "a mish-mash of the tacky and the tony."

14. Laura Millard, "Tootsie's Was Never Like This," *Nashville*, June 1990, 10.

15. Beth Monin, "Cowboys Ok'd for Broadway Corral," *Nashville Banner*, June 2, 1990.

16. Peter Jordan, "The Heart of the City," *Nashville Business and Lifestyles*,

January 1991, 26–31. See also Bill Carey, "Lower Broadway in for Change," *Nashville Tennessean,* February 20, 1994, for similar commentary a couple of years later from a honky-tonk bar owner: "I'd hate to see this place turn into a row of commercial tourist traps and fern bars."

17. Jim Constantine and Hunter Gee, "Nashville Invests in Riverfront to Stimulate Downtown Redevelopment," in *Community Renewal through Municipal Investment: A Handbook for Citizens and Public Officials,* ed. Roger Kemp (Jefferson, N.C.: McFarland, 2003), 143–47.

18. Historic Riverfront Association, "From Classic Nineteenth-Century Charm to the Authentic Honky Tonks of Broadway, You Can Have It All in the District," "The District" Clippings File, Metropolitan Government Archives, Nashville Public Library.

19. Tammie Smith, "Metro Joining Ryman Project," *Nashville Tennessean,* December 21, 1990.

20. "Broadway to Get a Facelift," *Nashville Tennessean,* May 22, 1987; Beth Fortune, "Check of Buildings on Lower Broad Set," *Nashville Banner,* July 15, 1987.

21. George Gruhn, "Broadway Merchants Desire Area Clean-Up," *Nashville Tennessean,* May 27, 1987; Lacrisha Butler, "Land Owners Wary of Ryman," *Nashville Tennessean,* February 7, 1988.

22. Don Hinkle, "Lower Broad Redevelopment Boosted by Ryman Center," *Nashville Tennessean,* February 4, 1990; Don Hinkle, "New Roof, More Parking Mark Ryman Progress," *Nashville Tennessean,* February 4, 1990; "Ryman Will Sing Again," *Nashville Tennessean,* October 21, 1990.

23. Mary Hance, "Bell Signs Today on Downtown Site," *Nashville Banner,* January 15, 1992.

24. Mary Hance, "Bell Project to Get Under Way in April," *Nashville Banner,* January 29, 1992.

25. Sharon Zukin, *Landscapes of Power: From Detroit to Disney World* (Berkeley: University of California Press, 1991), 187–95; Neil Smith, "New City, New Frontier: The Lower East Side as Wild, Wild West," in *Variations on a Theme Park: The New American City and the End of Public Space,* ed. Michael Sorkin (New York: Hill and Wang, 1992), 61–93; Dennis Judd, "Visitors and the Spatial Ecology of the City," in. *Cities and Visitors: Regulating People, Markets, and City Space,* ed. Lily Hoffman, Susan Fainstein, and Dennis Judd (Malden, Mass.: Blackwell, 2003), 23–38.

26. Robert Palmer, "Nashville Sound: Country Music in Decline," *New York Times,* September 17, 1985; Jess Cagle, "Corn Again," *Entertainment Weekly,* February 7, 1992, 34–37.

27. Don Cusic, *Discovering Country Music* (Westport, Conn.: Praeger, 2008), 110–23.

28. Laurence Leamer, *Three Chords and the Truth: Hope, Heartbreak, and Changing Fortunes in Nashville* (New York: HarperCollins, 1997), 8.

29. Peter Applebome, "Hank Williams. Garth Brooks. BR5-49?" *New York Times,* October 27, 1996.

30. Peter Applebome, "Country Graybeards Get the Boot," *New York Times,* August 21, 1994.

31. Applebome, "Hank Williams."

32. "All About the Cover," *Music Row,* September 8, 1990, 2.

33. According to Peter Applebome, "The high-stakes race for new acts is compounded by the degree to which the amalgam of light rock, folk and country that gets dubbed country these days is filling a lucrative new demographic niche of whites from high school youngsters to aging baby boomers who find rap, metal and most of the other contemporary music either inscrutable or off-putting. In effect, outside of a few metropolitan areas, particularly New York, country has become white America's music of choice, with all the marketing potential that comes along with it." Applebome, "Country Graybeards."

34. Bruce Feiler, *Dreaming Out Loud: Garth Brooks, Wynonna Judd, Wade Hayes, and the Changing Face of Nashville* (New York: Avon Books, 1998), 98.

35. Jon Pareles, "Garth Brooks, Genial Superstar, Plays for the Folks up North," *New York Times,* September 7, 1992.

36. Ken Tucker, "This Is Garth Brooks," *Entertainment Weekly,* January 17, 1992, www.ew.com.

37. Cagle, "Corn Again."

38. Karen Schoemer, "On the Tube, Country Music Can't Go Down-Home Again," *New York Times,* February 9, 1992.

39. Ken Tucker, "Hot Country Nights," *Entertainment Weekly,* December 13, 1991, www.ew.com.

40. Michael Hight, "Gaylord Goes Downtown," *Music Row,* May 8, 1993, 7; Joe Rogers, "Opryland's Plans Likely to Transform Downtown," *Nashville Tennessean,* April 8, 1993; Mary Hance, "District Realizing Potential," *Nashville Banner,* May 10, 1993.

41. Joe Rogers, "Whole Lot of Shakin' Going On," *Nashville Tennessean,* April 8, 1993.

42. Mary Hance, "Opryland Planning to 'Sell' Downtown," *Nashville Banner,* May 10, 1993.

43. Brice Minnigh, "With Wildhorse Opening, Boom Begins in Earnest," *Nashville Banner,* May 31, 1994. See also Hance, "District Realizing Potential," for more commentary from Second Avenue shopkeepers who refrained from denigrating the tourists but emphasized that the avenue had a more neighborhood feel, which was bound to be transformed by an influx of tourists.

44. Sometimes one person's tacky tourist is another person's fancified version of a country music fan. A 1992 article on Tootsie's and Lower Broad quoted a patron's declaration that "Nobody likes Opryland and that fancified stuff. These are the last real honky tonks in town." Kym Gerlock, "Lower Broad's New Day," *Nashville Banner,* November 9, 1992.

45. David Fox, "Gaylord Stretching Its Muscles," *Nashville Tennessean,* May 30, 1993.

46. Thom Duffy, "How Nashville Goes Pop," *Entertainment Weekly*, January 25, 1991, www.ew.com.

47. "There's No Place Like Home," *Nashville Business and Lifestyles*, June 1991, 29–38. The chamber purportedly commissioned a study which found that "Music City USA" was the second-most recognizable city moniker in the country, behind New York's "The Big Apple." Marjie McGraw, "Making Chamber Music," *Nashville Business and Lifestyles*, June 1992, 52–57.

48. Andrew Wright and Nadine Post, "Steel Trusses for Steel Strings," *Engineering News-Record*, November 1996, 24–27.

49. Chet Flippo, "Honky Tonk Beat: Nashville's Lower Broadway: Tootsie's Back Room on Front Burner," *Billboard*, July 15, 1995, 1; Jim Bessman, "Dial BR5-49 for Alternative Country," *Billboard*, July 15, 1995, 1.

50. Bessman, "Dial BR5-49," 1.

51. Jon Johnson, "Hitting the Number with BR5-49," *Country Standard Time*, September 1996, www.countrystandardtime.com.

52. Bessman, "Dial BR5-49," 89.

53. Phil Fuson, "Honky-Tonk Heroes of the Western World," *No Depression*, Spring 1996, http://nodepression.com.

54. Amanda Petrusich, *It Still Moves: Lost Songs, Lost Highways, and the Search for the Next American Music* (New York: Faber and Faber, 2008), 120–21.

55. This sense was echoed retrospectively in Bill Rouda and Lucinda Williams's 2004 photo book *Nashville's Lower Broad: The Street That Music Made* (Washington, D.C.: Smithsonian Books, 2004).

56. Bill Carey, "Inez's Broadway," *Nashville Tennessean*, June 16, 1996.

57. Ibid.

58. Carrington Nelson and Mary Hance, "'Shoppertainment': Opryland Will Become Mega-Mall Centerpiece in 2-Year Makeover," *Chicago Tribune*, November 9, 1997.

59. Peter Applebome, *Dixie Rising: How the South Is Shaping American Values, Politics, and Culture* (San Diego: Harcourt Brace, 1996), 246.

60. Applebome, *Dixie Rising*, 254. See also Marjie McGraw, "They Come to Play and Decide to Stay," *Nashville Business and Lifestyles*, November 1991, 26–31, for a similar description of migrants from Los Angeles who prefer the laidback pace of Nashville.

Conclusion

1. Taylor Holliday, "Thirty-Six Hours in Nashville," *New York Times*, May 7, 2004; Tim Ghianni, "Music Still Packs the House," *The Ledger*, September 16, 2011.

2. Laurence Leamer, *Three Chords and the Truth: Hope, Heartbreak, and Changing Fortunes in Nashville* (New York: HarperCollins, 1997), 394.

3. Jay Orr, "Fans' Jury Still out on Downtown Fan Fair," *CMT News*, June 16, 2001, www.cmt.com/news.

4. "Fan Fair Draws Record Crowds," *Billboard,* June 20, 2001, www.billboard. com.

5. Michael McCall, "From Down-home to Big-Time," *Nashville Scene,* June 9, 2005.

6. Diane Pecknold, *The Selling Sound: The Rise of the Country Music Industry* (Durham, N.C.: Duke University Press, 2007), 211–18.

7. Bruce Feiler, *Dreaming Out Loud: Garth Brooks, Wynonna Judd, Wade Hayes, and the Changing Face of Nashville* (New York: Avon Books, 1998), 289–98.

8. Karen Schoemer, "On the Tube, Country Music Can't Go Down-home Again," *New York Times,* February 9, 1992.

9. Jon Pareles, "Garth Brooks, Genial Superstar, Plays for the Folks up North," *New York Times,* September 7, 1992.

Index